A Place in France

Nigel Farrell is a journalist, writer, television documentary producer and, latterly, restaurateur. He was educated at the charity-funded Christ's Hospital School in Sussex, where he was inspired to experiment with writing and story-telling by two outstanding English teachers, Roger Martin and Dickie Dawes. This equipped him to earn a living and enjoy a remarkable range of experiences and travel for the next thirty years.

Among his television production credits are: *The Village* (ITV); *On The Road To Monkey Bay* (Channel 4); *Copshop* (ITV); *Country House* (BBC); *A Place In France* (Channel 4); *A Country Parish* and *A Seaside Parish* (BBC).

A PLACE IN FRANCE

AN INDIAN SUMMER

NIGEL FARRELL

WITH REZA MAHAMMAD

First published in 2004 by Pan Books
an imprint of Pan Macmillan Ltd
Pan Macmillan, 20 New Wharf Road, London N1 9RR
Basingstoke and Oxford
Associated companies throughout the world
www.panmacmillan.com

ISBN 0 330 43139 0

A CIP catalogue record for this book is available from
the British Library.

Typeset by Perfect Bound Ltd
Printed and bound by Mackays of Chatham plc, Chatham, Kent

This book accompanies the major Channel 4 television series
A Place in France: An Indian Summer made by Tiger Aspect Productions.

To Sally Ann

～ ACKNOWLEDGMENTS ～

The authors would like to give special thanks to Katie Thompson, who has worked tirelessly to edit and complete the manuscript against a very tight deadline; to Claire Parkinson who copy-edited the original text; Dan Newman who provided the book's elegant design; Emma Marriott who commissioned and editorially managed the book, and Penny Price who provided invaluable editorial assistance; to Sir Terence Conran and Conran Octopus Ltd, for permission to use such inspirational extracts from the book *Terence Conran on Restaurants*; to Paul Sommers, Jo Boylan, Lynsey Neale, and the long-suffering Dave Harries at Tiger Aspect, and Jo McGrath at Channel 4, all good friends as well as colleagues; to Darrell Vydelingum, whose pictures and artefacts did so much to enhance the restaurant, and who deserves to do well despite Christiane's reservations; to Christelle Porter, who bravely dropped everything to help out at a critical moment, and kept us afloat; to Piers Allen, who just pitched up and worked his clogs off without a word of thanks; to Henrietta, Duchess of Bedford; to Anita Land; to Vivien Green, who Nigel would love to meet one day; to Nigel's family, especially Pam and Angela, and Tom, Al and Georgie, who've put up with so much; to the Tochous, without whom none of this would have been possible; to Margaret Clowes, whose long-term contribution proved most attractive; to Redina, Larrissa and Xenia; and finally to Gow Gibson, whose specialist advice on haberdashery proved invaluable.

~ *Dramatis Personae* ~

Nigel Farrell

Self-obsessed out-of-work journalist, television producer and divorcee. Living in the south of France at a loose end, accruing large debts and coming to terms with a mid-life crisis. Hopelessly in love with gorgeous mortgage broker Celine Cavaillez.

Reza Mahammad

Petite Indian genius of a restaurateur with an enormous zest for life. Has an ability to create a drama out of any problem, however insignificant. Travels with a wardrobe that would shame Elton John.

Nippi Singh

Striking Indian Sikh with a keen business eye. Runs the post office and stores in a small village in the south of England and bravely agreed to buy the house at Les Fabres with Nigel. Makes memorable chicken curries.

MANU TOCHOU

Unpredictable but utterly charming French estate agent. Sold the house at Les Fabres to Nippi and Nigel for £15,000 over a glass of Chardonnay, promising that in time he would become their best friend in the whole of the Ardèche, which, amazingly, turned out to be true.

MONSIEUR GOLETTE

Small, ageing French builder with unusual sense of humour who, despite enjoying the most extravagant lunch breaks ever seen in the construction industry, promised Nippi and Nigel he was the best builder in the whole of the Ardèche. Amazingly also turned out to be true.

CHRISTIANE TOCHOU

Manu's mother. Dominant matriarch with a powerful but emotional personality who for twenty-five years has run one of the finest small restaurants in the Ardèche. Once an Air France stewardess, she has a dazzlingly beautiful smile and a propensity for tears, both of joy and of sadness.

MARCEL CARBENERO

Diminutive French neighbour to Nippi and Nigel with an inexplicable sense of humour and huge walrus moustache. Obsessed with anything to do with concrete or cement, he wears unfeasibly large underpants, which his wife, Elise, hangs with pride on the washing line outside Nigel's bedroom window.

CELINE CAVAILLEZ

Stunning-looking mortgage broker invariably clad in an outrageous selection of avant-garde couture. Well aware that she's adored by most of the male population, astonished everyone by taking a genuine romantic interest in the lovelorn Nigel. But will she ever really fall for him?

SALLY ANN FITT

Attractive, blonde, theatrical thirty-something, impossible to dislike (it states on her CV), who has honed an ability to 'back into the limelight' into a fine art. Old flame of Nigel's.

CHARLIE FORMAN

Extremely plummy Anglo-Ugandan cameraman and director who in the past has worked on many brilliantly successful television documentaries (it states on his CV) with Nigel. Great athlete and rugby fanatic, he has sadly developed a hearing problem after an unfortunate incident in Brittany.

~ INTRODUCTION ~

Celine was looking at me with incredulity. I'd never before seen her looking even remotely serious.

'You really mean to do this thing?' Since we'd been together I'd shamelessly abandoned further attempts to improve my French in the face of her growing confidence in English.

I nodded.

'Let me understand this once more. You have no money? And no normal income?'

I shook my head.

'You know nothing about cooking. You know nothing about France. Your French is terrible. You have never been a manager. Of anything.'

'No.'

'You know nothing about cuisines. You know nothing of Indian culture.'

'You've got it.'

For a moment her unique look of seriousness and concern was replaced by the familiar flash of sultry humour.

'So you have decided to borrow thousands of pounds, come to live in the south of France, and open an Indian restaurant?'

She had a point. Stated so dramatically, it didn't sound like a project that crowds would be exactly falling over themselves to invest in. And yet when I'd first stumbled across the idea, it had seemed like a lifesaver.

I first met Nippi Singh more than a decade ago when he arrived with his wife, Bimmi, and twin daughters to rescue the ailing post office and stores in the small Hampshire village where I had lived since the early 1980s. Two years ago, after my painful divorce, I had suggested to Nippi that we pool our resources and buy an old farmhouse in the Ardèche mountains in the south-east of France, just north of Provence. The renovations were a nightmare and cost five times more than we'd planned. I ended up heavily in debt, and decided the answer lay in renting out my little flat in England and moving out to live in France on a more or less permanent basis. Nippi had his doubts about my sanity but agreed to let me use the house. This turned out to be a mistake.

Not that the house was a disappointment, far from it. I was thrilled with the place. We'd fallen for it the moment we saw it, a crumbling old ruin of a farmhouse on the corner of a row of terraced barns, tucked in a little hamlet of four or five houses called Les Fabres. It was utterly unsuitable. It had a relatively new tiled roof, hastily stuck on by a uninterested owner who knew only too well that if no remedial action were taken soon, the 300-year-old stone walls would simply crumple into a heap. He'd made it just in time.

Inside it was like a cave. The walls were constructed of pitifully small stones that immediately announced the poverty of the farmer who had built them. Now they were seared with great cracks formed over decades by trapped rainwater freezing during icy winters, and some sections were in imminent danger of disintegration. The floors looked and felt like bare rock; in fact this was the granite-like product of centuries of excrement from the sheep and cattle that would have shared the house with the family. In one little room with a lovely but crumbling vaulted stone roof, this residue had raised the level of the floor so dramatically that Nippi and I had to stoop almost double to enter it.

But it was the views that instantly won us over. On an upper level there was a stone terrace – which inexplicably could be reached only by a rickety ladder – and from here the great valley of the Ardèche lies spread before you, its slopes speckled on high either side by clustered oases of orange-tiled houses, and set against a backlit range of mountains silhouetted in the Mediterranean azure of the sky. Way down below, slicing its way through a huge valley of pines, flows the famous river itself, its ripples occasionally catching and deflecting the light, blinding the eye. In the early morning breeze, the sun dispatches iridescent rays through the branches of cherry blossom in the neatly planted orchard beside our terrace, and in late spring and summer the heat is strong enough to melt butter by 6.30 a.m. Yes, this was it.

We had to wait a year just to find a builder. The Ardèche is only two hours' drive from the Côte d'Azur, and with prices there and in Provence soaring, people were beginning to look further afield for affordable property. This has caused a building boom locally. When we found our mason, the wonderful Monsieur Golette, he told us we were fortunate – some people wait two years. Like every other French person we met, he assumed we wanted to tear the old ruin down and build a spanking new house in its place, and expressed astonishment when we showed him our plans to renovate it instead.

We got off to a wobbly start with Monsieur Golette. He arrived one Friday mid-morning with his two Spanish labourers, José and Ricardo, unloaded a small mechanical hand-digger, rigged a generator and set to work amidst a swirling fog of stinking dust, frantically cutting and hammering out the rock-like floor of the little arched *cave* beside a large hole that must have one day been the front door.

After an hour or so the noise of the digger stopped abruptly, and Monsieur Golette emerged covered in thick grey dust like a little ashen ghost and holding a small metal pin which turned out to have sheared from the digger. Whereupon he, José and Ricardo piled back into their rickety old blue truck and set off to find a replacement.

Nippi and I didn't see them again for nearly five days. We waited at Les Fabres for the rest of that Friday, and again – rather optimistically in hindsight – most of the next day. On Sunday we killed time knocking around bars and eating too much in Vals before returning to Les Fabres at eight o'clock sharp on Monday morning. Not a sign. Nor on Tuesday. And then finally, at about ten on Wednesday morning, we heard the distant clonking sound of the truck as it groaned up from the valley below.

Monsieur Golette's explanation was straightforward. They had discovered a replacement pin for the digger on Friday but it was too late in the day to return to Les Fabres. They never work at weekends. And Tuesday had been a bank holiday.

'Why didn't you come on Monday?' I asked him.

'Monday was *le pont*,' he explained.

'*Le pont?*'

Monsieur Golette looked at me with something akin to pity.

'*Le pont* . . . the bridge.'

'The bridge?'

'The bridge between the weekend and the bank holiday. Nobody works on *le pont*.'

Oddly, most bank holidays in France appear to fall on a Tuesday.

But Monsieur Golette and his loyal Spanish workers turned out to be far from the stereotypical idle French builders so fixed in the English imagination. There were all the usual problems over planning permissions, of course, disputes with the neighbours, endless rows over money, but in the end, thanks to the astonishing dedication and application of Monsieur Golette and the boys, having taken the best part of a year, our house was finished on time, and it looked sublime. Nippi and I threw a big *Pendaison de Crémaillère*, the traditional housewarming party, at which our dashing, Clint Eastwood-lookalike neighbour and shepherd Yves Monteil persuaded the local mayor, Monsieur Fleuri, to cut the ribbon across the lovely arch that formed the entrance to our house. During the party we got through seventy-eight and a half bottles of champagne, much of it on endless rounds of toasts in honour of the outstanding masonry skills and meticulous attention to detail of Monsieur Golette. Afterwards, Yves moved his sheep from his field for the first recorded game of cricket ever to be held at Les Fabres, which ended in an ignominious thrashing of the English team, most of whom were having trouble standing.

No, the house was all that I'd dreamed. The problem was that I was broke. Moving out to live in what we had only ever seen as a holiday home seemed to be a good idea on two counts. First, I could raise an income from renting out the flat in Farnham on the Surrey–Hampshire border, where I'd lived alone since my divorce. This would give me the chance to earn a living as a freelance journalist, producing stories and ideas from the south of France for an eager audience back home. And, after all, my three children were almost grown-up, I needed a fresh start, and in Les Fabres the sun always seemed to shine.

Secondly, there was Celine.

I fell for her the moment I set eyes on her. She has a pencil-thin figure, a hypnotic, beautiful face and an instant, bewitching charm. She flirts with the confidence of one who knows it, so our inability to communicate properly (in either my stumbling schoolboy French or her apparently non-existent English), far from being a problem, in fact proved a provocation and a delight. If I'd ever had a twinge of doubt that Nippi and I had chosen the right place to buy a house in France, the discovery of the dazzling Celine Cavaillez put an end to it like a sudden burst of wind extinguishes a candle.

She works in a rather dull little banking and insurance office in the Rue de Victor Hugo, which runs down from the Boulevard Gambetta, the main street in Aubenas. It's a very provincial hilltop town dominated by a towering château built by the Vogue family, who owned most of this part of the Ardèche before the guillotine caught up with them in the Revolution. Their château is now a rather splendid Hôtel de Ville, or Town Hall. Over the centuries Aubenas has developed into a sizeable regional centre where one finds estate agents, notaries, banks and, latterly, sprawling out-of-town hypermarkets and vast Mr Bricolage DIY stores. They've cleverly sat Celine at a desk in the front window of the office from where she tantalizingly smiles and winks at passers-by and from where she told me she hoped to *trouve un mari*. She called me *chéri* almost from the start of our first meeting to discuss my loan, and the way she sucked in her cheeks and seductively mispronounced my cringingly English first name sent an odd shiver down my spine. In her late twenties, Celine explained that she'd split up from her partner of ten years and was now living alone with the little boy she'd named Quentin after the particularly bloodthirsty Hollywood film director Quentin Tarantino. I was mesmerized.

I told myself that maybe she saw in me something more interesting than she found in the claustrophobic life she leads in the Ardèche, still a remote and in many respects primitive region well off the beaten track. Perhaps a well-travelled, middle-aged man full of rather exaggerated stories about the exciting world of journalism and television documentaries offered a mild escape from the endless round of parties and dinners where she sees exactly the same small group of gauche young men every weekend of the year. It was abundantly clear that the lovely Celine wanted something more out of life. Whether I was the person to provide it, only time would tell.

Either way, it was Celine, much to my utter astonishment, who first suggested I move out of my flat and live in France. 'You could buy a flash Cabriolet and see me every day, *chéri!*' she smiled. Was she teasing? Alas, as always, the subtleties of our courtship were in danger of being lost in the confusion of language.

But said it she had, and the prospect of living every day just a few miles away from the adorable Celine had me packing up a few possessions, waving a cheery goodbye to the grey, grid-locked roads of southern England, and embarking on a life I would have believed impossible just a year or two before.

I set myself up beneath a huge faded-red umbrella on the magnificent terrace at Les Fabres, overlooking the bobbing cherry orchard, surrounded by piles of French language books and CDs with which to woo Celine before someone else did, and started phoning around all my old buddies back in London looking for work.

Journalists and television producers as a breed tend to generate ideas through personal contact, which often involves copious quantities of alcohol. I may have been only a couple of hours away by plane, a journey which often costs less than my return rail ticket from Farnham to Waterloo, but as far as my peers were concerned, I was now living in a different solar system. I realize now that I shouldn't have told anyone what I'd done and just kept in contact exclusively by mobile phone so they'd be none the wiser. But I didn't.

Within a few weeks I was bracing myself for the bleak prospect of slowly going bust, when I was struck, like a thunderbolt, with what seemed at the time an idea of such inspiration and simplicity that I couldn't believe I hadn't thought of it before. I called Nippi and suggested he might like to join me in opening up an Indian restaurant in the town just ten minutes' drive down the valley from Les Fabres, Vals Les Bains. He said he thought it a ridiculous suggestion and put the phone down.

In fact, superficially at least, there was some merit in the idea. Vals Les Bains, reluctantly subsidiary to Aubenas a few miles beyond, is a slightly faded holiday town that became fashionable at the end of the nineteenth century when the advent of the railways meant rich Parisians could travel down to sample the delights of the town's natural thermal springs. In high summer its hotels are still packed, with mainly French holidaymakers now, here for the spectacular canoeing, abseiling and climbing on offer in the dramatic volcanic peaks and valleys of the Ardèche. The most prolific foreign visitors are the Dutch, whom the French hate with an extraordinary vehemence because they never spend a sou locally if they can avoid it. They've bought up second homes in great enclaves, slicing off whole sections of villages, and making little effort to speak French or use local shops or restaurants, arriving instead in great convoys of cars and caravans groaning with produce bought in their local Dutch supermarkets. In one village a few miles south of Vals, the mayor has decreed that the refuse collectors should not empty the Dutch dustbins on the grounds that there's never anything French in them.

The locals, however, regarded us as something of a novelty. Most had never seen an Indian Sikh before and tended to rush out into the streets waving their arms in the air whenever the immaculately clad Nippi and his turban hove into view. Our estate agent, Manu, had nicknamed him the Maharajah of Les Fabres. Surely, curiosity about the two crazy guys from England setting up a weird restaurant in Vals would provide an avalanche of custom. Based back in Hampshire, Nippi could raise the finance and administer the running of the place and its accounts, and I could manage the restaurant day to day.

I arranged to meet Manu in one of his favourite restaurants, where his first glass of Chardonnay arrives on the table at 10 a.m. prompt. The restaurant is a short walk from his splendid old office across the main square, where, beneath its rows of pollarded plane trees, the old men of Vals stagger from the bars after lunch every day of the year come rain or shine for a few hours of boule.

'How is *la belle* Celine, my friend?' he began, as he always did, arching his eyebrows and flashing his wicked smile. Everyone knows about Celine – I had become a figure of some considerable interest locally because of it, and no doubt a figure of fun, too, had I seen the winks and been able to understand the softly spoken jokes that often greeted me as I entered the bars of Vals and Aubenas.

Manu is in his mid-thirties, tall, with long skinny legs, like pipe cleaners, but with a huge torso and chest, and a large, perfectly bald dome that makes him look like a character from a Desperate Dan cartoon. He held his smile, awaiting an answer.

We were sitting in Le Square restaurant beside the old concrete bridge that links the main part of the town to the sadly shabby art deco entrance to the Bains Thermale, still in use today. Even in summer, when it hasn't rained for months, you can hear the constant splashing of the water of the river Volane on the rocks beneath the bridge as it tumbles effortlessly down to join the mighty Ardèche itself, less than half a mile below us.

I swigged the wine and sighed. 'I'm taking Celine out to dinner on Saturday. To Le Fournil.' Le Fournil is without doubt the best restaurant in Aubenas, a legend throughout the area for its piping-hot *pâté de foie gras*, and is – even by Ardèche standards – extremely expensive.

'You really shouldn't concern yourself too much with Celine, you know. It's not good for the health of a man of your years.' He giggled and waved over the patron, the overweight young Sebastian, to top up his glass.

The winter sun had moved round and was glowing warmly on the glass of the window. I shifted my chair back into the shadow. Above us, a pair of enormous hawks cartwheeled through the cloudless sky, their keen eyes raking the walls of the tree-lined valley for lunch. There was a distant echo of hunting dogs, the bells on their collars ringing through the chill air, forever chasing wild boar. Across the bridge, the gentle swish-swish of a team of Arab workers from the *mairie* raking the gravel, as they did every morning, even Sundays. Downstream, a man with a thick Cossack-style hat was standing in the middle of the river, fishing, his shadow dancing across the bubbling water.

The place looked quite lovely.

It was exactly a quarter past eleven. In England it would be a quarter past ten, and in my old office in Soho people would just be arriving for work, fighting their way through the masses disgorging breathlessly from the Underground, red-eyed and clutching vast cardboard cappuccinos after another heavy night. In Farnham the awful early morning traffic would only now be beginning to clear. The rubbish in the bin on the street outside my flat would be overflowing, and the Safeway trolley would still be there, rusting away, as it had for weeks. It would probably be raining.

The contrast could not be greater.

'I have come up with a really good idea. It could change our lives.'

Manu looked suspicious.

'I want to open up a restaurant.'

Manu frowned.

'A restaurant? You're not serious?'

'An Indian restaurant.'

'An Indian restaurant? Where?'

'Here in Vals, of course.'

There was a long silence. A single shot rang out across the valley. The hunting dogs were suddenly still. The fisherman cast his line and the hawks were carried away by the gentle breeze funnelling down the valley.

'You are joking?'

I shook my head. 'I really think it could do well. Don't you?'

For once Manu looked genuinely surprised, shocked even.

'You're crazy. It wouldn't work, it couldn't.'

'Why on earth not?'

'You don't understand this place. You buy a house here and you think you know everything. You know nothing.' He was still smiling, but there was a different tone to his voice. 'You are my friend. I can't let you do this. You know nothing of the people. You are crazy. Do you know how many restaurants there are already in this place?'

It may have been a combination of the warmth and the wine. It may have been my own sheer desperation; my real love for this place and the despair that I knew would come if I had to give it up. But for once I wasn't going to take Manu's advice.

'No, Manu, it's you who are wrong, it is you who don't really know me. I understand exactly what I am taking on. You don't understand my resolve. I will open an Indian restaurant here, and it will be a great success.'

Sebastian waddled into view, clutching a new bottle.

'*Un autre verre, Manu? M'sieur l'Anglais?*'

I'd better get started. There was a lot to do.

One week earlier Nigel had returned to France
after a brief Christmas break with his children.

❧

∼ 3 JANUARY 2003 ∼

New Year's blues.

Back home at Les Fabres after Christmas in that strange and already slightly alien country, England. Although this place is remote, at the same time it seems to be much more at the heart of things . . . closer to Africa than Hampshire, Italy is three hours' drive away, Spain just four – Barcelona is signposted from the motorway half an hour from here.

Yet just two hours' drive north of the Côte d'Azur and despite a low, hazy Mediterranean sun, it's breathtakingly cold. On the narrow, hairpin corners up the road from Vals Les Bains which haven't seen the sun all day, the glistening white waterfalls which spring out between the rocks are frozen into eerie white horizontal statues, as though the world had suddenly stopped for a moment.

It's minus-five degrees inside the house, too cold certainly for attempting Frank Sinatra's 'I Am a Rover' on the old upright piano in the stone-vaulted study on the ground floor, which is how I'd passed most of the weeks waiting for Christmas to arrive. Weighing over a ton, the rather lovely iron-framed Edwardian beast of a piano was already hopelessly out of tune before the bumpy 600 miles across France, and now it really does sound like the death throes of an animal under torture, yet irritatingly determined to hang on to life.

Not that it matters. My neighbours, the Carbeneros, have very sensibly decamped for the winter months to their family in Marseilles. I call Celine, but no response. I think she's still on a skiing holiday with her family in the Alps (two hours' drive).

I am alone.

～ 5 JANUARY ～

Awoke to a strong smell of damp.

The north wall of the house is built into the road above us, and since autumn there has been a slightly musty smell, but today it's overpowering.

Call Monsieur Golette, our builder, and explain. He said the smell was indeed probably caused by damp, chuckled, and put the phone down. At least, I think that's what he said. His accent is so strong that even Manu has trouble understanding him.

The house is just too big, much larger than I'd ever imagined from the architect's plans, and much too large to heat adequately in conditions like this. All the warmth from the expensive electric radiators downstairs disappears straight up into the roof via the huge stairwell. Architect has now sensibly left the area.

Fortunately surrounded by woodland, so I'm keeping alive by spending five hours a day chopping and sawing wood, and eleven hours huddled in front of the absurdly small wood-burning stove that had seemed so vast when we bought it six months ago.

It had all seemed so perfect back in the summer.

～ 7 JANUARY ～

Suddenly very worried about my finances.

I should have paid a 947 Euro local tax bill to the Trésor Public's office in Privas, the administrative centre in the north of the Ardèche, but simply can't afford to do so. Manu says they'll come round to the house soon and start removing anything they can lay their hands on. This may include a frozen corpse.

The hamlet of Les Fabres is at the end of the little road that winds up the valley of the Ardèche river itself from Vals. Today it consists of six houses but only one inhabited permanently, by the reclusive, fearsome-looking boar hunter Monsieur Tessiaux, whose language – and expression – remains impenetrable.

In search of warmth and company, I set off on foot to the next hamlet down the valley, Vasselent, to seek out Yves. He's an extraordinary shepherd who, with his poncho and cowboy hat, looks as though he's stepped straight out of a hurriedly thrown together Spaghetti Western. His moving jaw completes the image as he chews his way through a small mountain of wood splints set aside specifically for this purpose in the corner of his little hut on the roadside. Yves' hut, a place where women are banned, is bedecked by faded black and white football photos of himself in unbelievably athletic contortions as a very handsome young goalkeeper. Yves spends all his spare time here, sipping caustic red wine and only moving on the rare occasions he hears a car approaching, whereupon he leaps up, grabs his shepherd's crook and stands posing shamelessly, shouting at Sandy his sheepdog, and casting surreptitious glances at the occupants of the vehicle to ensure they are taking full account of his presence.

After being warmed by his ever-welcoming smile and two huge glasses of wine that I could almost hear stripping off the lining of my intestines, we chatted amiably for a few minutes. Yves articulates slowly and clearly, and as my French slowly improves I can spend more time chatting with him. Our conversations gradually reveal a completely different and much more likeable personality to the one I'd assumed I had met when we bought the house at Les Fabres over two years ago. This is one of the unexpected delights of learning a language, when first impressions are for once utterly irrelevant.

Yves' neighbours, Eric and Christine, speak good English and always promptly dine at 7.30 p.m., so I 'coincidentally' drop round at 7.20 p.m., to spend a pleasant evening eating boar stew, being reassured about life in general by good friends. Eric is a tax inspector, so wisely decide not to mention outstanding Privas tax bill, and am relieved when he doesn't mention it either.

~ 8 JANUARY ~

Early morning call from Eric. My outstanding tax bill has been sitting on his desk for over a month and he is demanding to know why I haven't paid it. He's asked me to report to his office in Vals at 11 a.m. tomorrow.

Know I won't sleep well tonight.

~ 9 JANUARY ~

One of the few compensations of growing older is the realization that the fears and terrors of the early hours almost universally fail to survive the scrutiny of the daylight hours.

Set off much too early for Eric's office in Vals, so drive slowly down the valley, through the corridor of leafless, skeletal chestnut trees that for the rest of the year obliterate the distant views across the Rhône valley to the Vecours mountains, the foothills to the Alps beyond. These mountains are still renowned for being home to the legendary network of hideouts for the French Résistance during the Second World War, despite saturation bombing by the Luftwaffe of the dozens of little hilltop villages which cling on to the grey granite summits. In a very isolated Little Englander way, I'm still always amazed at the number of German visitors who each summer flock to holiday in this area, and to the rapturously warm welcome they receive from the locals. In our astonishingly stable country, last invaded in 1066, it's easy to forget that this area of southern France and northern Italy was traditionally a chaotic region where new leaders and invading armies were being changed and replaced almost as frequently as the national and canton borders which enclosed them. Very mind-broadening.

The chestnuts, or *marron*, have been big business around here for centuries. In autumn they carpet every square inch of the hills in their spiky yellow greatcoats, historically capable, along with goats, sheep and boar hunting, of sustaining the economy of the entire valley-side farming community, and still prevalent today in sauces and ice creams – and of course the ubiquitous *marron glacé* – in every restaurant in the area.

Below lies Vals itself, with swirling winter mists mingling with the teased strata of smoke from the lone chimney of the glass factory established to bottle the famous Vals thermal water for generations of pale, liverish visitors to buy at outrageous expense.

Apart from the neat rows of pollarded plane trees along the square, the dominant feature of the town seen from above is the enormous pale blue swimming pool, which in summer attracts many beautiful, tanned and topless girls as well as schools of athletic, begoggled swimmers pounding up and down the lanes. Beside it is the little casino, which, Eric says, is the most profitable, per person, in the whole of France.

After an anxious ten-minute wait at reception, I'm ushered into Eric's bleak, blindingly white office. He is utterly charming. I have been charged a large amount of interest because of the late payment of my tax bills, but Eric says that if I write to the tax office at Privas and explain that I've been away in London much of the time and have therefore missed the reminder letters, I can avoid paying the excess.

To my surprise and gratitude, he spends forty-five minutes drafting the letters in his own hand for me to sign, and then posts them. Afterwards he suggests lunch at Roget and Joel's riverside restaurant just down the road, La Clementine. Only wish tax officials were like this back in Blighty.

Eric is a little dark-haired wisp of a man – despite a vast appetite – who, unusually amongst the Ardèchoise, relishes the chance to speak English. Sadly, his poor vocabulary fails to match up to his relentless enthusiasm for telling terrible jokes, which usually end with him roaring with laughter amidst a sea of bemused English faces. Eric chatters away, chuckling, as he works his way conscientiously through a vast pile of food, nodding occasionally at the arrival and departure of a large coterie of acquaintances who eat every lunchtime at La Clementine. Stubbornly dining at the same place every day, come what may, seems to be another very inflexible French habit. I've recently taken to eating steak tartare, which I would never have even contemplated a year ago, but under the skilled, manipulative fingers of Roget the chef, beautifully lean, raw steak accompanied by the equally raw egg has become a treat to relish. I thank Eric profusely and promise I will pay my outstanding tax bill within the week.

'You like the food here?' he asks, with a mischievous grin.

'*Bien sûr.*'

'Then you are, after all, just like a kangaroo . . . no?' says Eric, bursting into laughter. I smile weakly. As so often at such moments there is an awkward pause.

'Of course,' he continues at length, enunciating his words carefully, 'nothing could ever be so good as the Indian food you gave us all at your *Pendaison de Crémaillère*...how you say this?'

'Housewarming party.'

'Yes, this food was truly a miracle.'

It was at this moment that I had the Big Idea.

It could change my life forever.

∽ 10 January ∽

Slept fitfully last night, but for all the right reasons.

I've become really excited about the Indian restaurant idea. I may know nothing about running a business, or Indian cuisine, but even I can see a great opportunity when it pops up, announced, before my very eyes.

As far as I can discover, there are no Indian restaurants in the Ardèche at all, largely because there are no Indians here and no history of Indian culture. I visit the lovely Madame Bossi at the old Hôtel de Vivarais down by the square in Vals, who confirms this. In fact, she said, the word *Indien* is so alien to people in this part of France, they would assume I'm referring to the Red Indians of North America – a rather dubious legacy of Hollywood, I presume.

We sit over the bar sipping tiny cups of espresso, a canary chirping away in a cage in the corner amidst a sea of faded flock wallpaper that looks as though it has been here since the hotel was built in 1927.

'I think the idea has some potential,' she says, which is encouraging since

Madame Bossi is acknowledged to be one of the finest *cuisinières* in the valley. She then rather spoils the effect by adding: 'But I think it is a very *strange* idea.'

∼ 15 JANUARY ∼

I'm taken aback by the extraordinary range of reactions to the Big Idea.

Trudged down through the snow to seek out Yves, who was in the woods with Sandy and *les brebis*, the bells around their necks echoing eerily in the chilled silence so that it took only a moment to track him down. He is most enthusiastic, grinning and clapping me on the back with his usual unabashed exuberance, and suggesting an immediate meeting to discuss the plan with *Monsieur le Maire* of Vals, Monsieur Fleuri, who had come up to Les Fabres to cut the yellow ribbon at our *Pendaison de Crémaillère* last May. I'd been most impressed by Monsieur Fleuri, who superficially appears to be that most unusual of creatures, a dynamic, intelligent and apparently open young politician who gets things done. Yves, one of his deputy mayors, agreed to talk to him, which suddenly made me wonder if his enthusiasm was merely political expediency.

Inevitably, Yves asked about Celine – like everyone else I've met in the past year of my life in the Ardèche, he's fascinated by the progress of our relationship. I told him that Celine is back from her holiday at last, and that I'm taking her out to dinner on Friday, and that of course I would keep him informed of developments. He said that wasn't good enough and asked if we were still in love. I said: '*Oui*.' And then added, '*Je crois*.'

But this is not the moment for prolonged contemplations on affairs of the heart.

I thought Nippi might have been keener on the BI but then I should have known better. As always with Nippi I took the carefully planned diplomatic approach, pointing out that it was the genius of his Indian cuisine which had fired the imagination of the locals in the first place, and appealing to his entrepreneurial flair to exploit such an obvious opportunity. He hurrrrrumped in a very Nippiesque way, and suggested I had the courtesy to at least do some basic research before he would consider joining me in the venture. It was only after I put the phone down that I realized I hadn't actually suggested that.

But, of course, I will do, in time. This is something I could never attempt alone. I arrange to do some 'basic research' over a glass or two of *moresc – pastis* and a generous slurp of the almond *syrop* – with Manu and my builder Monsieur Golette, who may indeed have a first name, but under that curious but deep-rooted French code of respect and belief in the innate superiority of the middle-class, middle-aged male, no one had ever dared ask. We arrange to meet at *midi* on Friday at the Bar de Château in Aubenas.

This evening I get a totally unexpected call that has the potential to change the entire landscape. It is from Charlie Forman, a television cameraman who lately has become a documentary director.

Charlie – in his late twenties – is an old friend with whom I have made a number of series over recent years for BBC 2 and Channel 4. One of the reasons for his success is his classlessness; he is the product of an ex-pat Englishman living in Kenya and a Ugandan princess, and – after being educated at both a Kenyan primary school and later an English public school – he has emerged as a most unusual individual with one foot firmly in Black Africa and the other equally firmly embedded in Europe, or more precisely, in the heart of middle England. With his combination of a big, trusting smile splitting wide a handsome black face, and an unmistakable upper-class twang, he presents no threat, nor feels inferior, to anybody, a key quality in a documentary maker, so that he can hold his own with a duke, doctor or dustman.

We've had a fair few adventures together, Charlie and I, not least in Brittany, where Nippi and I had started our search for the first series of *A Place in France*. We'd arrived in the attractive little medieval market town of Domfront, an hour's drive south from the ferry terminal at St-Malo. I was visiting estate agents in the town and filming with Charlie, whilst Nippi was in England waiting to join us.

A Place In France

Charlie and I had just finished shooting a few picturesque scenes about town, put away the camera and were standing on the pavement in a corner of the main square when a battered old blue Peugeot, driven by a wild-looking young man, reversed towards us at high speed, braked so hard the tyres looked as though they might almost burst into flames through the heat and smoke, and then roared off up the road just a few feet from where we were standing. Seconds later, a police car screeched to a halt beside us, and two *gendarmes* leaped out, pistols in their hands, and started shooting repeatedly at the disappearing, runaway car. The smell of cordite was overwhelming.

Then an extraordinary scene unfolded. An old woman, with a relative or friend on her arm, suddenly emerged on to the street from a shop doorway. We watched, transfixed, as she was gunned down by a stray bullet. She fell forward, clutching a gaping hole in her abdomen from where a long, powerful jet of blood was streaming, and crashed face down on the road. A second bullet hit her screaming companion in the arm, and another stream of blood shot across the tarmac.

We discovered later that both women had survived their ordeal after emergency surgery, but Charlie and I were shaken, nonetheless. Someone who had seen us filming earlier and witnessed the appalling events came across and asked us the name of the movie we were shooting. He didn't believe us when we told him it was all very real. And the young man the police were attempting to shoot? Apparently all he had done was try to steal five hundred francs from a small bank across the border in Normandy.

It was all very surreal. And it's left Charlie with impaired hearing in his right ear, which is extremely irritating.

Of course, Charlie wants to know all about the Big Idea, and as soon as I start to explain the details, he falls ominously quiet. This is a sign I immediately recognize from years of working with the guy, which is why I know exactly what is coming next. Charlie's in the process of having his own Big Idea. Strangely enough, his Idea itself takes me completely by surprise.

'Nige, this would make a brilliant documentary series. Following someone like you trying to set up an Indian restaurant in the south of France? It's got Channel 4 written all over it.'

Now since I've been living in France, I guess my mindset has altered beyond recognition. The journalist inside me is still alive, it's true, but recently it has proved precious little help in finding me an income. The concept of 'going back' to anything in life I have decided to move on from somehow fills me with dread – I've never returned to my old schools, old homes, to former places of work, to ex-girlfriends. If I could really make the restaurant work, documentaries are history.

'Now hold on a minute, Charlie, not so fast,' I say quickly.

'Pardon?'

'I'm trying to move on, to make a new start, a new life. I don't make documentaries any more.'

'You don't need to. You open the restaurant, I make the movie.'

Now this needs serious consideration. I'm a creature who over the years has become used to existing *behind* the camera, asking the questions, directing the action. Then, a couple of years ago, Channel 4 heard about Nippi and me looking for a place in France to buy and renovate as a holiday home and we made a series about it. Suddenly the tables were turned. Charlie, along with a second cameraman/director, a Swiss German guy with the seriously aristocratic name of Claudio Von Planta, filmed us relentlessly twenty-four hours a day, and many of the tensions, rows and disasters that ended up in the final programmes made, for me at least, uncomfortable viewing. Do I really want to put myself through all this again? On top of everything else?

'I'll let you know, Charlie,' I shout down the line.

'Don't leave it too long.'

～ *17 JANUARY* ～

The Ardèche is an angry sea of limestone and basalt outcrops, mountains and fabulous gorges, its landscape twisted into random contortions by centuries of volcanic eruptions. Slicing its path through the weakest points of the rock is the Ardèche river, helped by thousands of years of floods which can swell its volume by up to three thousand times, creating valleys, cliffs and dramatic natural bridges that lead all the way down south to where the Ardèche joins the mighty Rhône at Mornas-Les-Adrets, twenty-five miles north of the wonderful Pont d'Avignon, and thence due south to the Camargue delta to empty itself into the Golfe de Fos and the warm, salty waters of the Mediterranean.

Aubenas is the dominant commercial centre to the south of the Ardèche, sitting astride a dramatic escarpment, the Coiron cliffs. A silhouette of its château, complete with machicolated round towers, pyramid-tiled summit, fairy-tale turrets and the hexagonal Dôme St-Benoit beside it, can be seen from miles around in every direction but most imposingly as one sweeps down from the Montélimar road, having come off the Autoroute de Soleil, the Lyons–Marseilles motorway which mimics the course of the Rhône. It instantly draws the eye, proud and confident in its military and financial superiority, the valley of the Ardèche dropping away from it like a huge cloak draped around the form of a sleeping giant.

Parts of the château date back to the twelfth century and it's now one of the most impressive Hôtel de Villes in this part of France. The Bar de Château looks out on to the château itself on one side, and the peculiar sixteenth-century House of Gargoyles, with its fine turret decorated by a range of odd and distorted stone faces, on the other. It looked as though Manu and Monsieur Golette were well into their second *moresc* by the time I joined them. Manu always looks slightly inebriated, even when he's stone-cold sober, but today Monsieur Golette, too, looked wild-eyed, and was guffawing with laughter and repeatedly banging the table with his hands in joyous abandon.

I had just settled down with my glass of *pastis* to quiz the two men on their honest assessment of the feasibility of the BI when a very familiar face hove suddenly into view.

Like me, Claudio, the Swiss German cameraman, has fallen head over heels for the charms of the Ardèche, and has also decided to buy a house and live out here. I've seen him only once or twice since I've been out here because he's still in the process of moving out of his home in Battersea and into the new house in Largentière, just down the road; but now, much to my astonishment, here he is.

'So what, Clouds,' I ask at length, 'brings you here?'

'I haff come to see you,' says Claudio, in his strong Germanic accent.

'How did you know I'd be here?'

'Manu told me. I spoke to him last night.'

This is all a bit baffling.

'Why do you want to see me?'

'Not *see* you, exactly. I vant to film you. Talking through the restaurant idea with Manu and Monsieur Golette. My camera is in the car.'

This, it transpires, is all the work of the devious young Charlie Forman. He's called up Claudio in Largentière and asked him to come down and shoot a few scenes to show Channel 4. To see if they want to commission a series. About me opening an Indian restaurant in the Ardèche.

I'm torn between cursing Charlie for his sheer cheek, and admiration for the professionalism of his approach. This is, after all, how programmes get made.

'Clouds, this is the first I've heard of any filming,' I protest. 'I told Charlie I'd let him know, he's got no right to call you about it behind my back.'

Manu and Monsieur Golette are not even trying to disguise their amusement.

'Nigel, think of the publicity value for the restaurant. And this is only a pilot. It doesn't commit you to anything. There's no harm in me shooting a few sequences, and if you don't vant to proceed, ve vill forget the whole thing.'

These are words I have spoken myself on so many occasions (without the accent, obviously). I can't help but smile. And, as I know so well, that smile is the first implicit signal of acquiescence.

'Well, if it is just for a pilot.'

Claudio, too, smiles. He gets the camera, and within a few minutes we are all wired for sound, and the videotape is rolling.

Manu's views on the BI have mollified a little after one or two of his friends have expressed a mild interest in the subject of Indian cuisine, but it was to Monsieur Golette that I looked for real encouragement. Although not a distinguished-looking man, short in stature, his thinning mop of grey hair constantly brushed brutally forward so that it has a slightly comical appearance as if he is standing with his back towards a force nine hurricane, he nonetheless has quite a standing in the local community. As a highly sought after and respected builder for thirty years, he knows the Ardèche better than most, and seems to be some sort of key figure in the Ardèchoise traders' association. He also loves his food. When he, José and Ricardo were working up at Les Fabres, at twelve noon on the dot they'd down tools, and whilst the Spaniards made a bench out of a few planks and munched their way through a slab of baguette and a large lump of cheese, followed by a gentle smoke on an obscure, foul-smelling rolled tobacco, Monsieur Golette would set about preparing his *déjeuner* as though he was entertaining royalty. He'd make a fire and cook the *plat du jour*, be it sausage, beef or lamb, with meticulous attention. Then he'd open his bottle of fine Côtes du Rhône and on top of a series of starched linen napkins would lay out the bread, salad or *légume*, salt and pepper and various shades of mustards each in their own little pots, and elegant, tall-stemmed wine glass. Then he'd simply eat, his eyes half closed, unable to converse for fear of breaking the concentration required to relish the range of tastes on offer. And all this on a building site.

This must be a man with his finger on the pulse of the Ardèchoise palate.

Unfortunately he finds the BI inexplicably amusing.

'The Ardèchoise love what they've always loved,' he tells me. 'Their goat's cheese, boar and potatoes. You will have a battle, *mon ami*, if you wish to tempt them into even sniffing another food.'

'But they loved what we gave them at the *Pendaison de Crémaillère*.'

'The Ardèchoise, they are also very polite ... and they didn't have to pay for it,' he says, with another mighty guffaw, crashing his huge rough-skinned builder's palms down on the table so that the glasses rattle.

'Listen,' says Manu, feeling, I sense, a little embarrassed on my behalf, 'your idea may be crazy, but you are my friend and I will do anything for you. I will help you.'

'What about putting some money into the restaurant, then?'

'I'm not that stupid,' says Manu, and both the Frenchmen roar again with laughter.

'Great!' says Claudio, beaming. A red ring has formed itself around his right eye with the pressure of the rubber eyepiece of the camera. 'Very good, well done, very, very good! Very amusing, very droll! Believe me!'

∽ 1 FEBRUARY ∽

Celine never ceases to bemuse me.

She looked radiant tonight when I met her for dinner at the little restaurant Le Pont d'Aubenas, her face alive with dancing shadows from the log fire casting its golden glow from the centre of the room. Outside, the flames were reflected in the foil wrapped around the palm trees to protect their delicate fronds from the ravages of the winter. Above, the Dôme St-Benoit, the former Benedictine chapel of Aubenas, and the lovely château beside it basked in the warmth of the floodlights.

Celine is a picture of rude health, her mass of purple hair, flecked with tinges of orange, exploding like a firework fountain around a face with a fine, defiant jaw line, wide, sparkling blue eyes and a perfect skin dappled with freckles kept alive by the winter sunshine. I haven't seen her for days.

Unusually, she ate a hearty meal, of *terrine de saumon aux épinards*, rounded off, to my astonishment, by a large *crème brûlée*. Celine is pencil-thin and, thanks to a dedication to the newly opened gym in Aubenas, which has become a Mecca to the fashionable youth glitterati of the town, very lithe-limbed.

And she's going out with me.

Once, when I'd spent the morning with her at the little red-bricked bungalow where she lives with her son, Quentin, in one of the dozen almost identical picturesque villages that seem to orbit Aubenas, and guarantee confusion from whichever direction you are approaching, Celine asked me if I'd like to stay for lunch. Inside the large American-style fridge was a shrivelled tomato and one small pot of yoghurt.

'I've been talking to my friends about your idea,' she announces. 'I think maybe it's not so bad . . . and you need something to keep your little mind busy now, *chéri*,' she adds, blowing me a kiss.

'I've missed you, Celine.'

'And me, you, *bien sûr*.'

One of the continuing difficulties of our relationship is that sometimes I simply never believe a word Celine says. On one of our very early dates, she said she'd pick me up at eight thirty to accompany her to a birthday party at the place we stayed before the house was habitable, Madame Bossi's Hôtel de Vivarais beside the casino in Vals. Eager to impress her young group of friends, I spent quite some time getting ready, borrowing an iron from Mme Bossi to run over my only clean shirt, and on impulse buying an incredibly expensive *eau de cologne* spray, something I've not worn since my pretentious and usually unsuccessful attempts to woo pretty girls at university nearly thirty years ago. By ten thirty there was still no sign of her, and I was just about to retire to bed when Madam Bossi rang the room to say *la belle* Celine had arrived. I stomped angrily down the five flights of stairs to reception, insisting to myself that I must demand an explanation and preparing for what could be our first serious confrontation.

She looked stunning, of course, in her long evening dress, and I felt myself weakening immediately. With a wave, a smile and a kiss we were in her car, heading up towards the dancing lights of Aubenas, and just as I thought it might be *cool* not to mention her late arrival, Celine yawned and the explanation suddenly plopped out uninvited.

'I'm sorry I'm so late, *chéri*, I've been sleeping all afternoon. I was at a party yesterday evening in Montélimar, and I met a very handsome man, and we spent most of the night making love.'

I was so shocked I couldn't speak. There was a long silence between us.

'Then, when we awoke this morning, we made love over and over again. Until lunchtime. Then we drank champagne.'

We'd been out together only once or twice at this stage, and certainly weren't a couple, but nonetheless this startling and heartless revelation completely ruined my evening. My mood wasn't helped when we arrived at the party and our gracious hostess, after embracing Celine, looked me up and down with a certain Gallic disdain, and said: 'Celine, I didn't realize you were bringing your father with you,' which caused great hilarity throughout.

I was seething with anger – not so much at what had happened to her, but that Celine had had the gall to tell me – but determined not to let her see it. I got slightly drunk on Scotch whisky, the only drink on offer, performed a solo Mick Jagger impression on the dance floor, and made up my mind to wait until tomorrow before making any decision about whether I really wanted to take this girl out on any other date.

The next morning I met Manu at Le Square for Chardonnay.

'How did the party go last night? Was it good with Celine? I'm sorry I couldn't be there,' he says.

'Not good,' say I. 'In fact, a total disaster.'

Manu holds up his hand to stop me continuing, and takes a deep draught of wine.

'Don't tell me. I know what happened. Celine told you she'd been making love all night to some handsome guy she met at a party, right?'

'How did you know? Have you spoken to her?'

Manu smiles his vast smile, and pats me gently on the arm.

'I don't need to. I know what happens. She always says this to a new guy. It's her standard line, designed to make you jealous and interested.'

For the second time in twelve hours I am rendered speechless.

'Don't worry about it. She was just joking.'

Some joke.

Charlie phones this evening in a state of high excitement. Channel 4 has offered £2,000 upfront for him to shoot a *proper* pilot, with the *stated* view of commissioning the series if it cuts the mustard. Just like that. It is all happening too quickly.

'Charlie, they never move this fast, not with the lightweight material you've had at hand to show them.' After the scene in the bar, Claudio had shot some interviews with me, and sequences around the towns and at Les Fabres, but it was hardly epic, earth-moving stuff.

'They loved it. We start immediately. Eight half-hours is what they've in mind.'

'Charlie, I haven't said I'll do it yet. Life's going to be stressful enough without you and Claudio trailing me around like lost sheep asking, "How do you feel about this or that?" all the time.'

'Farrell, you won't even notice us, it'll all be *end of lens*.'

'And how much editorial control do I get over the material you shoot?'

'Pardon?'

'Do I get to vet it?'

'Mate, you know the rules!'

I am to be treated like any other contributor. I must either sign a consent form to be filmed, or give an 'on-screen' consent to the producer whilst the camera is turning over, which also entitles the production company to all rights to the material in perpetuity, and total editorial control over the way the programme is edited and finally put together.

And I know Charlie's methods of working only too well.

'How do I know you won't stitch me up?' I ask after a long pause for thought.

'Farrell! How long have we been working together?'

'Exactly.'

If the series really is commissioned, which it sounds from their initial response it might well be, this is how it will probably work: there would just be the two of them, Charlie and Claudio, shooting all the pictures and sound between themselves, the ultimate, highly flexible two-man crew. They would be with us for weeks, maybe even months, filming everything that was unfolding before the camera, but they would be very discreet, Charlie assures me. So discreet, on past experience, that I'd 'forget' they'd be there at all much of the time, and they'd 'certainly never get in the way'. Oh no.

Almost everything, therefore, will be caught on video. And putting the BI into practice is almost guaranteed to be a traumatic experience for anyone involved, let's face it. There'll be triumphs, with luck, but big mistakes, too; there'll be the disagreements, the feuds and the rows and, yes, no doubt there'll be tears.

'But I do get to see it before it goes out?'

'Of course, Farrell. Don't be so flaky about it. You know exactly how it'll work.'

In the past, Charlie and I have always started to edit our documentaries whilst we are still filming them, which on a practical basis gives us the flexibility to go back and shoot extra sequences to drop into edited programmes. It is also a way to keep the contributors on board, because if they like the first few finished programmes we show them, they will continue to cooperate. It's a kind of insurance policy for them: if they don't like what they see on the editing bench, they simply won't continue to play ball. I know all this. I know too that we normally like to develop a second and maybe third series from the original, so it's also in our interests to keep the contributors happy.

And, ultimately, there's the matter of trust between director and contributor. Whatever else I can say about my relationship with Charlie, I do trust him. I think.

'I'll let you know if I want to go ahead.'

'Farrell, you just can't turn this one down. It's there for the plucking.'

'I'll call you tomorrow.'

'Sorry?'

'Be by a phone at 9 a.m.'

∼ 2 FEBRUARY ∼

Nippi suddenly seems oddly fired up by the BI.

'Manu and I have set aside time for research,' I tell him. 'I am doing my homework. As soon as we've uncovered places that might be worth investigating for potential purchase or rent, and conversion into an Indian restaurant, maybe you could jump on a cheap flight and come over to recce them. See what you think.'

To my surprise, he seems genuinely enthusiastic.

'Nigel, listen to me. You and I opening up an Indian restaurant down there? In the Ardèche? Why not? It's got many things going for it.'

I'm puzzled. As so often, Nippi appears to have undergone a volte-face. But why?

'Nippi, I'm delighted. I have somehow been under the impression that you didn't think this was exactly one of the top ten greatest ideas of modern history. But you really are interested?'

'Nigel, of course. Why do you always doubt me? I could be over in a couple of weeks. Just let me know.'

'That's wonderful. Thank you so much. I'm really pleased you're so keen on the idea.'

'I'll let you know about the flight details. It'll be Lyons airport, I'm sure, within the fortnight.'

'Fantastic!'

There's a short pause. Nippi hasn't put down the phone.

'Will Charlie and the film crew be there to shoot my arrival?' he asks, after a few moments' silence. 'Or will the filming begin once we get to Les Fabres?'

It takes me a minute or two to figure out what's happening here.

This morning, I called Charlie. I have agonized about the programme idea. On one side, I'm desperate to cut away the flotsam and jetsam of a previous life, enjoy a new dawn, unencumbered by the physical and emotional baggage of a film crew. I certainly don't want to spend each and every day filling the lens of a Sony DSR 500 camera as I weave my way, cursing and spitting, through the minefield that surely lies buried somewhere between here and the success of the restaurant idea. But, on the other side, a bit of filming could be fun, I trust Charlie and he knows what he's doing, and it couldn't be bad for publicizing the restaurant. So I said, yes; but only on the strict understanding that the crew never, *ever* gets in my way. Charlie seemed unsurprised by my decision. It turns out he's already booked the plane tickets.

'How do you know about the filming?' I ask Nippi.

'Charlie called me.'

I hadn't thought this through, but of course Charlie had called Nippi. And that's irritating; I'm not in control. But, knowing Charlie, it was entirely to be expected. And perhaps it could work in my favour. There's nothing Nippi likes better than to swan about like the Maharajah of Les Fabres in front of a television camera, and if the by-product of that is an increased willingness for him to invest in my restaurant idea, then so be it.

So, the decision is made, come hell or high water, and perhaps Charlie et al will now allow me to concentrate on the real issue.

I need a restaurant, and I need one quickly.

~ 4 FEBRUARY ~

Wheels around these parts sure turn slowly.

Meet Manu at 10 a.m. for Chardonnay. Despite his deep misgivings, this most loyal of friends has agreed to help me draw up a list of premises in the area which are reasonably priced and could have real potential. There are several places in Vals Les Bains itself, but Manu knows many other estate agents in the area and suggests we cast our net much wider – to Largentière, the wonderful medieval market town where Claudio lives, some miles to the south-west, and Antraigues, ten minutes north up the Volane valley. This is another majestically located hilltop village, made famous in the sixties and seventies as a fashionable retreat for artists, writers, musicians and stoned hippies, many of whom are still there, balder, fatter and often poorer, but most still eschewing the values of *la belle vie*. They might just have more imaginative palates, too. He thinks there may be a dozen or so suitable places worth a visit by Nippi and me, and agrees to check them out on our behalf within the next few days.

I look at Manu as he starts work on his third Chardonnay. His eyes are constantly flicking around the restaurant, as people come and go for coffee or drinks. Most of them he knows, so he spends a lot of time nodding, smiling or exchanging little jokes. Amusing, exuberant, and immensely affable, it's no surprise that Manu knows everyone in town. He's thirty-six and lives in a one-roomed flat in Aubenas with his beautiful, wide-eyed girlfriend, Olivia, who's just turned twenty. They've been going out since Olivia was seventeen.

Manu may be bald and gangly but there's no doubt women find him attractive. And now, already beginning to sip his fourth Chardonnay, he had the chance to prove it.

He was nodding across to a pretty girl of maybe thirty-five, who was sitting a few yards away playing with an espresso and reading a copy of *Le Dauphine*, the local newspaper.

'*Belle!*' he said admiringly. 'Forget Celine, Nigel, she's more your sort. Shall I ask her if she's free?'

'I bet you can't get a date out of her.'

'Of course,' said Manu, meaning it. 'I can get a date out of anyone.'

I eyed up the girl. She looked vulnerable, rather sweet, a curtain of rich black hair shielding her pale features. Manu's large, laughing eyes slowly turned to meet mine.

'Go on then,' say I. 'I'll buy you lunch if you can get a date out of her.'

I was reluctant to admit it, but his technique was brilliant.

It goes like this:

Manu walks over to girl and asks to borrow the sports section of her newspaper because he wants to check the result of a weekend game. Girl, being politely brought up, smiles and nods. '*Bien sûr.*'

Manu returns to table, pretends to look at paper, winks lasciviously at me. Returns newspaper to girl.

After a couple of minutes, Manu summons Sebastian for more Chardonnay. Says to girl that he is indebted to her for loan of paper, now owes her a favour, would she like *un verre de vin*? Girl looks horrified, checks watch, explains that it's much too early, and buries herself in newspaper blushing furiously.

Nothing happens for five minutes.

Manu summons Sebastian for more Chardonnay. He loudly instructs our patron to get another glass and pour wine for the girl, who protests.

Sebastian, smiling (I sense he's been here before), pushes a glass in front of her nonetheless. Short of creating an embarrassing scene, she has no choice but to accept.

Girl sips wine, and Manu engages her in conversation. Now feeling in his debt, she has to respond. After a few minutes, we know all about her, she's a secondary school teacher from Lyons, called Sofie, staying with her parents for a fortnight at Antraigues a few miles upriver, actually a little bored with life here.

Sofie swigs Chardonnay and becomes animated.

Sofie suddenly joins us at table, summons Sebastian for more Chardonnay.

Sofie and Manu exchange telephone numbers. Sofie leaves with a wave, agreeing to go with Manu to a weekend party in Montélimar. She didn't bother to say goodbye to me.

'Now where shall we go for lunch?' said Manu.

Nippi arrives on Sunday. I am apprehensive, unsure as to his motives or his commitment.

And even if it goes swimmingly (which, based on our previous experiences together, is frankly most unlikely), do I really want to go into business with him? Should friends ever do business together under any circumstances? And especially friends like Nippi and me?

～ 9 FEBRUARY ～

Still desperately unsure about the wisdom of all this, but have drawn up a schedule for the next few days so there's no room, or point, now for worry. Let's just get on with it.

Nippi's here at last, the big man with the big turban and big personality, his presence filling every room and every space, his personality almost overwhelming.

I picked him up at Lyons airport. Claudio was late, so, after standing around awkwardly for a few minutes whilst we were fitted with radio mikes for the filming, Nippi had to go back into the *douane*, and arrive again. I wish Claudio could work faster. We can't keep wasting time like this every time someone wants to do a bit of filming.

It is good to see Nippi, though. We've had many rows and disagreements over the house at Les Fabres in the last two years, but beneath it all there appears to have survived a solid bedrock of mutual respect and friendship.

In many ways I admire Nippi. He came to England from the Punjab when he was in his early twenties, and trained as an accountant. When news reached the wealthy and very traditional village of Crondall in north Hampshire, where I then lived, that an Indian Sikh was taking over the village post office and stores, there was consternation amongst certain of the more reactionary retired brigadiers, and stockbrokers who commute, first-class, to their jobs in the city. In fact, when this tall, handsome, immaculately dressed and obviously quite well off Sikh arrived with his beautiful wife, Bimmi, and their young twin daughters, they immediately became the toast of the town. A curious example of inverted snobbery took place, in which the very same of Nippi's detractors began falling over themselves to fete, wine and dine him and his family.

Since then he's metamorphosed to become more middle class than most of the villagers themselves, becoming a member of the parish council and a governor of the village primary school. When I get particularly frustrated by his foibles and idiosyncrasies, I try to remind myself of this question: how on earth would I have fared as a green-gilled, twenty-two-year-old Englishman arriving to forge a new life for myself in India?

Within a few minutes of hitting the Autoroute de Soleil, we are arguing.

His erstwhile enthusiasm has evaporated. Nippi's already listing dozens of potential problems with the restaurant idea. What I find particularly infuriating about the man is his inability to see, or at least put forward a view on, the bigger picture. He would argue, no doubt, that I'm the complete opposite, hurling myself headlong into the whirlpool without a second thought to the consequences.

The list of doubts and worries is obvious, and of course I've considered most of his points, but the relentless negativity of it all I find depressing. Where was the money going to come from? What about the language problem? Was I really up to managing a restaurant? Did I realize that Nippi was a busy guy and couldn't devote much time to all the responsibilities involved?

He also complains constantly about the cold, in much the same way that in the summer he complains constantly about the heat.

'Thanks, Nippi,' says Claudio, when we pull up at Les Fabres. 'Good scene. Charlie vill be joining us the day after tomorrow. Great stuff.'

Inside, I dowse Nippi with enormous gin and tonics, and curiously the mood lightens rapidly. However, I'm not too hopeful about the next few days.

~ 10 FEBRUARY ~

Awoke to the sounds of creaking wood.

This turned out to be Nippi stretching his turban on the staircase.

Preparing himself to face the world each day seems to take Nippi about an hour and a half. He washes and blow-dries his long, uncut hair, and twists it into pinned spirals on his head. He then ties one end of the turban around the banister and pulls the other end to iron out the wrinkles and folds, before carefully wrapping the thing around his head. The cloth is an astonishing six metres long. Before we bought Les Fabres we looked at a number of smaller houses which were immediately ruled out by Nippi because there just wasn't the room to stretch his turban each morning.

Despite the cold, Nippi seemed quite chirpy when we set off to Largentière to inspect the first restaurant I'd lined up, the exotically named Le Cep d'Or – the Mushroom of Gold. The little Arab lady whom I met a couple of days ago when I checked out the place was there to greet us, although she spoke no English. Much to my surprise and delight, Nippi seemed genuinely taken by the place. Although it's small with no space for outside seating to take advantage of the lovely view across the old bridge and the château on the hill behind, it is in immaculate condition.

'We could just about move in and begin business right away,' said Nippi, coming dangerously close to sounding slightly excited.

The kitchens are pristine and relatively large, and Nippi spent a good half-hour opening cupboards, examining fridges, counting glasses and cutlery and working out where the tandoori oven could go. We counted out the number of seats, or covers. There could be forty with a squeeze.

'And all this for a *Fond de Commerce* of £18,000?' asked Nippi.

I've already discounted the notion of buying a property outright as simply too expensive. To buy a restaurant freehold – the building as well as the contents – would cost a minimum of £80,000. To buy a building and convert it into a restaurant would cost at least £100,000, with the added headache of complying with the nightmare of French health and safety regulations – Manu says a new kitchen would have to be examined by no less than twenty-five government or quasi-governmental organizations. Most businesses in France simply don't own their premises. If you are taking over an existing restaurant, say, you'd pay a monthly rent, and a large payment upfront to buy 'the business' – this sum is called the *Fond de Commerce*.

'Yes £18,000, plus £300 weekly rent.'

Nippi had suggested we think in terms of trying to raise around £20,000 to set the business up. Once we are open presumably there will be at least some income to pay for outgoings like rent, and staff wages.

Nippi's eyes were getting wider by the minute. I could see he was starting to imagine us really moving in. Just like that.

I couldn't believe we'd found the right place at the first attempt.

'I think we're interested,' I said to the Arab lady in faltering French.

'What in?'

'In buying the *Fond de Commerce* to this place.'

'Ah, *M'sieur, je suis désolé*. We sold the *Fond de Commerce* to someone else. Yesterday.'

Nippi's eyes narrowed dramatically and swivelled slowly from her to me like the gun barrels of a battle cruiser.

'Why didn't you tell us this before?'

'You didn't ask, *M'sieur*.'

We walked in total silence to the next restaurant, La Bodega, a much bigger place, in the old centre of the town. Nippi was trying unsuccessfully to hide his exasperation, which didn't bode well for the remainder of the day, and as always, presumably, I was to blame.

Manu was waiting for us there, alongside the pony-tailed Spaniard with the black-toothed grin who owned it. La Bodega is an altogether grander place with two main dining areas, which together can make up well over a hundred covers. The *Fond de Commerce* was around £25,000.

'Just make sure it hasn't been sold already, will you?' hissed Nippi as we went in.

The Spaniard speaks good English and is quite an astute salesman, but no words could disguise the fact that the place is a bit of a tip.

'I guess we'd have to spend a bit doing up the kitchens,' I proposed diplomatically as the four of us stood around discussing details.

'Spend a bit?' demanded Nippi, seemingly unaware that the Spaniard was standing right beside him, grinning darkly. 'Spend a bit? This place needs ripping out completely, it's a disgrace!'

The black-toothed grin evaporates. We are shown rapidly to the door. Things didn't get any better.

The next two places we rejected out of hand. The fifth restaurant, Les Arcades, seemed to me to be more promising. It's the oldest restaurant in Largentière. Dating from the early fifteenth century, it has a wonderful vaulted terrace looking out over a small square in the old heart of the town, which in warm weather can accommodate thirty or forty tables. Inside there's only a dark little bar and a small, murky, grimy kitchen. But even though no specific figures had been mentioned, I now knew enough about local prices to know what to expect, and I believed this place had real potential.

Naturally enough, Nippi didn't. Sadly, it was still freezing cold, which didn't help him to imagine investing in a restaurant that only had tables and chairs outside. Some restaurants in the Ardèche remain open throughout the year, but most open in April or May, and close in September or October. Many of the proprietors make enough money from the season to avoid having to work for the rest of the year.

Nippi seems to have trouble believing me when I point this out.

A heated discussion then ensues over a cup of minty black tea in a little café round the corner. There was nowhere else. Largentière seems so cold and damp and empty, I have to admit that it's hard to picture it heaving with hungry visitors basking in the piercing June sunlight.

'Les Arcades is out of the question,' decreed Nippi.

When I had the gall to question his judgement, he said imperiously: 'Why is it you always find it so hard to be realistic about life?'

'Great,' says Claudio. 'I just love the vay you two guys bicker like an old married couple. The viewers vill luff it. Let's call it a wrap, shall vee?'

Went for a walk in the snow glowing beneath a blood-red sunset to try to compose my thoughts. I feel feisty and determined: if this thing were easy to do, someone else would have done it long ago. And there will be a certain gratification in proving to the ever-sceptical Nippi that the idea really is a good one. He had broken into a new bottle of gin, so later we sit around the old piano singing silly songs. As always, there are no hard feelings about the row. It's very strange, but our arguments seem to evaporate as quickly as they arrive, almost as if they weren't really rows in the first place, just play-acting.

∼ 11 February ∼

I've said goodbye to Nippi really none the wiser. This is all proving teeth-clenchingly frustrating.

The day started promisingly enough at Claudio's dream-like hilltop house, ten minutes' drive up from Largentière, overlooking the Disneyesque château at Montréal – today, as so often, dramatically shrouded in an extraordinary glowing-orange mist given life by the early morning sun. He bought it a few months ago entirely by mistake – well, perhaps more accurately, without the slightest intention of doing so.

It had been owned by a rich British banker, in his fifties, who had bought it to share as a love-nest with his beautiful young girlfriend. The guy's business was based in the Bahamas, so he was away a good deal and, predictably, the girlfriend, unable to speak French and growing increasingly isolated in their magnificent but very remote hilltop idyll, became bored. After only a few months, she left him. He responded by walking out of the place, driving to Largentière and, in tears, handing over the keys to the first estate agent's he came to, instructing them to sell it quickly, and with all its contents intact. He never once went back.

When Claudio first saw the place it was as if the original owner had just popped out for a minute to buy a newspaper. CDs still in the player, books on the shelves, sheets on the bed, coins in an ashtray, cupboards full of brand-new cooking implements, lawn mowers, hammocks, even the car in the garage – all were to be included in the sale.

The main house is small, consisting of a large living room and single, galleried bedroom above, but – with its vast windows and sweeping vista across the valley – is utterly, seductively charming. Along with a fabulously equipped kitchen and large bathroom, I'd have bought it for this alone.

But there's much more. A two-bedroom annexe with its own bathroom, like a giant play-house, perfect for Claudio's two young daughters; a second single-roomed annexe, with an even more sumptuously equipped open barbecue kitchen and outside shower; a long terraced garden surrounded by pools and small reservoirs to irrigate the apple orchards which fall away in carefully crafted steps down to an old ruined farmhouse and the river below; and a small tower, like the cornerstone of some miniature castle, ripe for conversion. Of course, Nippi loves it too, which gives him the perfect opportunity to bring out all the usual moans about Les Fabres – it's in the wrong place, too close to the Carberneros, cost far too much to renovate. Nigel, just look at Claudio's views! Look how much land he has! What potential!

Later, Charlie arrived from the airport, beaming, and started bouncing around like a puppy, unpacking his camera cases, simply bursting with enthusiasm for the filming, and the project.

'Farrell, don't you see, it's got everything! Lifestyle change! Aspirational! Interior designs, makeovers! Damn it, it's even got food and cooking! It's *No Going Back* with Nippi and Nigel, and a dash of Carol Smilie and Nigella Lawson thrown in! It's a winner!'

Nippi looked positively ecstatic.

'Charlie, we're having problems even finding a place.'

'What?'

'Nippi and I aren't exactly seeing eye-to-eye on what we're even looking for.'

'Fantastic!'

He looked at us all in turn, his face alight with energy, his whole body burning and twitching to get started.

'That's Programme One sorted, then! Clouds, get the radio mikes rigged on the boys, I feel an interview coming on.'

Next stop was the Hôtel de Ville in Vals for a meeting with *Monsieur le Maire*, Monsieur Fleuri. Our neighbour Yves the shepherd is there, too, in his role as deputy mayor, along with Manu. It is hugely gratifying to hear their real enthusiasm for the BI. The mayor wields great political influence and his backing will be an important calling card into the local community. We explained some of the difficulties we'd been having in our search and Monsieur Fleuri suggested to cut costs we should consider going into partnership with an existing French restaurant, maybe serving alternative French and Indian menus. Oddly, we've already considered this, which makes me think it's probably a good suggestion.

'How refreshing to find someone genuinely keen on the idea,' I said afterwards to Nippi, sardonically.

'Nigel, listen to me. They would be keen, wouldn't they?' he said. 'They're desperate to promote anything which broadens the interests of the town, anything that might help pull in more tourists.' Oh so sceptical, as always.

Just down the Rue Jean Jaurès, a typically narrow town street, presumably designed, like so many in this part of the world, to block out the heat of the cruel midday sunlight, and just a short walk from the *mairie,* is La Petite Maison, a rather dull-looking restaurant made up of two large and over-decorated rooms, and a terrace with a striking view overlooking the river. But it has potential. The proprietor is a friend of *Monsieur le Maire* and they had already discussed the idea of a partnership – the larger front room would be the French restaurant and the smaller back room and the terrace we could use as an Indian restaurant. It would require an investment of between £25,000 and £30,000. I feel it is a real possibility. Irritatingly but predictably, Nippi is non-committal.

We move on to Antraigues, fifteen minutes' drive north up the Volane valley, sitting astride its limestone hilltop like some picture-village illustrating a book of medieval fairy tales. We park in the idyllic little square where two almost identical competing restaurants glower at each other from opposite sides. One of them, La Montaigne, stands next to the home of the 1960s and 1970s heart-throb, singer Jean Ferrat, which is the explanation for the frequent presence of small gaggles of moist-eyed middle-aged ladies hoping to catch a glimpse of their idol. La Montaigne's walls are filled with photos of its famous neighbour amidst a few other token local characters. It has a little garden at the back with glorious views and a large kitchen, which serves the tables upstairs by way of a dumb waiter. Would Yvonne, the lady who runs the place, be interested in a partnership? She thought this could have potential, with the French menu acting as an insurance cover on our investment if, as so many people had predicted, the Ardèchoise really don't take to Indian food. When they arrived, diners (unlike at La Petite Maison, with its clear division between Indian and French) would all sit in the same room and would only then be offered the choice of a French or Indian menu.

'So we'd have to have two different chefs preparing two completely different sets of food with no clue as to where anyone is sitting,' grumbled Nippi. 'Sounds like a recipe for disaster to me.'

'Sorry, everyone,' said Charlie. 'Battery's just gone on Nippi's radio mike. Clouds, have you got a replacement? Thanks. Can you say that again, Nippi?'

We had lunch at Joel and Roger's wonderfully situated La Clementine; its huge glass windows overlook the turbulent weir, and the constant monotone of crashing water was strangely soothing. A week or two ago I raised the delicate subject of the BI with Joel to test his reaction. Far from trying to discourage me at the prospect of competition, Joel slapped me on the back and said it was a great idea. Furthermore, to my surprise, he said most of the other restaurateurs in Vals would probably react in the same way. Variety would intrigue visitors, and visitors are good for us all. Unusually enlightened, I'd say.

Today, as usual, the place was packed. This is one of the most successful businesses in town.

'The food here is adequate but nothing special,' said Manu. 'Yet it's always full of people. Why? Because of the location. You two should bear that thought in mind in your search.'

'Exactly what I was thinking,' said Nippi.

We had *crêpes*, several bottles of Chardonnay and then Manu cleared his throat as if to make a short announcement. 'I've been thinking, the *maire*'s idea to collaborate with a French restaurant and produce two menus is crazy. If you really want to get people excited about your idea you've got to offer them something new, something different, something that will surprise their palate. Having a restaurant that's neither fully French nor fully Indian will excite nobody.'

'I was just about to say the same thing myself,' chimed in Nippi helpfully.

Before going to the airport I took Nippi to a little restaurant built into the back of a huge medieval building, the bulk of which makes up the Hôtel de Ville of the village, Joannas. The restaurant is run by a *gérance* – that is a system under which the proprietor can give a licence to anyone who wants to run the place in exchange for a flat-rate weekly rental. The disadvantage is that it's not your own business; you are directly under the control of the owner. The advantage is you don't need to find a large amount of money for the *Fond de Commerce*. We had a splendid *omelette pipérade* and sat down for a conversation with Marcel, who is both manager and chef. He explained in detail how the place operated.

Nippi was already shaking his head.

'There's no way I am going to be involved in running a place where I'm not the boss,' he said, with an awful air of finality.

Since the *gérance* wouldn't involve him risking a penny of his own money, I rather naively hoped he would agree to come into it for my sake, to give me a job, an income, a way of staying in France. But that's not Nippi's way.

Well, at least we now know the options. But where to go from here?

The terminus at St-Exupéry airport at Lyons is most extraordinary, an enormous curved metal and glass structure like the folded wing of a giant bird. We'd been chatting away rather merrily on the two-and-a-half-hour drive about families and friends, and all the gossip from Crondall, and as we approached the airport I noticed again how odd it was that Nippi was in such good humour after such a failed trip, such an apparently depressing experience. I put this down again to what I think is his systematic approach to all problems or difficulties – rigorously assess every negative aspect, one by one, and only then, having exhausted everything that could conceivably go wrong, then – and only then – consider the positive, and thereby make a decision.

Presumably it's this coldly dispassionate approach which has made Nippi a successful businessman. Over the years, I've had a few insights into his business methods.

One day, over lunch at his home, I'd been describing a drive from London on the main A3 road. Nippi asked if I was familiar with a particular junction on the road, and when I said I was, he said if I turned left there, and driven on for another twenty minutes, I'd have arrived at a small row of suburban shops, one of which he owned, along with a flat above. I was already well aware that Nippi had interest in property.

'What's the shop like?' I asked.

'What do you mean?'

'What sort of a shop is it? What does it sell?'

'I haven't the remotest idea,' said Nippi. 'I've never been there.'

At the check-in desk at Lyons, we give each other a brief hug, then an affectionate shake of the hand, and suddenly, with a wave, he's disappeared through Gate 15.

He's promised to think things over, talk to his accountant, bank manager, family and friends, and let me know what he thinks we should do about the BI as soon as possible.

'What exactly is going through your mind now?' asks Charlie. Behind him, Claudio, clad in enormous earphones, dangles a long boom mike just above my head.

'To be honest, I've no idea what's going to happen—' I begin, suddenly sucking in my stomach and jutting out my chin in an attempt to improve my profile.

'Sorry, everyone,' says Charlie. 'Out of tape. Clouds, chuck over a new one, will you?' The thin blue cassette is ejected by the camera, labelled and boxed, and replaced by a shiny new one.

'Once again, please!'

'To be honest—'

'Vait! Vait, vait!' This time it is Claudio. 'Channel one or two, Charlie?' There is a brief discussion, something to do with sound levels, and then I am told to continue.

'Again, please!'

'What was the question again?' I've been putting people through this for years. I had no idea it was so tough.

'What's happening with you and Nippi?'

'To be honest, I've no idea—'

Charlie is holding up his hand.

'Farrell, don't try to remember what you said before, on the first take. If you do, it becomes a test of memory. Spontaneity is key. You must just answer the question. Again, please!'

'Well, Nippi and I have seen a number of possibilities, a range of potential restaurants and ideas, but we really need now to look again at the financing, and the way we want to go forward. So who knows where we go from here? I really have no idea.'

It doesn't sound too exciting to me, but Charlie is delighted.

'Fantastic, real cliff-hanger! Great end of Programme One! This is all about *anticipation*, Farrell. Must tune in next week. Brilliant, well done!'

And with that, Charlie, too, disappears through Gate 15. He's on the same flight as Nippi. He'll edit the material he's got and let me know what

Channel 4 says.

I wonder when I shall see either of them again.

～ 16 MARCH ～

There's really nothing on earth I can do about the BI until I hear from Nippi, and there's been an ominously stony silence from that direction. He's a guy who looks to work things out in a very methodical way, and he'll have spent days doodling with bits of paper and calculators, and no doubt will have had numerous appointments with his bank manager and accountant, and endlessly canvassed opinions from friends and family. But I'm running out of time in the sense that I'm running out of money; if the restaurant isn't ever going to make it, I will have to think of something else to do with my life, and pretty quickly, too.

My brain appears to be of the type that requires worry of some kind in order to function efficiently, and if I can't worry about the restaurant, I need to find something else to worry about, so right now I've decided I should be worried about Celine.

I told Manu that I haven't seen or spoken to her for several days – so unlike just a few months ago, when we were in contact two or three times each day, and when she'd seemed so keen to join me for weekends away in Carcassonne, and in an utterly charming little seafront hotel at St-Maxime, just a short ferry ride across the bay from St-Tropez.

Is she deliberately distancing herself, or is she really bowed under by the work of expanding the mortgage business in what she told me she saw as a unique 'career' opportunity?

'Take a look at yourself in the mirror,' Manu says, but with kindness. 'You have many worries, and the future is unknown. Money is short. Maybe you have lost some of your humour and youthfulness. Lighten up. Remember she is a young woman who wants some fun from life.'

I decide to have a savagely short haircut at Manuel's, the tiny *coiffure homme* in Vals, where Yves goes to have his long, luxurious locks regularly tended.

I look a completely different person, although whether more likeable and attractive or not, it's hard to say. Encouraged by the potential of the new look, I steam off to the appallingly named Jeans 'n' Tonic, a trendy men's clothes shop in Aubenas, where the dashing young owner, Olivier, persuades me to part with a large section of my dwindling pile of Euros and buy a long brown leather jacket – never owned one before – and a raft of expensive shirts and tight-fitting but surprisingly comfortable trousers.

Trying hard to assume the expression of a Greek god I wave imperiously through the window at Celine sitting at her desk in the mortgage office. She sees me and, after a moment's hesitation, throws me one of her all-encompassing smiles and beckons me to come in.

She says she *adores* the new look, seems really thrilled to see me, and is genuinely affectionate. NB: Buy Manu champagne.

She also says that after much thought, she will find the time to help me in the restaurant venture – a gesture which has never been offered before – and agrees to find a babysitter and come over for dinner at Les Fabres tonight.

Must go now. She's still here.

~ 19 MARCH ~

Charlie called. Channel 4 have apparently signed us up.

'But Charlie, nothing's happened, there've been no developments. I've not heard anything from Nippi. It's gone dead. The waiting's killing me.'

'Fantastic!' says Charlie. 'Tension building. What on earth is Nippi's decision going to be? Edge-of-seat stuff. Superb end of Part One, Programme Two!'

I'm neither pleased nor disappointed. My future lies here in France. Making an appearance in a British television documentary which no one here will ever see means nothing to me.

'Just so long as it doesn't take up too much of my time.'

'Come again?'

'Charlie, you'll just have to film what happens, as it happens. I can't spend hours doing stuff just for you.'

'Of course, no other way it can be done. You won't even know we're there. When shall I come over?'

'I'll call you when there's something to film.'

I've been emailing Nippi every other day. At last I manage to get hold of him on the phone; he announces that he only checks his emails once a week, I say it would be more efficient to write to him by post, or even by carrier pigeon. So much for *technologie moderne*. He promises to let me know what he wants to do about the restaurant by the end of the week.

I'm oddly full of optimism, the sun feels warm on my skin again and there are buds on the cherry trees at the front of the house. Also, the Carbeneros are back from their winter sojourn with their family in Marseilles; it's reassuring to hear the sounds of human activity next door again. They are generous neighbours, always asking me over for drinks or meals, and Marcel is constantly offering his DIY skills to do jobs around the house. He put up a letterbox for us, fixed a shower curtain and unplugged a blocked drain. Apart from his obsession with mixing cement – the apron of concrete that surrounds his house seems to encroach on the garden more and more, month by month – they are the neighbours from heaven. So it comes as a shock when he tells me over a glass of *pastis* that he is disliked, even reviled, by a large section of the local community.

'It's because we're from Marseilles,' he says dolefully, taking a swig from his glass and apparently chewing the *pastis* before eventually swallowing it. His statement is bizarre. It's not as though Marseilles is on the other side of the planet; in fact, it's just a two-hour drive down the A7. Suddenly I'm reminded of a conversation I had with Alain from the little Citroën garage in Vals, from whom I'd bought the old Deux Chevaux, or 2CV. After I handed over the 6,000 Francs, he asked me where I lived and I said at Les Fabres.

'My neighbours are the Carbeneros. Maybe you know them?'

Alain looked at me with deep suspicion,

'*Oui*, I know them,' he said. Then, after a pause, 'You know they're from Marseilles?'

I quizzed Manu about this. He said that like the Carbeneros many Marseillans had bought little houses in the Ardèche as weekend homes, and for use later as retirement homes. A lot of the renovation work was botched, done so cheaply that the result was often a painful embarrassment for those who lived nearby.

'Also,' he said, 'they're gangsters.'

Lying midway between the two huge metropoli of Lyons and Marseilles, the mountains of the Ardèche are apparently well known as ideal for providing haunts and hideouts for robbers, drug dealers and murderers. People originating from either city but living here therefore tend to be regarded with deep suspicion by the locals.

Manu drove me out to the spectacular Château de Ventadour, which figured largely in the Hundred Years War because of its strategic location totally dominating the entrance to two large valleys. Up a narrow road in a tiny village on the hill opposite the château he showed me a small house, the scene of a gangster gun battle in 1974 in which a *gendarme* was killed and another was wounded. A more unlikely site for such a major crime is hard to imagine.

What an extraordinary place this is turning out to be.

Still no word from Nippi.

～ 22 MARCH ～

It's a wonderful spring morning when I awake. My thoughts turn instantly to *la belle* Celine. I intend to take her in hand.

With Quentin spending the weekend with his father in Montélimar, I announce assertively that I have decided to take her out for the day. She has ten minutes to get ready.

'*Fantastique.* I'll take the roof down on the sports car,' she says.

'No,' I say, pulling my shoulders back and stretching to my full height. 'I'll drive. We'll take my car.'

I've bought another 2CV from Alain, even cheaper and more battered than the last. The engine is extraordinarily reliable but it has a few flaws. There appears to be a hole in the pipe carrying fluid to the brakes because the only way I can get the car to slow down is to pump the foot pedal repeatedly; when sufficient pressure is reached the car comes to a sudden and extremely abrupt stop. Worse still, the bottom of the chassis has been completely rusted away and with the force of such a sudden stop the pressure causes the chassis to buckle, and all four doors open simultaneously. This is quite an arresting sight – in fact, it nearly became one, literally. I was driving along at some speed downhill on a narrow lane when an enormous juggernaut roared past me going in the other direction. Looking up, I saw that the canvas roof of the old car had all but disappeared. The slipstream of the speeding juggernaut had dislodged the two rusting clips holding the roof to the front windscreen, tearing the canvas so that it was trailing behind the car, flapping like a loose sail in a force ten gale. I pumped up the brakes as hard as I could, and about ten seconds later the car stopped dead, and all four doors flew open. It was then that I noticed the police car with a flashing blue light racing up behind. Mercifully it sped past me, clearly on a higher mission, though there was an interesting expression on the faces of the two *gendarmes* as they flashed by.

'Do we really have to travel in that thing?' says Celine.

'Get in,' I say.

It is one of the first days of the year that's warm enough to eat outside, so we take a table and munch pizzas at The Beatrix, overlooking the lovely Volane river in Vals. The sky is so clear that after lunch, I drive Celine to the Mont Ste-Marguerite, the highest mountain in the area which, curiously, she's never visited. I suffer badly from vertigo, but from ground level the slopes of the mountain look gentle and unthreatening, carpeted by a huge forest of pine – and anyway my curiosity got the better of my weakness.

Ever since moving to Les Fabres I've wanted to know what the view is like from the summit.

The journey starts well enough, with Celine and me still glowing with the after-effects of a good bottle of rosé. As we climb higher, however, the road becomes narrower, and the hairpins more contorted. Soon the little stone walls, built to prevent cars from tumbling into the ever deepening ravine, disappear altogether, leaving long stretches of winding road with nothing but a sheer vertical drop falling away down the rocky side to the fields of sheep that are becoming smaller with every turn. I begin to sweat profusely, the blood draining from my face, and soon I can feel my heartbeat increase dramatically. I can't stop thinking about the problem with the brakes. I reduce our speed from five to two kilometres an hour. Celine thinks I'm joking, just pretending to be frightened, but when I turn to look at her and she sees the drops of perspiration on my face, she, too, begins to become alarmed.

'Just keep going, *chéri*, we can't turn around.'

After what seems like a further half an hour creeping along at a snail's pace, we enter a pine forest and immediately I feel fine; the view is obliterated and we could be driving anywhere. I force myself to smile, and feel my heart rate drop.

'Not so bad after all,' I mutter with relief.

Just then we suddenly emerge from the trees, and into the most dramatic, breathtaking view I have ever seen. I am overawed. We are at the highest point for as far as the eye can see, the peaks of the mountains and hills slipping gently down to the Rhône Valley and then up towards the Alps on the other side, stretched out below us like a frozen sea. We are almost touching the sky. The little exposed road runs up ahead to the summit at an extraordinary gradient, falling away unprotected to the left, in a sheer vertical drop of several hundred feet.

Somehow I make it to the top. There are moments of such giddiness and palpitations that I panic I might simply pass out and drive over the edge. Worse still, there's an ominous tingling – and then a series of sharp pains – in my testicles. This is a sensation I recognize from other moments in my life when I've been in mortal danger. I guess it's nature's early warning system of impending danger to life and soul, but it's certainly not helping here.

When we finally manage to park up at the top, I make the mistake of telling my beloved all this, and she collapses with laughter, then suddenly leaps out of the car, and runs around like an excited teenager, savouring the exhilaration of the altitude. It takes me ten minutes to get out of the car, and even then I find that a combination of light-headedness and the severe pain in my groin means I can't walk at all, but instead have to stand, legs trembling, clinging to the vehicle like a storm-tossed ship to its anchor.

There is a large black viewing tower right at the rocky summit, which I can see from Les Fabres. It's run by the *pompiers* in summer as a lookout for forest fires. Beside it is a tiny chapel. It's open only one day a year, on the first Sunday of September.

'They have a service there then. Shall we go, *chéri*?' she asks, smiling.

'I don't think so somehow, *chérie.*'

I keep my eyes firmly closed as Celine drives the old bus back down the valley, a merry tune on her lips.

'Next time, *chéri*,' she said, 'we take my car. For the sake of your *testicules* and our future together.'

~ 23 MARCH ~

Word from Nippi.

And it's not good.

Despite all his fears and concerns about the BI, despite his relentless negativity, for some reason I had assumed that in the end he would simply go along with the idea. After all, he always has in the past. The path to completing the renovations at Les Fabres was littered with endless problems, rows and disputes over what we should be doing and the way we should be doing it, but in the end my ambition and enthusiasm invariably won the day, so that Nippi, amidst much protestation and grumbling, would at the last possible moment agree to go ahead, presumably licking his lips with relish at yet another verbal punch-up.

Not this time.

He tells me over the phone that he likes the idea, is intrigued by the concept, and thinks an Indian restaurant might do well, but on balance he isn't prepared to risk any of his own money in the venture.

I've been banking on the fact that Nippi would agree to us at least forming a liaison with La Petite Maison in Vals, where one room could have been French and the other Indian. I know this isn't ideal but because the season is not far away and time is running out, I thought that for a relatively low initial expenditure we could use it as an experiment to see if there really was a demand for Indian food in the Ardèche. If so, maybe we could have made enough money to keep my head above water and to use the experience to plan and develop a properly funded Indian restaurant of our own at the beginning of next year. But Nippi wants a guarantee against any investment, and that I simply can't – and won't – agree to.

So that appears to be that.

Charlie and Claudio had been in the house and had started turning over as soon as they had heard the nature of the conversation. They were right in there to film my reaction at the end of the call: the shock, the disappointment and the sudden, new insecurity over the future. Then Charlie took off his headphones and put the camera down.

'That's utterly brilliant!'

'What?'

'Well, what on earth are you going to do now?' said Charlie with that big, excited smile.

'I've absolutely no idea.'

'Exactly! Don't you see, Farrell, this is much more than just about a telephone call, it's about a struggle for success against all the odds, it's about ambition and endurance of the human spirit. It's about friendship and betrayal! We're all gagging to know what happens next, real edge-of-seat stuff again. This is panning out perfectly, don't you agree, Clouds?'

'Very very very vell.'

I told them they were both heartless bastards feeding like a pair of vultures on the misfortune of others, and went inside and had a large *pastis*.

Take the long walk down the valley to Vasselent and Eric and Christine's, timing my arrival for exactly 7.20 p.m.

I really can't do this restaurant thing on my own.

I consume an enormous plate of *filet mignon aux oignons*, and countless glasses of Christine's gratifyingly toxic homemade orange wine.

It's an even longer walk back up to Les Fabres.

It's a chilly but beautifully clear starlit night, and as I walk slowly up – I'm in no hurry – I can see the ominous black silhouette of the Mont Ste-Marguerite and the little fire tower on its summit backlit by a vast beetroot moon.

I have absolutely no idea what to do next.

∼ 24 MARCH ∼

Oddly (under the circumstances) I slept like a dog, and awake consumed by a new and fiery resolution.

I'm determined to make a go of the project despite Nippi's fears, a determination underpinned by the knowledge that I have no option – the horizon is otherwise quite desolate and empty.

I meet Celine in Aubenas for Quentin's tennis lesson. He's six years old, with that wonderfully flawless olive skin that so many Mediterranean children possess by divine decree. I have no idea at all what he makes of me. He has an insatiable appetite for football, which exhausts me, and he's always begging me to fight with him, an activity that usually results in me emerging covered in welts and bruises. He also seems to get much pleasure from kicking me in the shins, which Celine never fails to find amusing. There are some flaws to my French Goddess after all, which to my (admittedly, probably perverse) state of mind makes her all the more human and, ironically, even more attractive.

Today she's in a diaphanous pale mauve silk dress and jacket, which tantalizingly wafts about in the breeze and which makes her look like an angel in a 1930s Hollywood B-movie. She gives me an unexpected boost in confidence. Isn't London full of Indian restaurants? Surely I could find someone else to invest in my idea? Despite her initial scepticism, many of our friends have convinced her that my idea would not only work, but could really make money, and the prospect of going out with a Nigel with bulging cheque book is clearly more interesting than a Nigel standing in the dock of a bankruptcy court. And of course she loves me and wants me to be happy. I think.

So I'm off to London (with Charlie inevitably following like a lost lamb) on another ridiculously cheap flight and armed with a handful of names and addresses of Indian restaurants in London that I've culled from those friends who know more about Indian cuisine than I do (i.e. all of them) – in search of a lucky break and a new business partner.

~ 27 MARCH ~

Can't believe how depressing it is to be back.

I mean, I'm as patriotic as the next ex-pat, but – oh dear! – I can't think of any aspect of life here that is superior to the French. They really do have better roads, railways, climate, food, women, alcohol, schools and hospitals. Yves showed me around the general hospital where he works in Aubenas a few months ago; it looks like Claridge's. The words 'ward' and 'waiting list' simply don't seem to exist in their vocabulary. Vowed only ever to have heart attack on French soil.

I'm hardly cheered up by a brief meeting with my son, Tom, in the rather glum students' union bar at King's College where, oddly enough (considering his genetic make-up), he's doing rather well at his degree course in French and Linguistics.

'Course is crap and I've still not got a girlfriend,' he announces gloomily, downing a pint in one and instantly demanding a *vodka chaser*, a phrase I've not heard since my schooldays and an abiding addiction to the novels of P.G. Wodehouse.

'And another thing,' he adds, leaning forward ominously. 'What exactly is the meaning of life anyway?'

After dozens of calls, thanks to a mutual friend I now have an appointment with someone called Reza Mahammad, who runs a restaurant on the Old Brompton Road called the Star of India.

He turns out to be quite extraordinary, small, almost waif-like in an Audrey Hepburn kind of way, slight enough to be blown away by the merest hint of a breeze, but with brightly burning eyes that alert you instantly to an unusual and powerful personality fizzing with energy. I explained my position and he listened intently, occasionally bursting into uncontrolled giggles and nodding frequently. I was just hugely relieved he didn't dismiss the idea out of hand.

The Star of India doesn't look Indian at all, with elegant murals in pastel shades depicting Rubenesque figures in fabulous Italianate scenes that are more reminiscent of the interior of a Greek temple. Reza had taken over the place at the age of just seventeen, twenty-five years ago, after the sudden death of his father, who'd come to England in the 1930s and had worked at Verusami's, London's first Indian restaurant. It was early evening and the restaurant was already packed with immaculately dressed Kensington poseurs, so this was a man who clearly knew precisely what he was doing. I ladled on the charm and hoped I wasn't overdoing it.

'I think you're slightly mad, but I'm always interested in adventure. Find some suitable premises and then we'll discuss it again,' he says with a little melodramatic wave of the hand and final farewell giggle.

I like his style.

Two steps down the pavement and I'm on the phone to Manu in Aubenas.

'Find somewhere, and find it fast, baby!' I say, with the air of someone who senses that after a very long voyage of rough seas and foul wind, the tide – in just the nick of time – was maybe about to turn in his favour.

REZA: My first meeting with Nigel was quite bizarre. My friend Zee just couldn't believe it. A total stranger, Nigel walks into my restaurant and without so much as a by-your-leave asks me to join him as a partner in a crazy business idea that is based on no research or business plan whatsoever – bar a housewarming party he once gave, serving Indian food to locals. Zee says it sounds like the crazy dream of a desperate man trying to extricate himself from a dire situation entirely of his own making. He speaks bad French, has never cooked in his life, knows nothing of Indian cuisine, has a slightly maniacal glint in his eye, and by his own proud admission is 'not exactly brilliant' with money.

Zee says don't touch him with a bargepole, but throughout our meeting I could hardly keep a straight face, it's just hysterical!

So I'm intrigued.

∼ 26 APRIL ∼

After weeks of searching, I've found the treasure, and – as so often – it has been right under my nose all the time.

Laurac is a typically roasted-looking little sixteenth-century hilltop village, a satellite to the larger fortified medieval town of Largentière, and like everywhere around here it developed as a base for the thousands of *paysans* who for generations plodded out each morning to labour in the fields beneath the full weight of the Mediterranean sun. When I arrived I couldn't help but notice that the beautiful church at the summit of the village rings out the hour twice. The bell tolls each hour once; and then rings it out again two minutes later.

I asked in the *tabac* about this.

'It's so that the labourers in the fields can prepare for their lunch, or to return home at the end of the day, or whatever.'

'Right,' said I. 'So why does it ring a second time?'

I noticed that vaguely patronizing expression the French seem to reserve only for the English come across the man's face. 'So they can then begin doing whatever it was they were preparing to do, of course!'

Like so many little places, Laurac boomed with the arrival of the silk industry, when local farms started to be adapted for the mass-production of silk from worms. The silk was then carted down to the huge mills by the river in Largentière a few miles to the east, to be woven into fabric. With the development of nylon in the 1950s the industry spectacularly crashed overnight, and today the population of Laurac – 700 – is a third what it was a century ago.

Just down the road from the main square with its standard coterie of *boulangerie/patisserie, pharmacie, café* and *le poste* is the tiny Square d'Externat, and beside that, built into a corner of the road, is Le Relais Fleuri, a small and oddly shaped restaurant that has one of the finest reputations in the area.

I know the place well. It's been owned for the last twenty-five years by Manu's parents, the Tochous, who took it over as a virtual ruin. Almost unchanged from the day it was completed in 1803, it had no staircases, no water, and no electricity – a state typical of many Ardèchoise homes of the 1970s. The transformation was complete, and included the addition of a roof over the little front garden to make a terrace. With the help of a huge vine, creeping rose bushes and dozens of trellises and pots spilling over with bougainvillea, fuchsia, daisies and geranium, they've cleverly managed to create a feeling of rustic tradition where certainly none existed before.

Christiane Tochou is a woman with so much charm and exuberance in her eyes that you feel a curious urge to embrace her and bury your face in her voluminous bosom the moment you first meet her. Manu had taken us to eat there on numerous occasions and every single time the wonderful Christiane had resolutely refused any attempt at payment, a fact even more extraordinary considering the quality of her food was famed far and wide, and she was booked up weeks in advance by gourmands desperate to sample her latest excursions into gastronomic paradise. A shyly produced photograph of herself as a young stewardess for Air France revealed a stunning youthful beauty, which is still only too vibrantly visible. Her husband, the portly, white-whiskered Jean-Bernard, who's universally known as JB behind his back but very formally as Monsieur Tochou to all but the immediate family, shares the apartment above the restaurant with her and works with Manu in the estate agency in Aubenas. With a beautiful daughter, Isobel, living with her husband and two young sons just down the road, they are indeed a formidable and charismatic family, the kind of people you meet once and never forget.

Le Relais Fleuri – the Restaurant of Flowers – is indeed perfect. Manu has for once (accurately this time) used a superlative with great accuracy. His mother is toying with notions of retirement after two decades of ceaseless, round-the-clock toil, and the concept of leasing out the place for a few summer months so she can take a break obviously holds a certain appeal. It is neither too big nor too small, and I can see immediately it would be very easy to adapt to an Indian style. If the Ardèchoise take to the food, we could take it over full time – and Christiane has even offered to stay on and guide us through *la transformation*. Too good to be true? It's just very strange that it has occurred to no one to approach her before, the most obvious solution, as so often in life, being so close to the lens of the eye as to be rendered invisible.

Charlie's thrilled. He thinks Le Relais Fleuri is perfectly photogenic; so compact and neat it could almost be a purpose-designed television studio.

'It looks so much better than the other places you've been looking at. And Christiane! What a character, the audience back home will simply fall in love with her!'

'Charlie, I don't care about what it looks like through the end of a lens. It has to be perfect for the naked eye.'

'Claudio and I can light it for you, we'll make it look sensational.'

Now this is a good idea. Claudio has a wide range of lights for television filming stored up at the house in Largentière, and both he and Charlie of course are experienced lighting cameramen. With a few strategically positioned *blondes* and *redheads* (as they're known in the trade) to give pools of colour across the terrace after dark, Le Relais Fleuri could look stunning.

In a way, though, I am pleased for Charlie that the project is at last progressing. He has a very low boredom threshold and, despite booking him into the Oxygym in Aubenas and bringing him along to swim with me in Vals, I've been growing increasingly concerned that he'll lose interest and enthusiasm if there are no developments.

Today's filming has left him in a very good humour. We all celebrate with a big dinner at Mme Bossi's hotel. Charlie orders three starters and two main courses, which he instructs the waiter should all be brought simultaneously. He doesn't appear to have an ounce of fat on his toned, muscular body, presumably because he burns up so many calories with sport. He is the ultimate rugby fanatic and announces he's already started his mental preparations for England's bid in the Rugby World Cup in November – seven months away. This amuses Claudio, but it doesn't surprise me.

We were filming in France a couple of years ago when England were due to play an historic match against Australia at Twickenham. Charlie spent days trying to find a hotel with satellite television so he could watch the match live. He'd announced weeks in advance that he would be unavailable for filming the day of the big match, and that he'd have to allow time in the days running up to it for mental preparations – quite what these involved he never really made clear. The game wasn't due to start until about 4 p.m. so I said to Charlie that maybe we could do a little filming in the morning and he was horrified. 'The morning,' he explained, 'must be set aside for *physical preparations for the match.*' This apparently involved cross-country running, press-ups and deep-breathing exercises followed by a stint of meditation and self-hypnosis in which he would focus his entire mind on an England victory.

'Charlie, you're only watching the game on television, you're not playing in it.'

Charlie is the most easy-going of guys but on this one topic he's not to be trifled with.

'If you say *"it's only a game"* to me ever again,' he said, his eyes flashing in anger, 'I might not be responsible for my actions!'

I'd never before seen him even remotely upset or ruffled by anyone or anything – his placidity is a most unusual characteristic in his line of work – but on this occasion I decided it might be wiser to keep silent.

When England finally won the historic match in the closing seconds, Charlie went completely berserk, running up and down the four-storey staircase over and over again, bellowing at the top of his lungs, much to the bemusement of the other guests in the hotel.

Reza has agreed to come over right away to see Christiane Tochou's restaurant. I have absolutely no doubt he'll love it.

～ 29 APRIL ～

This morning I enjoyed what some would argue was a truly telepathic experience. Also rather disturbing.

I've started to do yoga exercises when I get out of bed each morning in an effort to prevent a recurrence of a prolapsed disc in the lower spine, which left me unable to walk for three weeks, a year ago. I was terrified at the time that I would never walk again. It took me half an hour just to crawl to the bathroom, leaving plenty of time en route to consider the fragility of my own mortality. Sobering.

My consultant had announced gloomily that it would take up to ten years for the damage to the spine to be repaired in full, and in the meantime I should make a real effort to keep my back as mobile as possible.

I've noticed a few twinges of pain in the last week or two and with time on my hands and the weather improving week by week, I've resolved to swim every day as soon as the splendid outdoor pool at Vals reopens after the winter, and stretch and bend like a newly awakened cat out on the terrace, so that whilst exercising I can watch the long fingers of the glorious dawn sun creep across the valley and reach out towards the cherry orchard below the house.

I've never quite got to grips with the mental exercises yoga promotes, so I've invented my own technique to cleanse the mind of the current stresses and strains I am subjecting it to. As I breathe deep and throw my complaining limbs into a series of prescribed contortions beneath the translucent Mediterranean sky, I instruct my brain to wander at will through the byways of my memory, stopping at random to consider, reflect, relive, savour or reconstruct any event it chooses, providing it bears no relation whatsoever to the pressures of the present day.

Which is why, this morning, I came to dwell on the subject of Sally Ann.

I met her last year in the bar of a West End theatre during the interval of a particularly dreary musical. My son Tom and I were just getting stuck into a couple of hefty gin and tonics, bemoaning the performance, when I suddenly noticed beside me a startling-looking girl, with striking blue eyes and a short mop of blonde hair, in animated conversation with a friend on the same sad subject. Our eyes met for a moment, during which I felt that unforgettable frisson of connection that I have only ever experienced once or twice in my lifetime (although dozens of times, of course, in Hollywood movies) and which is the instant flicker of realization that *I could love this person*. It's an utterly compelling, yet strangely dispassionate sensation, like the certainty of an algebraic formula or chemical reaction.

She asked me if I agreed with her assessment of the musical, and I said that indeed I did. We chatted for a few moments and then suddenly she and her friend had disappeared into the throng.

Tom and I finished our drinks and when the three-minute bell went to tell us to return to our seats, we decided we couldn't face any more pain and bailed out. We left the theatre and in the wet darkness of the street outside I saw Sally Ann and her friend hurrying away, having clearly come to the same decision.

I ran across, stopped her and said I'd love to hear more about her views on the state of musical theatre in England today (OK, not very inspired, but time was short) and gave her my email address. A week later she contacted me, there was a brief exchange of bizarre emails, the last of which included her phone number. We met for a drink, went out on a few dates and then I went to France and met Celine. Just ships passing in the night.

So there I was this morning, touching my toes, in the glowing and growing warmth of the sun rising over Les Fabres, when my brain elects to summon up an image of Sally Ann in the shadows of a wet winter night in London, and I hold it and ponder on the fate of its owner, and on what may have been, when suddenly the phone rings and Sally Ann's voice is on the other end of the line.

'Hello, gorgeous! How are you?' Despite it being a bad line I recognized the voice immediately. It's just one of those voices.

'This can't be the wonderful Sally Ann?' say I. 'How extraordinary, I was just thinking—'

'How about a late lunch on Thursday, after I finish my shift at the BBC?' In between acting jobs, Sally Ann does temp work on various radio productions at Broadcasting House. 'There's a new little Italian on Mortimer Street which you'd love!'

'But Sal, I can't – I'm in the south of France.'

There was a long silence.

'Is that you, Simon?'

'Sal, it's Nigel.' And then, just in case, I add: 'Farrell.'

'Well, how simply bizarre, I didn't mean to call you at all,' she said, after a time. 'How the devil are you anyway?'

Now young Sal is not only unusually good company, with a fast, witty mind and a slightly raucous but highly infectious laugh (like one of those fearlessly dynamic young debs in a Wodehouse novel), she's also a real ball of energy. It turns out that she's growing bored with her present BBC job and with no acting in prospect, she is clearly at a loose end. I told her all about Le Relais Fleuri.

'If you ever need any help getting it organized give me a ring and if I'm free I'll lend a hand,' she said. 'Providing the food really is as good as you say.'

'Sal, that's a wonderful idea!'

'You know, I've done quite a lot of bar and restaurant work while waiting for the big call from Hollywood.'

It is good to hear her voice again. I don't know whether she's serious but I shall certainly call her when the time is ready.

We're going to need all the help we can get.

∽ 3 MAY ∽

Disaster! Dame Fortune is playing cruel jokes: Reza thinks Le Relais Fleuri could never work and wants to fly straight back to London.

It had all started so well. I picked him up from the airport and we drove straight to Laurac. I could tell by the look on his face he was enchanted by the terrace of Le Relais Fleuri, and within a few seconds of entering the restaurant itself, his experienced eyes were flashing and darting to every corner, shelf and cupboard to assess its potential. When Christiane appeared, full of hugs and smiles and laughter, in my mind the deal was as good as done. I'd rarely seen two people get on so well so quickly. They were like a pair of young lovers, flirting, teasing, laughing, in complete synchrony, incessantly touching, holding, kissing each other. For the first time in the four years I've known him, even Manu looked slightly embarrassed, but he quickly recovered his composure and in very Manu-esque style asked how long it would be until he had to address Reza as *'Papa'*. It was a truly happy moment, and no one was happier than me.

Then Christiane took Reza into the kitchen. Instantly the mood changed.

Even I have realized the *cuisine* is rather on the small side. It is minimally equipped and, because of the peculiarly triangular shape of the place, I suppose it does feel slightly like being rammed into the tiny fore cabin in the bow of a very modestly sized yacht – particularly if Christiane is already in there ahead of you.

But I'd been so swept along by the simple and exhilarating joy of the previous ten minutes that it had never entered my mind he'd turn the whole project down.

He was too polite to say so in front of the Tochous, of course, but whilst they appeared to be popping a cork in celebration of our potentially successful partnership, Reza took me out on the terrace, shaking his head slowly. He'd spent twenty-five years carving out a reputation with a highly regarded restaurant in London, and he wasn't about to throw it all away on a kitchen that may just be useful on a small camp for Boy Scouts equipped with army survival rations, but couldn't physically accommodate even the tiniest of tandoori ovens.

REZA: I just couldn't wait to get on the phone to Zee. She couldn't believe ANYONE could ask ME to work in a kitchen that SMALL. I like Nigel, I admire his creativity and ambition, and I find him quite amusing, but you couldn't swing a chapati in this place. I know of course he has no experience in the food world but even so I can't believe ANYONE in their right mind could consider turning this place into an Indian restaurant. I don't think he's even looked in the kitchen. For starters we'd have to limit the menu severely just to suit the kitchen. Zee says the problem is a) Nigel knows and likes the Tochous, and wants to do them a favour, a very dodgy starting point for any business, which he could and should be aware of, and b) he regards all this as a bit of a game. Zee says this is an approach not recommended by the Harvard Business School.

But then I don't want to just abandon him, like a young puppy frolicking on the edge of Beachy Head. He says there is nowhere else; he's seen every other available place, that this is our only option.

Reza and I had been in heated discussion about all this, outside on the terrace, and I was furious to discover that Charlie had filmed the whole episode through the glass window of the door to the dining area.

The problem with wearing a radio mike all the time is that you forget it's on.

'Charlie, there is no way I will agree to you using that material. That was a private discussion between Reza and me. If people see it they'll think how unprofessional we are.'

'Hmm?'

'I don't want you to use it.'

'Farrell, don't you understand this is great stuff? This is *real* life. Don't you understand that the people will associate with you; they will sympathize with you and thereby be drawn into the story. These are the kind of arguments that everybody has every day of their lives. Do you want to sterilize my programme? Do you want to neuter it? Let me edit it into the programme and then we can make a decision.'

Charlie's clearly feeling very chipper about the material he's getting. I overhear him on the phone to his girlfriend up at Les Fabres; with his usual unbounded exuberance, he's telling Katie he's sure the series will *press all the right buttons* with viewers in England and could pick up a big audience.

Charlie's personal life at last seems to have settled down after several turbulent years and numerous girlfriends, and I've never been more glad of that than now; this isn't really the moment to be dealing with yet another of Charlie's personal crises. When you are working with people on location you get to know them pretty well indeed.

A few years ago, Charlie started to tell me about the rocky patch he'd entered in his relationship with the then girlfriend, Anna. Each evening in the pub he'd lament about the woes that he was going through, and constantly ask my advice as to what he should do next. It was clear he thought things had run their course with Anna and what he really wanted to do was to split up. But this wasn't a discussion I wanted to become involved in.

'Come on, Farrell, what do you think I should do? I badly need some advice.' This was a question he asked almost every time the subject came up.

'Charlie, I've made a complete horlicks of my personal life, there's no way I'm going to give advice on matters of the heart to you or anyone else.'

Every night we would ritually go through the same exchange, Charlie insisting that I must be able to form an opinion on the evidence he provided; me equally resolute in not wanting to get involved.

Back in the office, when filming was over, his quest for my advice as to what he should do continued relentlessly.

'Farrell, just answer this simple question: if you were in my shoes what would you do now?'

I was so bored and irritated by this stage that I cracked.

'Oh for God's sake, Charlie, if I were in your shoes, I'd dump her. Now I'm going for a pint, so don't ask me again.'

The next morning in the office Charlie gave me a wink, walked over and said: 'I've taken your advice.'

'What advice?'

'I told Anna last night that you thought I should dump her.'

'What?!'

I was horrified. I knew Anna quite well.

'So I have.'

'What?'

'Dumped her.'

So thank heavens he's not putting me through all that again.

'I've had an idea,' says Charlie when he comes off the phone. 'About Reza. To get him round to the idea of Le Relais Fleuri. You've got to charm him. You've got to make him fall in love with the area, with the Ardèche, then he'll change his mind.'

Maybe there's some merit in being miked all day after all, with Charlie and Claudio – like a silent invisible pair of M15 operatives – listening to every word that's being spoken. After all, three minds are better than one. And Charlie's idea is a great one.

~ 4 MAY ~

Not that he's aware of it, but following Charlie's advice I am indeed organizing a massive charm offensive on Reza.

It's curious how perverse life can be. The tougher this project becomes the more determined I am to achieve it. I know I have a reservoir of strength, ambition and will somewhere deep inside me, but more often that not it's difficult to locate, and even harder to tap in to. But I feel it now, chafing, pulsating, exhilarating, impossible to ignore. I sense Reza will be won over in the face of a really focused and powerful onslaught.

My campaign got off to a dodgy start. Reza's agreed to stay on as planned for a couple of days so this evening I took him up to the house at Les Fabres. Nothing was right. He thought the view from the winding little road up was ruined by the smoke from the glass factory down in Vals. Les Fabres is too remote. It's too quiet. Too close to the neighbours. On the wrong axis, no sun after noon.

I know Reza's a city boy but he seems genuinely surprised that we are on mains electricity and water, he expected it to be much more primitive, which I find slightly insulting. It's a pity, he said, we hadn't renovated more of the original stone walls. He hates plasterboard. So do I, said I, but it's cheap. Yes, says he, it looks it.

The wooden staircase, which I took such pride in when it was installed and which I still consider to be a minor miracle of engineering, he decided would have looked much smarter in wrought iron. The windows are in the wrong place, the frosted glass looks tacky, the view from the terrace spoilt by the overhead power lines, and that from the main bedroom by the telephone lines. Nippi's framed woodblock images of Indian life, which he had so proudly and so meticulously positioned around the bedroom walls, were in appalling taste, the decorating in the upstairs bathroom was just too ghastly, and the whole place reeks of damp.

Could I really work with a guy like this?

Slightly more encouraging was a quick meal with Roget and Joel at

La Clementine. Reza is razor thin and has been told by his doctor he must put on weight, but he only managed half the Clementine salad – local cheese, olives, diced tomatoes and a selection of chopped meats from the mountains. I assumed that Rez, being a *gourmand*, would be sniffy about the meal, but he praised its simplicity – it turns out he's not a food snob at all. I ordered a bottle of white Louis Latour, which has become standard fare in most restaurants around here. When the Chardonnay grape was introduced to the area a few years ago it was found to thrive in the local soil, producing a cheap and deliciously dry wine which has made small fortunes for the local farmers previously struggling on a crop fit only for the production of industrial vinegar. Reza announced that he never drank alcohol, then proceeded to consume most of the bottle, ending the evening in a seamless sequence of chortles, giggles and high-pitched laughter which left his eyes running with tears, and his poor asthmatic chest gasping for air.

He certainly is a bundle of contradictions.

He's also completely cool and unfazed by the presence of Charlie and Claudio constantly lurking in the background with their cameras, which is just as well because Charlie thinks Reza is an *absolute star*.

REZA: Oh Lordy, may the saints preserve us! Nigel was so po-faced and pompous showing me around his house, he looked like a slightly seedy estate agent from the Home Counties. I just could not resist teasing him about the place, it was hilarious. He's so deliciously gullible. I actually rather like the house at Les Fabres. I admire the guts it took Nigel and Nippi to transform what was a ruin carved out of the rock face into what is now clearly a spacious, cool, unusual and a rather pleasant house. They seem to have had a ridiculously low budget and an almost complete ignorance of the language and local customs.

Zee and I had a right old giggle over Nigel's transparent attempts to charm me into liking the place. I certainly haven't told him, but

*he really doesn't need to bother – on first glance it's just enchanting!
Zee and I have only ever been to France once before, to Paris, so Zee
says I should try to appreciate the 'raw and brutal' beauty of the
Ardèche landscape described in the guidebooks. Not hard to do, it
takes the breath away. The Tochous are a SHEER delight. Manu is
unique, a real find. Charlie and Claudio make it all fun, too. I'm
enjoying myself. The only obstacle to my delight at the visit is the
continuing doubts about the minuscule little kitchen at Le Relais
Fleuri. Quel horreur!!!!*

~ 5 MAY ~

Poor Reza's had a dreadful, sleepless night, endlessly wheezing and
spluttering through what he describes as a sea of dust and bedbugs in the
downstairs bedroom, followed by a shower which has flooded his en suite
bathroom and formed an impressive sea of bubbles and foam right across
the kitchen floor. He seems surprisingly stoical in the face of such adversity,
though, and cheers up after a modest petit déjeuner on a sun-bathed
terrace based on my only two, vital concessions to English life, Tetley's tea
and Marmite.

Manu has nobly agreed to take Reza on a charm-offensive tour of the
gastronomic as well as geographic highlights of the region, ending at
Madeline, a wonderful restaurant overlooking Largentière, converted from
a fourteenth-century goat farm and specializing in superb goat's cheese
dishes, whilst Celine drives me upriver in her racy little two-seater Peugeot
for a drink at La Beaume, where early groups of tourists are already basking
on the rocks like Mexican lizards or even dipping hesitant, pale limbs
into the chilly waters of the Ardèche itself.

Celine has been working seven days a week opening up her new
mortgage and insurance office in Montélimar, but despite having seen
so little of each other in recent weeks, she seems genuinely caring and
loving and insists, much to my silent gratification, on holding my hand as

we walk across the low stone bridge towards the two identical little restaurants that sit side by side in apparent rivalry beneath the ubiquitous plane trees, and which, curiously, turn out to be owned by the same family.

I explain to Celine that everything now depends on Reza. If I really can't win him around to Le Relais Fleuri the BI is effectively dead. I then take a deep breath and say the words that have been circling ominously around my mind over the last few days like gathering vultures.

'This is my final option, *chérie* . . . if Reza says no, I am lost. I may have to give up and return to England.'

Celine then said almost exactly what I had known she would in the endless mental rehearsals with which I had been preparing myself for this scene.

'You know I can't come with you to England, darling. Quentin, my work. . .' Her words trailed off in an unspoken mutual understanding.

Oddly, it feels better now it's been said, out loud, in the warm, damp air beside the river at beautiful La Beaume.

～ 6 MAY ～

I have passed most of the day afloat on a sea of adrenalin and exhilaration.

Reza had a *simply divine* day with Manu yesterday and at noon today he announces that he has made up his mind about what to do, and says he'll take me out for an early supper to discuss his decision. I know immediately from his mischievous grin that my unswerving belief in the future of the BI has paid dividends. I have to suppress a surge of excitement to get started right away on all the practical details involved in starting work on Le Relais Fleuri. Clearly, though, Reza must be allowed his little moment of triumph.

Over a plate of fleshy, pink *crevettes* in oil and garlic, and a bottle of house red, my hero and saviour explained his reasons for the change in mind. It's not been easy to rationalize these, but on reflection I think they are broadly as follows, though possibly not in any order of importance:

a. Reza clearly relishes an adventure and is intrigued by the challenge of selling a new concept to a sceptical populace.
b. Reza has decided that because the locals know nothing of Indian cuisine the menu could be small and very simple and therefore he could learn to live with a tiny kitchen.
c. Reza finds the Tochous *adorable*.
d. Reza seems to find me hugely amusing and thinks the project could be *hilarious*.

After supper we drive straight over to Le Relais Fleuri and announce the news to Christiane, who does a short but unbelievably energetic tango around the terrace of the restaurant in the arms of Reza before opening a bottle of champagne and going upstairs to find JB. Christiane is like a schoolgirl, grinning with excitement at the prospect of such an unpredictable and bizarre summer ahead. JB eventually appears, bleary-eyed and grumpy, but after a glass or two of bubbles he too begins to smile.

'Monsieur Nigel!' he says, and such is his stature and authority that all fall silent. '*C'est vraiment des bonnes nouvelles! Santé!* And, Monsieur Nigel, one more thing?'

We wait in silence. After several more swigs, the big man eventually continues.

'After much thought I have arrived at an important decision. It is not the kind of decision reached lightly.'

Another swig. Like so many Frenchmen I have met, Monsieur Tochou has an innate sense of melodrama.

'I have decided that you may now call me *Jean-Bernard*.'

There was a short, stifled gasp from the assembled company.

I had finally made it. And I've known him only three years.

REZA: Sometimes, heaven knows, despite one's better judgement, one simply HAS to just go with the flow! I am quite overwhelmed by everyone's enthusiasm to make the project work. Nigel has turned out to be one of those guys who, once he gets the bit between his teeth, just won't let go – and I admire that. And of course it will be fun. Apart from the risibly small kitchen my one major concern is Nigel's total inexperience, but in this I have found an important reassurance. During my sanity-saving midnight calls to Zee in London, she pointed out that the locals hold Christiane Tochou in high esteem and that Le Relais Fleuri is a well-known and highly regarded established restaurant, which could save the day whatever. And she is SOOOO right! For instance, I was amazed to meet a Dutch couple on holiday in the restaurant last night who have been coming to Le Relais every single blessed summer for the last twenty years solely because of Christiane, her food, her personality, her aura in the place. If she really is prepared to stay on as a paid consultant and see us through the first turbulent weeks of the transformation, I know I could in time return to London and let Nigel and her get on with it in some confidence. Zee agrees absolutely. Providing it's been set up properly. Providing we can find the finance. Providing we can staff it. Providing the French take to the food.

I must be COMPLETELY insane.

∼ 7 MAY ∼

On the way to the airport, Reza – who rather irritatingly is apparently not suffering a hangover – is for once deadly earnest. I am quite shocked.

There must be clear and unequivocal agreement between us. Reza will do all he can to help set up the restaurant, and will use his expertise to find chefs and devise and source the menu. He will be in charge of transforming the *décor* of Le Relais. He will share any financial investment required, providing he agrees the figures. It will be a fifty-fifty partnership and the agreed sum we will each put in is £10,000. He will remain in France until confident the new venture is working, but then must return to his real life in London and his restaurant, the Star of India. He will make short trips to Laurac to advise and help throughout the summer as and when necessary. If there are any profits, we will share them equally, but he won't be holding his breath.

I'll do everything else.

Do I agree?

He is so focused and confident that suddenly I understand why the Star of India is one of the most successful Indian restaurants in Britain.

Of course I agree, of course, of course, of course. I will live in France, I will manage the place, I will run everything, I will work twenty-four hours a day, seven days a week, I will do anything and everything to make it a success.

All agreed on the simple shake of a hand. I am starting a new life.

REZA: Oh God, what have I done?

⌒ 8 MAY ⌒

Basking in the after-glow of achievement. After yoga on the terrace and a Marmite baguette, I'm glowing physically, too. The sun is shining, as it always is when I feel like this.

Eventually managed to get hold of Celine on the phone last night and, just to add icing to the cake, she seems genuinely relieved and happy. This must mean she really does want me to stay on. She then rather spoils things by firing off a series of detailed questions about the restaurant costs, and I say I don't really have much clue and she says the project sounds doomed already, and laughs for a moment or two longer than she should.

Well, she is a mortgage broker. And she has a point.

Have a strong urge to phone Sally Ann but decide it's too early and I must wait until I have firmed up a few more details.

Over an enormous lunch of mussels in garlic and local pork sausage, it's down to business with the Tochous, including Manu, with a vengeance.

Eventually we hammer out what could form the basis of a reasonable deal, but I'll clearly need to check out everything with Reza.

We will rent Le Relais Fleuri for a trial period of four months – June, July, August and September. At the end of September we can either renew the contract for the winter, if things are going brilliantly, or hand the place back to the Tochous with an option to reopen next spring. We will pay 2,000 Euros a month for the building – that's about £1,400 – and 600 Euros a month (£420) for the little flat above the Tochous' apartment. We are committed to paying this even if the idea's a disaster and we have to close. We will redecorate and re-equip the place and do everything required to convert it into an Indian restaurant. Christiane Tochou will stay on to help us with the transformation, and we will pay her a consultancy fee. The current French chef will leave, to be replaced by an Indian chef, who we will find. Ramsa, Christiane's beautiful young North African waitress, who we will find will look splendid in Indian costume, has agreed to stay on. I will be *maître d'* and manage the place. Even though the restaurant is only forty covers, we will probably need another pair of hands to help with the waiting. They would like to hand over Le Relais Fleuri to us at the beginning of next month.

It really is going to happen. I feel dizzy. I look around for Charlie and Claudio. If ever there's a moment I would like to be interviewed, this is it; but they seem to have become bored by a sequence of four people sitting around a table exchanging figures, and wandered off. This is odd; surely this is the key to the main story? Don't people want to know the principal details?

JB is very much in charge of negotiations. Christiane may run the restaurant (in a charmingly haphazard and disorganized way – the table where she sits making reservations and sorting out the bills is a mountain of hundreds of little pieces of paper with endless hieroglyphics and long lists of figures scribbled all over them) but it's very clear that her husband runs the business and, eschewing his normal uncompromisingly Franco-macho stance, is charmingly protective about Christiane and her interests in every aspect of the discussion. Even with Manu translating for JB's benefit, we talk for at least three hours. JB speaks no English whatsoever, and my French is just about sufficient to exchange basic concepts with him, and maybe share a joke – strangely, humour seems the easiest universal emotion to translate. But a complicated business transaction is rather more challenging. Each phrase or sentence must be explained, queried, translated, explained again.

It suddenly reminds me of a Mediterranean cruise ship I did a feature about a few years ago, with a passenger complement made up of at least a dozen different nationalities. On most evenings, the cabaret consisted of a smoochy singer and a four-piece band, but on one mad night, the entertainments officer had an aberration and decided to hire a comedian, who had to tell each joke in English, then French, Italian, Spanish and finally German, so that each group would laugh one after the other (except the Germans, who remained stone-faced throughout), which for the first ten minutes was considerably more amusing than the show itself. We ended up sitting there from ten in the evening until about three o'clock in the morning.

Call Reza, but irritatingly had to leave a message. Once again my fate hangs on his whim.

Celine thought the figures sounded good, but she, like me, knows nothing about the catering industry. But she did add how pleased and relieved she is that I am beginning to take control over my own life, and I am reluctantly forced to agree.

Played 'I Am a Rover' better than ever, before going to bed. Must get piano tuned now I'm on the verge of becoming a multi-millionaire.

~ 9 MAY ~

Surprisingly, Reza seems quite excited by the deal I've brokered.

We've divided the tasks. Reza will find a chef, organize the re-equipment, and oversee the redecoration. I'll do the rest. He says he's already started on the retail therapy and is doing rather well! I'm impressed by how fast he moves.

There's one gnawing problem. The season's well underway. The Ardèche is gradually filling up with tourists with money in their pockets and empty bellies. They come in their thousands from all over France, from Germany, Holland and Belgium, drawn year after year by the hypnotic charm of the mountains, to walk or swim or pursue that uniquely French obsession with the bicycle, to abseil, hang-glide or bungee-jump down the endless fault-lines of limestone cliffs that throw themselves skywards all around us.

I had originally planned to open a restaurant with Nippi in time to catch the Easter trade. It's now May. According to the Tochous, the earliest we can take over Le Relais Fleuri is Monday, 2 June – and even that depends on the notoriously pedantic French lawyers moving a little faster than a snail's pace. Presumably it will take several weeks to redecorate so at best we'll open mid-July.

The season is effectively over with the departure of the grape pickers by the end of September.

Marcel Carbenero, who's erecting a series of concrete pillars on the terrace outside Reza's bedroom window downstairs, invites me over for a *pastis* or six. Elise fusses about with nuts and olives and *petits oignons*, unable to sit for a moment. As always, the serious talking is left to the men. Marcel's been considering our restaurant. He says it'll be a disaster. The Ardèchoise are perverse; they will come once, so we will think it's a success, and then they'll never return. They'll never allow an outsider like me to triumph. I should abort now.

And he should know. He's from Marseilles.

~ *10 MAY* ~

Time for a serious reassessment of my financial landscape.

This is a predictably dreary journey I know I hate to make and which I have postponed for as long as I can, but I will endeavour to view it like a trip to the dentist, something that has to be done only to spare pain and anguish in the future.

Need to somehow come up now with my half of the money.

Manu arrived to value the house this morning, as usual bouncing around full of boyish enthusiasm for the project in hand, making wildly optimistic declarations of the huge prosperity that lies ahead for us all, and suggesting we begin by opening a bottle of Chardonnay, which, since it's already well past 10 a.m., I am only too glad to do.

FACTS:

Nippi and Nigel's original and naively low budget to buy and renovate a holiday house in France:	£30,000
Cost of purchasing ruined house at Les Fabres:	£15,000
Nippi and Nigel's estimated cost of renovation:	£15,000
Actual cost of renovation:	£65,000
Shortfall:	£50,000
(*Somehow Nippi and I managed to scrape this together, but Nippi has a bigger shovel than me so he did most of the scraping*)	
Total cost of project:	**£80,000**

Now I'm no accountant, but the words *'business plan'* were clearly nowhere to be seen during the entire enterprise outlined above; this is an omission I plainly cannot afford to make second time around.

Manu wandered around for a bit scratching his bald pate, made a few token measurements, then disappeared next door for a long discussion with Marcel Carbenero.

When eventually he returned, smelling strongly of *pastis*, he announced that he was confident he could get £110,000 for our house – a possible profit of £30,000.

'This is unusual for France,' he said. 'But as you know, prices on the Côte d'Azur and Provence are sky high, so they are rocketing here too . . .'

We opened another bottle of Chardonnay, whereupon Manu announced once again that if we ever wanted to sell, he would waive any commission on the sale of Les Fabres, just as he'd waived all his charges on its purchase. Manu apparently offers this to most of his clients, which is why he's permanently broke, living in a tiny one-bedroom flat with Olivia and driving around in a battered old Rover with no back seats and a constantly exploding exhaust, so you can hear him driving up the valley from Vals long before he hoves into view.

'So I can borrow money against the house?'

'You need to ask your girlfriend,' said Manu, with a grin. 'How much are we talking?'

'Ten thousand pounds?'

'Of course! There'll be no problem. And if there is a problem, there'll still be no problem, because she loves me, baby! And she loves you!'

'Does she?'

'That's what she says.'

Resolve that on balance it's probably wise not to mention the loan to Nippi.

REZA: Ooh la la! Having another crisis of confidence! Still losing weight. I'm down to nine and a half stone. Zee is convinced more than ever that Nigel hasn't the slightest idea of what he's doing; she says I really need to be out there supervising what's going on. God knows what he's up to on his own! And all this being recorded for posterity by Charlie – he must be mad! But I can't do a thing until I find a chef, and that's proving a problem. Much harder than I thought. Oh, tripetti-dee! Many of the Indians I've approached seem nervous, even slightly frightened of moving to France, which they see as a bit of an alien culture. And it's hard for me to leave the Star for long periods. Business is down, particularly at lunchtimes; Zee says many of the City people just can't afford to come out west as they used to. In the last few months, several good friends in the restaurant business in London have gone bust. It's just a tragedy! This is probably the worst moment to be investing £10,000 in a new restaurant venture, but I guess I'm committed, or should be.

Bought some heavenly pink silk shirts at Harvey Nicks. Charlie says pink will look great on me for the programme.

~ 13 MAY ~

Who says France is a bureaucratic nightmare?

Within just twenty-four hours of our discussion, the Tochous' *notaire* has drawn up a contract. Through my old office in London I found Marie, a bilingual lawyer in Lyons, so today I was invited to the restaurant for champagne, a formal signing session, and an unfeasibly large lunch with the whole family to celebrate this momentous occasion. From 2nd June I am to be the new *propriétaire* of Le Relais Fleuri. Or rather, as it states boldly on the contract, *L'Été Indien au Relais Fleuri*.

It was a week or so ago that Manu had the brainwave for the new name for the restaurant.

'Why don't you call the restaurant "L'Été Indien" – the Indian Summer? L'Été Indien au Relais Fleuri.'

This is an inspired idea. It means we can utilize the original name and hold on to the interest of Christiane's large number of existing customers by simply plonking the temporary and very seasonal words *L'Été Indien* above any signage that's already in place. Sheer genius. Fantastic, brilliant, gloriously wonderful genius. And now here it is, in print, in a legal document. L'Été Indien really exists.

JB staggers upstairs for his siesta. The rest of us, half-comatose already, find dark cool corners of the restaurant and, like a posse of over-fed cats, curl up in balls and are instantly asleep.

I sense the next few months aren't always going to be so luxurious, so best enjoy *la belle vie* whilst I can.

∾ 14 May ∾

A dilemma.

Sally Ann.

I want to phone her but I'm confused by my motives. Did I mention Celine to her? My memory fails me, but I suspect I did not. Is she really serious about coming out to help in the restaurant? If so, why?

But I need help and maybe Sally Ann can provide it.

Oddly, I'm nervous dialling her number.

'How ya doing, Freckles?' she says, in that typically hearty way of hers (dizzy toff gall endlessly trying to hook a rich bachelor friend of Bertie Wooster).

I tell her it's all going spiffingly, and that we take over the restaurant in just over two and a half weeks' time.

'It's a tense but gripping plot, SA. With lots of romance.'

'Romance?'

'Did I mention my girlfriend, Celine? Late twenties, divorced with young son, works for a very successful mortgage and insurance company in Aubenas. Strange taste in clothes but very glam.'

Quite a long pause.

'How long have you been going out?'

'Best part of a year.'

Another pause.

'You old rogue.'

'Do you disapprove?'

'Why on earth would I disapprove? Good for you, Freckles, just look after the heart. Do you still want me to come out? I'd love to meet her.'

So it's settled. I'm collecting Sally Ann from the Eurostar train at Montélimar a week today.

It'll be bizarre and wonderful to see her again.

Charlie seems gripped. 'Two girls? Fantastic! You can never have too much love interest. Jealousy. Victory. Rejection. Brilliant. What's Sally Ann like?'

'Attractive.'

'Did you say attractive?'

'Charlie, she's lovely. But it's not like that. We went out together for a short time. And she's great to have around. But I'm not available, and for all I know she's not either.'

'For the moment.'

'What do you mean?'

'Just joking.'

Have stern words with Charlie. He's in mortal danger of overstepping the mark. If there's any suggestion SA is anything other than an old mate who's here to lend a hand, I'll withdraw all cooperation. It would look dreadful, not only for Celine, but also for me: I'd come over as an ageing Lothario.

'You underestimate me, Farrell. I'd never do that,' he protested.

'Oh no?'

'Listen. Whatever else happens, however the restaurant fares, it is essential one thing remains constant: the viewer *must* sympathize with you. If you lose their sympathy, even for a moment, I don't have a programme.'

No news from Reza about a chef. If he can't find a chef, I don't have a restaurant.

∼ 15 MAY ∼

Of course, France really is a bureaucratic nightmare.

I've spent most of the day with Christiane Tochou, squashed into the restaurant's old white battered Peugeot van that Manu, thoughts of alcohol never far from his mind, has wittily nicknamed *Vin Blanc*. When I formally take over the restaurant at the beginning of June I must also take responsibility for all the utilities, so the first stop is the local office of EDF, the state electricity company, which is closed because all its employees are on strike. Next stop, the Hôtel de Ville in the wonderful château at the top of Aubenas, for what Christiane says is a vital document before I can begin trading: the *carte de séjour*.

'Sort of a work permit,' Christiane explains.

'But I don't need a work permit. Britain's a fully paid-up member of the European Union.'

'Really? I thought you British people didn't want to join up.'

'That's the Euro. But we've been members of the EU since 1973.'

'I didn't know that. But you will still need a *carte de séjour* anyway.'

This exchange reminds me again how utterly irrelevant Britain is to people living in this part of the world. For example, I'd assumed that all French schoolchildren visit England at least once, in the same way that all British kids visit France. But in fact that applies only to children in the north of the country. To people like Christiane, it's Spain, Italy and even North Africa that are close neighbours – ours is just a faraway island which matters not one bit. On one of my earlier trips I told Celine I'd just flown in from Heathrow and she had actually said: 'Where's that?'

We stagger up two huge sets of stone staircases inside the château. It amazes me that this ancient, lovely building, which would make a fantastic set for a re-shoot of *The Three Musketeers*, is still a working office. We tap on the glass window of the office's front desk and a tall man with a large black beard appears and asks us to wait a minute. We wait nearly half an hour, then the beard reappears and goes through a list of documents which Christiane helped me prepare for my *carte de séjour*, including a letter from her to me explaining the new business arrangements, and proof of my official residence at Les Fabres. These he checks most thoroughly. Then he smiles broadly.

'All is in order. Now I just need proof of your date and place of birth, M'sieur.'

'Have you brought your passport?' asks Christiane.

I've long since learned it's best to travel everywhere in France with your passport readily to hand. I produce it, and the beard scrutinizes it most closely.

'But this is not proof of your date and place of birth.'

I point out that on the last page of the passport it clearly states my date of birth, 22 January 1953; place of birth, London.

The beard shakes his head sadly.

'This is not sufficient. I need your birth certificate.'

'But I don't have my birth certificate with me, it's in England.'

'No birth certificate, no *carte de séjour*,' he says to me conclusively, closing the glass window.

'No *carte de séjour*, no restaurant' says Christiane.

I sigh, wearily. 'I'll have it sent over.'

Next stop, the Bureau de Poste. Christiane explains that before I can begin trading, a temporary change of ownership of Le Relais Fleuri must be officially registered at the Chamber of Commerce. For this we need two forms which have to be filled in and paid for at the post office. It's only a short walk from the château but it takes us a very long time to get there because Christiane, the big-hearted personality with the most beautiful smile in the Ardèche and the proud owner of one of the area's truly delicious restaurants, is something of a local celebrity. Everyone knows Christiane; she's virtually mobbed by friends and acquaintances, anxious to exchange news and family stories. At last we make it to the post office where we join a long queue, which is just great for Christiane as she is able to catch up with all the gossip, but pretty damned dull for me. Just as we get to the front of the queue Christiane suddenly realizes that she's left her handbag at the Hôtel de Ville. So we rush back to the beard, who smilingly hands it over, and then rejoin the back of the queue at the Bureau de Poste.

'You must watch me like a big bird. I always leave my bag wherever I go.'

'Like a hawk.'

'Yes, you watch me like a bird with big eyes.'

When we finally reach the front of the queue, we are served by an official with a very large head on very small shoulders, called Pierre, who Christiane knows very well, so there's quite a long exchange of pleasantries before we can get down to business. Then, after she's explained what we want, the man disappears for a moment and returns brandishing a form, which he then proceeds to fill in in very slow, large, childish handwriting.

'Name?'

The tone of voice has changed completely. Gone is the jocular friend, keen to know all the news from the restaurant. This is clearly a man at work. Important work. And even though he's known her name for years, he still makes Christiane spell it and writes it out in his agonizingly slow crawl across the paper.

'Address?'

We go through all the points on the form. At the end he stamps it, tears off the perforated edges and hands us the top copy, only to reveal a further four carbon copies beneath. The first he files in a drawer beneath the desk, the second he gives to a woman working beside him, and the third to another woman working behind him. The fourth he takes with a flourish through a mysterious-looking door at the back of the office, returning some minutes later.

'That'll be 35 Euros.' And I pay it, gladly.

Now the official transaction is complete we are best buddies again. He wants to know about JB's dyspepsia, Manu's girlfriend, and sister Isobel's little boys. Eventually Christiane says: 'Is this form all we need to re-register at the Chamber of Commerce?'

No, he explains, this is merely half the documentation required. He then disappears through the door at the back and returns some minutes later with a form that looks suspiciously like the one we've just spent twenty minutes filling out.

Unbelievably, we then go through the entire process all over again.

'Name? . . . Address? . . .' One for us, one for the drawer, one for the woman on his left, one for the woman behind, one for filing somewhere deep in the bowels of the office behind.

'That'll be 39 Euros.'

After a bit more gossip, Christiane asks: 'Do I now have everything I need?'

'Indeed you do. These two forms will be accepted by the *Chambres de Commerce* as evidence that as of 2nd June you are no longer the *propriétaire* of Le Relais Fleuri.'

'And Monsieur Farrell here?' says Christiane.

The man with the big round head looks at me for the first time in forty-five minutes.

'And the M'sieur, who precisely is he?'

'Monsieur Farrell is the new *propriétaire*.'

'The new *propriétaire*! Why didn't you say so before?'

Whereupon he disappears out the back, and eventually returns, waving a third form.

'Name? . . . Address? . . .' We go through everything all over again, but this time with my details: two sets of forms, eight duplicates. By the end of our session the patient queue of customers behind us has stretched right out of the door and into the square beyond. But nobody seems to mind.

'One final question, Pierre,' says Christiane, when at last the ordeal is over.

'Monsieur Farrell has to send a fax to London. Can we send it from here?'

The man looks me up and down with the disdain of a detective finally unmasking a much-hunted sexual deviant.

'Of course you can send a fax from here. What do you take us for? This is a Bureau de Poste!'

I pull out the paper, a modest invoice for some work I'd done for a company in London, and Pierre hands it to the woman behind him, who then proceeds to feed it into an ancient-looking fax machine.

'That'll be 60 cents.'

I hand over the coins, whereupon, for the nth time since we've arrived, Pierre disappears through the back door, only to return a few minutes later with a payment form for the fax, which bears an uncanny resemblance to the four previous ones.

'Name? . . . Address? . . .' This is almost beyond belief. Once more, all the details are painfully written down, and once the four copies have been distributed around the office in the usual way, Pierre hands me my copy with an expression of pride and slightly manic fervour spread across his enormous face.

I have it here beside me now as I write. My official French government receipt for sending a fax: 60 cents.

When we get back to Laurac and park the *Vin Blanc* in the little open garage at the back, Christiane looks at her watch and announces: 'It's *Ricard moins quart!*' This roughly translates (from Tochou-speak) as: it's quarter to twelve and time for our first *pastis* of the day. Christiane looks around her for a moment and says: 'You'll find the *Ricard* bottle in the scullery, use lots of ice. We'll have lunch as soon as I get back from Aubenas.'

'Aubenas? That's where we've just been.'

'I must have left my handbag in the post office.'

The preparation of food, along with the meticulous organization of its consumption, is the reason God put Christiane on the planet. To say she is obsessed with cooking is to do her a disservice. For her it's the only reason to get out of bed in the morning, and the only consolation in going to bed at night is that in only a few hours' time she'll be getting up again to prepare more food. At whatever the time of day, the command 'Now we eat' cannot be disobeyed. She simply ignores any protestations, however strong, before disappearing into the kitchen and emerging sometime later with a feast made up of anything she's been able to lay her hands on. It begins with a huge bowl of hot black coffee at *le petit déjeuner* and continues throughout the day virtually unchecked as friends, family, customers and even tradesmen drop by and are instantly force-fed from a plate of delicious *terrine de foie gras aux poireaux et brioche chaude* or *cassoulet au confit de canard*.

Phone my son Tom and he promises to go to the flat in Farnham tomorrow and locate the missing birth certificate.

～ 16 MAY ～

An absolute catastrophe!

Tom has searched through every file in my office cabinet, through every bookshelf, drawer and cupboard in the flat and then right through the filing cabinet again.

No birth certificate.

No birth certificate. No *carte de séjour*. No restaurant.

And I'm supposed to be taking over the restaurant in seventeen days' time.

'Fantastic,' says Charlie. 'What a drama!'

'Get stuffed, Charlie.'

Am trying hard not to panic and decide to mop the kitchen/dining room tiled floor to calm myself down and have time to ponder the consequences. Since the floor is very large, it is littered with an odd assortment of insects and flies among the dust and also, rather to my alarm, what appears to be a small scorpion, which I poked gingerly several times to ensure it really is dead. This allows quite a lot of thinking time.

Apart from a dull and dumbing disbelief that I could have actually lost the precious certificate, I have no idea whatsoever how to begin going about finding a replacement. I presume it's something that has to be done in person. A trip to London will be expensive and time-consuming. Where do I go? What proof of identity will be required? And, most worrying of all, how long will the whole process take? I can think of only one person who might conceivably be able to help me in my hour of need.

'You complete nincompoop,' says Sally Ann, when I call. 'Where, exactly, were you born?'

～ 17 MAY ～

I can't believe what's happened.

Even though we hadn't been out together for long, I was always well aware that they don't come more streetwise than Sally Ann. In between her acting and theatre jobs, SA has worked in numerous bars, restaurants, shops and on reception desks, often on appallingly low wages, yet still able to exploit the best that London has to offer by simply using her wits. Free art galleries, cheap West End theatres and cinemas, cut-price meals – if anybody on the planet could help me get a replacement birth certificate at short notice, it was Sally Ann. And that's exactly what she's done.

I was born at Guy's Hospital in the London borough of Southwark, and armed with that one fact plus the date of my birth, Sally Ann went this afternoon to the Southwark registry office and simply asked for a copy of Nigel Farrell's birth certificate. At no stage was she asked for any proof of identity either for herself or for me. She must return next Tuesday whereupon, on receipt of £7.50, the replacement certificate, signed by the registrar, will be available. She'll have it with her when I pick her up from Montélimar station on Wednesday morning.

I'm torn between eternal gratitude and incredulity at the ease with which any criminal or terrorist could have done exactly the same thing.

I explained all this to Celine, who laughed rather a lot and then asked, with her usual disarming frankness: 'Was Sally Ann your lover?'

'Why don't you see if you can guess when you meet her?' I say.

I am rather pleased by this response. The childlike side of Celine relishes playing games and Manu never fails to remind me that it is very important to keep her entertained.

～ *21 MAY* ～

Minor hurricane hits Ardèche.

The wide smile, the raucous laugh, the big, burning blue eyes – the moment I saw her walking down the platform beside the departing TGV I remembered that everything about Sally Ann is slightly larger than life. We chatted away like old mates as V*in Blanc* roared us back up to Laurac. She appears genuinely enthusiastic about L'Été Indien, which is reassuring – when Sal gets involved with anything, she gives it all she's got. She's even brought a gift: a book by Sir Terence Conran, full of tips on how to set up your own restaurant.

'I really thought you might find it quite helpful,' she said. 'Now I realize how hopelessly ill-prepared you seem for everything, maybe it's better you don't read it.'

She's hit it off immediately with Christiane, which shouldn't surprise me because they are quite similar characters with an almost identical sense of humour. Sal's arrival has suddenly brightened up the place, like the switching on of an electric light. Even JB is appearing more animated in her presence. He's constantly winking, smiling, flirting with her; and an impeccable set of manners I've never seen before has miraculously appeared. Can he really be seventy years old?

But then Sal has a *penchant* for the older man, and they for her. She's chosen never to have had a long relationship with anyone, and has certainly never married or had children, although she's never been short of admirers or boyfriends. There're fifteen years between her and me, which worried me for a while when we started going out; then one night in a pub we ran into one of her ex-boyfriends, who looked like a Chelsea Pensioner, which made me feel like a young boy. I must ask her about this sometime.

Although we don't take over Le Relais Fleuri formally until two weeks' time, the Tochous have said Sal can use the little apartment above theirs, which is ideal.

'I can certainly stay for a few weeks, maybe longer,' she said. 'It depends on how they're fixed at the BBC. I'll do anything you need me to. Pay me when and if you've got some money.' I feel buoyed up by her presence.

Good news from London. The genius Reza has located much of the equipment that we are going to need, on the cheap. Fifty oriental cut glasses, £3.50 a piece. Fifty wicker place mats trimmed in deep red, £6.50 each. Ten cupped-glass candleholders, in vivid oranges, greens and yellows, £2.75 each, which he wants to hang at different heights from the beams on the terrace on fishing hooks. Forty floral-styled fairy lights, £18. Four metallic Indian table lamps at £70 each, but Reza likes them so much he's bought them out of his own pocket and is loaning them to L'Été Indien for the duration. Best of all, he's bumped into a talented young Indian artist, with a studio in Notting Hill, who he has somehow persuaded to lend us thirty-five works of art – paintings, woodblock prints, table lamps, candleholders – all in a very modernistic Indian style, which we'll display in the restaurant with price tags for anyone interested in buying. He's even borrowed a Thai Buddha from a mate around the corner from where he lives in Chiswick. He wants to redecorate all the walls in a pale lime green, which sounds ghastly to me, but then who am I to quibble? Reza believes we can totally re-equip the restaurant, including all the new kitchen utensils we require, for less than £1,500. The man deserves an *Legion d'Honneur*.

We're keeping all the Tochous' tables and chairs and using all their crockery and cutlery. I've agreed to buy *Vin Blanc* from them for just over £2,000, which is more than I intended to spend on transport, but it's a goodwill gesture and they have agreed to buy it back from me if things go badly. Sally Ann's been included on the insurance policy. I wonder if the local French drivers know what's about to hit them.

All we need now is a chef. And with an experienced and well-known restaurateur like Reza at the helm, I'm sure this won't be a problem.

～ 24 MAY ～

Had a panic call from Reza in London, which instantly panics me too.

He can't find a chef.

We'd already discarded any notion of finding one in India on the grounds that we don't have the time or the money, and now he is struggling to find someone available in England. He'd been talking to a chef who only had an Indian passport and this will break French labour regulations. He has some friends in Paris who he is trying to contact, but almost certainly – even if he does find someone suitable – they'd have to give a month or two's notice to their current employers. It's nearly June and we are both well aware that by September the season is over. If we don't find someone damn soon our season won't even start.

After a strong *pastis* I break the news to Christiane. She's still running Le Relais Fleuri, which will remain open until we officially take over next week, but she's very conscious of the fact that her future livelihood is at stake too, as well as her formidable reputation. I know her well enough by now to know that she wouldn't be angry, but it is obvious she's worried. It is financial lunacy to keep a restaurant closed for one day more than necessary. Friends and customers have already been phoning, asking when Le Relais Fleuri would reopen after we've taken over. She is clearly embarrassed that she can't tell them what's happening. 'If you don't find someone soon I may begin to get upset,' she says in her wonderfully understated manner.

She isn't the only one.

～ 26 MAY ～

Sadly no news on the chef front, but in every other respect things are starting to move quickly. Charlie and Clouds are delighted. Lots to film.

SA and I spent several hours in the DIY store in Aubenas armed with a French dictionary trying, unsuccessfully, to make sense of the instructions on the back of the cans of undercoats and white spirit that we need to get started on the decorating. Along with brushes, cloths and tape, we've bought an all-white zip-up zoot-suit complete with elasticated hood for Sal to wear when painting, which she says makes her look like a giant sperm from Woody Allen's film *Everything You Ever Wanted To Know About Sex*. The store is called Mr Bricolage, a strange name somehow for a nation with so much disdain for the English language. Why not Monsieur Bricolage? Everywhere around us – even in this remote part of rural France – there's evidence that defiance of Anglo-American culture is slowly being eroded. A McDonald's appeared a year ago and in March a huge American-style Buffalo Grill appeared on the southern outskirts of town. No doubt some *nerd* will be opening up an Indian restaurant next.

Sal drove back from Mr Bricolage in *Vin Blanc*, and we travelled through the narrow winding lanes to Laurac averaging about 100 mph. It was a terrifying experience. Because she lives in London and doesn't need, or can't afford, a vehicle, SA has scarcely driven a car at all in the last eight years, and certainly never before on the right-hand side of the road. When we finally, miraculously, got back to Le Relais Fleuri unscathed, despite a number of potentially fatal near-misses, I asked her why on earth she had driven so fast.

'Because I was nervous,' she replied.

Now this is a curious characteristic of young Sal. Whenever she's tense or on edge about anything, she behaves completely opposite to the way most people would react. I once took her to meet my mother and aunt, both formidable ladies and products of an Edwardian marriage who expect good manners and admire polite conversation. She was so nervous she became louder than ever, drinking half a gallon of wine, shouting out appallingly rude jokes across the room, then roaring with laughter and slapping everyone on the back, ending the evening by gleefully relating to my mother a sexually explicit story which so shocked her she's never been able to repeat it to anyone, even me.

This afternoon Tom arrived at the restaurant from London, in a hired van full of Reza's acquisitions. Amidst much excitement the Tochous help Sal and me unload and unpack. Christiane is very enthusiastic about everything Reza had bought; it is all superb, perfect, wonderful. She confides in me later that she thinks the loaned paintings are a bit bizarre, and I am forced to agree. One of the bigger pictures is of a beautiful woman in traditional Indian dress sitting in the Lotus position on a rug. She's holding a German Luger revolver in one hand, and above her is the Union Jack. Baffling, but I guess quite eye-catching and very, very different to anything one would see in a traditional French restaurant. And the more I consider it, the more I'm convinced that above all we have to be *different* if we're to stand any chance of success.

I'm also aware, for the first time, that beneath all her compliments and praise for Reza's taste and ideas there's a real ambivalence in Christiane's mind about what is happening. She's handing over the product of twenty-five years of love and toil into the hands of two comparative strangers, so there really is a lot at stake for her, too. If we fail, she fails.

It's good to see Tom; he seems to have cheered up considerably since our last meeting in London. The trip seems to have given him a real shot of adrenalin.

By four o'clock we are all dripping wet in the heat of our exertions, so Christiane phones an old friend, Marie-Elise, who lives with her husband, Marcel, in a lovely old farmhouse surrounded by vineyards just past the Pompe Funèbre on the road leaving Laurac and heading out towards the old market town of Les Vans to the west. Funerals are clearly big business in France – even the smallest villages are often seen to boast their own Pompe Funèbre, which perhaps gives them a certain bizarre status in the regional hierarchy. Here, with its acres of very prominent churches and graveyards filled with hugely ornate gravestones and elaborate memorials festooned with grimly smiling photographs of its victims, death is something of which to be proud. The more I get to know France and the French, the more the huge differences with England and the English appear.

Crucially, Marie-Elise has a swimming pool.

We all pile in the back of *Vin Blanc* and soon we are being introduced to the welcoming and incredibly tanned Marie-Elise, a dark, tousle-haired woman, probably in her mid-forties but with the figure of a woman twenty years younger. This fact is not difficult to ascertain at our first meeting since she is standing there shaking our hands stark naked, but for a very modest thong. I was so taken aback by her appearance and utter lack of self-consciousness that I stood, transfixed, unable for a moment to speak or even breathe properly. This inevitably embarrassed everybody, including her, and made me, yet again, curse my wretched Englishness.

Sal hasn't swum for years and splashes about, laughing, like a young teenager on a first visit to a Mediterranean beach. Tom swims up and down with a strangely grim determination. Christiane belies her size and moves through the water with the agility and beauty of a predatory shark. Marie-Elise drifts expertly on her back, motionless, a basking mermaid. Behind, the mountains and medieval spires of Les Vans shimmer in the late afternoon heat of a baking sun. I feel I'm in a dream.

Afterwards we are joined by Marcel, a handsome carpenter – with a lush dark beard and head of hair despite his imminent sixtieth birthday – brandishing six glasses and two icy bottles of white wine. We laze on the poolside loungers and watch as the sun bends to brush the top of the mountains. I try hard not to think about the fact that we will start paying rent and staff wages in just one week's time and that the season is starting to slip away from us and that we are facing, potentially, a real disaster – we have no chef.

～ 28 MAY ～

No chef.

Meanwhile this morning, minor hurricane met lover. I don't know what I expected, but it wasn't quite this.

Sal was clearly nervous about driving again, because we made the journey from Laurac to Aubenas, which normally takes half an hour or so, in what seemed like five minutes. She threw *Vin Blanc* about like a fighter jet, constantly overcompensating for misjudging the distance between the right-hand side of the van, and the verge. Whenever it looked like we were about to collide with either animate or inanimate objects, SA thrust the throttle relentlessly to the floor so we shot off like a bullet from a rifle. Amazingly we seemed to get away with it every time. But I do desperately need her to drive for the restaurant, so I've decided the only way she can overcome her inexperience is to insist she drives as much as possible, whilst the rest of us can only watch, stunned, from a distance, and brush up on our prayers.

We meet Celine and the gang sitting in the dusty sunshine having drinks outside Le Bureau, a curiously popular drinking hole for the Aubenas glitterati considering it's a rather ghastly foreign-inspired snub to the French way of life; it's a dark and shabby imitation of an English pub, full of old sporting memorabilia depicting men in droopy Edwardian moustaches and long white flannels drifting aimlessly around Wimbledon and Lord's.

Celine greets me with a passionate embrace and I can't help noticing, with a pang of gratification, that she's mesmerized by SA, who greets her with a cordial smile before turning away quickly to meet the rest of the group. There's Manu, who greets her, of course, like a long-lost friend; his silent but ever beautiful girlfriend, Olivia, who gives a distant smile and wave as though she were on a live satellite link from a different continent; her equally tall and lithe brother, Jean Baptiste, taxi driver and token local Lothario; and one or two other vaguely familiar faces, who seem to be ever present, chain-smoking, in the periphery of the Manu–Celine social axis.

There's a spare seat next to Celine, and SA plonks herself down whilst I summon the waiter for drinks. The body language could not be more antagonistic; Celine turns to her right and absorbs herself with Quentin, always a useful distraction at awkward moments because he constantly demands her attention, whilst Sal, who's discreetly in the opposite direction to her left, is for a moment looking uncharacteristically lost and even a little bit shy, before the gallant Manu rides to the rescue and engages her in animated conversation.

It shames me to say it, but the obvious frisson between the two girls made my heart skip a beat. Can Sal's presence make me more glamorous to Celine? Should I flirt with Sal a little?

Charlie saunters over.

'Flirt with Sal a bit,' he whispers. He seems fascinated by Sally Ann.

'Don't be ridiculous, Charlie. What do you take me for?'

At this point my mobile phone bursts into life, and there's an over-excited Reza jabbering away so rapidly that it takes me a moment or two to understand what he's saying.

He thinks he's found a chef.

'That's fantastic, Reza, you really are a genius,' I enthuse, genuinely overjoyed. I could see Charlie focusing in on me from beside the door to the pub. 'When are you going to see him?'

'Just as soon as I can get a plane ticket.'

'A plane ticket?'

'He's in Paris.'

I pause for a moment. For some reason I assumed the chef would come from London.

'There's nothing in the budget for you to fly out to Paris.'

'You've worked out a budget? Now you really are joking.'

On reflection, a France-based chef may be no bad thing. Flying someone out from London would cost more than bringing a chef down from Paris. And presumably he would speak French and understand the French way of life.

'OK, Rez, I agree, go ahead and book the tickets.'

'I already have.'

When I return to the table and announce the good news to Manu, he claps his hands with glee and without a moment's hesitation summons the waiter for more wine. 'My mother will be so relieved, she can't sleep for worry.'

'I know. But Manu, don't start celebrating too quickly. The guy's not hired yet. There may be a problem.'

Manu's face lit up with a smile of pure, undiluted confidence.

'Reza will hire him. Our dreams are answered. Drink!'

At the other end of the group I notice, with an almost physical twinge of irritation, that Celine and Sally Ann are chatting away like old friends, occasionally flicking glances in my direction, and laughing. And, of course, Charlie's there, recording everything.

REZA: Zee and I are in ABSOLUTE agreement. It's perfectly obvious that Nigel has never employed anyone in his life before. He thinks I should simply steal away one of the chefs from the Star of India to work in Laurac for three months (honestly!) and I keep trying to explain to him that this is impossible. The Star is a tightly run and extremely efficient machine with each chef and sous-chef specifically trained in a speciality, so that to remove even one would mean that the whole wheel would start to wobble. Anyway, we'd never get the work permit through in time. Nigel doesn't believe me, but poaching a chef from another restaurant won't work either – most must give three months', or at least one month's notice. As Zee keeps pointing out, there just isn't a pool of unemployed Indian chefs floating about in London – most are flown over direct from India by employers with specific vacancies in mind.

So now, after at least thirty-seven EXHAUSTING phone calls, I've managed to track down Ramesh, an Indian chef who's been in Paris for six years, so one hopes he knows what he's doing.

Tomorrow I fly to Charles de Gaulle and scrutinize him as he prepares a meal for me. It's all too frantic. I love Paris and if Zee was free we could skim around the Bois de Boulogne with a few empty bags, but I don't want to go there under these circumstances. I don't know my way around and my French is terrible. There are widespread strikes throughout the transport system. And what happens if Ramesh is not up to scratch? Should I lower my standards? Will food writers be coming over from London to test the quality of food at L'Été Indien? What about my reputation? What about Christiane's reputation? And why, oh why, am I asking myself so many questions? It's driving me mad! My doctor says I should be putting on weight, but I can't face eating a thing, so my trousers remain constantly hanging off me like a flag flying at half-mast.

And Nigel said this would be FUN.

∼ 29 MAY ∼

I hate even to utter the word, but Christiane has been pestering me about *les administratives* – the paperwork.

Le Relais Fleuri has continued to function as a normal French restaurant at lunchtimes and in the evenings all the time I've been here, of course, and whenever I can I've been watching and learning from Christiane as she moves about the place. Both in the kitchen and amongst the guests she is the consummate professional. But I've stalled from enquiring about the paperwork. I've asked her if she will continue to do it once L'Été Indien is up and running, but she argues it is my responsibility, and of course she's right. It is.

As I've already painfully discovered, the French are obsessed by paperwork and Christiane says that if I don't start to get on top of it the business will perish. And Celine agrees; she gives me one of those very rare expressions of earnest concern which involves wagging the finger a lot and putting her gloriously lush red eyebrows through their paces in a series of formidable frowns. Surely I knew the bureaucracy in France is so ridiculously complicated? It's an international joke, no? Like Christiane, Celine says if I don't get on with it, I won't be opening any restaurant. She looks incredibly sexy when she's *really* serious. Celine, I mean, not Christiane.

One of the immediate and pressing issues concerns the temporary change of ownership of the business. To begin trading legally, I must formally register as the new *propriétaire* of L'Été Indien. This must be done at the Chamber of Commerce in Aubenas, and it's a completely barmy procedure. I need to produce:

❑ Passport, birth certificate, *carte de séjour*, the two sets of paid-for Bureau de Poste certificates and a copy of my contract with the Tochous. (*All of which, mercifully, I now have.*)

❑ Details of a business bank account, which I should have opened but haven't. (*NB: Make appointment to see manager of Banque Marze in Largentière asap.*)

❑ A detailed written description of the 'enterprise'. (*What on earth does that involve?*)

❑ A letter from the Tochous authenticating the temporary handover of ownership, plus their last three EDF electricity bills and evidence of recent payments for oil and water. (*This could be tricky: Christiane's*

paperwork lies scattered in little piles all over the restaurant and her
apartment above, as though someone has blasted off a bomb beneath
her filing cabinet.)

❏ Evidence of ownership of the house at Les Fabres, plus copies of
invoices as above. (*Why? And inevitably, these are all buried
somewhere deep amidst the chaos of my flat in Farnham. NB: Before
Tom leaves to go back to England tomorrow, give him stern briefing
on need to root them out asap.*)

❏ Evidence of ownership of the flat in Farnham. (*Again, why? NB: Brief
Tom, as above.*)

❏ Letter from Monsieur Champetier, the Mayor of Laurac, authenticating
transfer. (*He's a pal of the Tochous so this shouldn't be too difficult.*)

❏ Letter from the *douane*, the customs office in Aubenas, authorizing
change in liquor licence.

❏ My mother's maiden name. (*And again, why?*)

❏ My late father's place and date of birth. (*Silly me.*)

Having listed all that needs to be done, and automatically put away the
list as something to be attended to another time, by an appalling
coincidence I pick up the Sir Terence Conran book about restaurants that
Sal brought over to help me get started.

> *This is the fine art of the restaurateur. And Terence Conran is one of the
> great exponents of the business. His early roots and his current collection
> of restaurants in London, Paris, New York and Stockholm put him in
> a unique position to shed light on the challenges that face the aspiring
> restaurateur.*

Sounds great. I happen to open the book on page 34.

> *Many restaurateurs almost come to the point of suicide before they even
> open their doors in their desperate attempts to unravel the nightmarish*

> *tangle of official regulations. It is important to be well-prepared for this assault on your nerves; it is one aspect of opening and running a restaurant that simply cannot be approached in a naive spirit of hopeful optimism.*

I can feel small beads of sweat breaking out on my forehead.

> *It is therefore essential for anybody who is planning their own restaurant to find out about the regulations that apply BEFORE they begin the project.*

Later Tom and Sal walked up with me through the idyllic little back streets of Aubenas towards the château, and stopped off for dinner at the best restaurant in the Ardèche, Le Fournil, where we shared a sumptuous feast of hot *foie gras* and *rillettes de saumon à la crème.*

It's Tom's last night. He's promised to send over all the documents for registration at the Chamber of Commerce the moment he gets back to the Farnham flat. I hope I've drilled into him the urgency of the situation.

I've never been good at saying goodbyes but tonight Tom's imminent departure back home leaves me feeling strangely uncomfortable and vulnerable, very much a stranger in a foreign country.

Resolve to make sure Reza never gets to see Sir Terence Conran's book.

～ *30 MAY* ～

Wake early after a fitful night, and throw my groaning muscles into a frenzy of exercises in the embryonic warmth of the morning sun on the terrace. I am doing this in an attempt to overcome my apparently unshakeable feeling of impending doom.

At the restaurant I check to see if Reza has left any messages on my mobile about the chef in Paris – the reception is virtually non-existent in Laurac but we've found that by hanging off the little balcony overlooking the Rue d'Externat beside the kitchen, it's just possible to pick up a signal. It's a position that is physically impossible to maintain for long, so conversations have to be brief.

No message from Reza.

'I've been thinking,' says Charlie. This is a familiar opening remark of his and, based on experience, it sets off alarm bells in my mind. 'Yes, I've been thinking.'

That worryingly blank expression has hijacked Charlie's face.

'I need some more shots of you and Celine in the Deux Chevaux.' Pause. 'Yes?'

'I have an idea.'

Now over the decades since it first came off the production line in 1948 the 2CV has proved itself the sturdiest and most resilient of vehicles. It was invented and designed as a car which could cheerfully transport a farmer, a pig and a barrel of beer across a ploughed field; today it is to be put to its sternest test yet.

After work, we pick up Celine. She and I are instructed to sit in the front two seats of the old banger. Charlie, camera on shoulder, stands on the front bumper and leans across the bonnet, so that he can shoot us through the windscreen. Claudio takes a yet more bizarre position, one that is impossible to imagine anyone but he would even attempt. Claudio trained in the Swiss Army and later carved out a career in roaming the world's most dangerous hotspots as a cameraman – he has lived like a native in Afghanistan, he's been imprisoned in Chechnya and has been a fugitive from the turbulent government of Papua New Guinea. He is lean, athletic, utterly self-sufficient and apparently fearless. Jolly good chap to have around.

He climbs up on to the roof of the car and lies across it, diagonally. With his right foot securing him on the rear off-side corner of the roof, he hangs his head down beside the passenger-door window (which is open) and holds the camera, the right way up of course, to his eye, so that he can shoot Celine and me from the side angle. Charlie then tells me to drive down to Vals, which I do, very gingerly indeed, aware that we are probably breaking every health and safety regulation in the book. Celine and I chatter away and the cameras roll, with only the occasional interruption from Charlie, who interjects with things like: 'Clouds, your right foot is just coming into frame through the back window of the car.'

We drive round Vals a couple of times, the car tipping forwards ludicrously (because of Charlie's weight on the front) and swaying violently from side to side every time we lurch around the corner (thanks to Claudio's weight on the roof) with me just hoping there are no gun-toting *gendarmes* around. Interestingly, the locals don't bat an eyelid. Presumably they just put it down to another example of the odd behaviour they've come to expect from the mad *Anglais des Fabres*, and therefore not really of any great interest.

Charlie's been pushing me to film as much as possible of Celine, but I'm wary of our relationship forming too big a part in his plans. I know that she and I have set many tongues wagging locally, and that for some I'm the silly old fool who inevitably, one way or another, will be publicly humiliated by the glamorous younger girlfriend. Do I really want all the folks back home to start thinking the same? Do I really want to come over as a *sad old git*?

On the other hand, as Charlie is quick to point out, it seriously ups the ante on my credibility with Celine, who finds the filming hugely amusing and clearly welcomes distraction from the routine of her daily life. I think she seriously believes the cameras have enhanced her reputation amongst the glitterati of Aubenas; and maybe I could be the principal beneficiary of this.

And, as usual, Charlie's sweet-talking me into doing more of it.

'Think what a real love interest is going to do to our story, Farrell. The joys and tragedies of the human heart. Everyone – but *everyone* – is going to be fascinated in this. What happens to Nigel and Celine? Stay tuned! It's got *everything*!'

Two days to go before takeover and suddenly I'm absolutely terrified. Le Relais Fleuri is incredibly busy at lunchtime and what unnerves me as I watch Christiane go about her business so skilfully is the realization that in just a week or two I will be standing in her shoes, knowing nothing about Indian food, nor running a restaurant, nor how to speak French properly. She has such a charming and relaxed way with the customers that the sudden thought of even attempting to emulate her fills my mind with a horrible black void. Every now and then she turns and smiles as I watch, giving me a little wave. I smile bravely back, feeling much as I did when my mother waved goodbye to me at the start of another long school term. It's a curious combination of impending abandonment and helplessness. One of the guests comes over to me and starts speaking machine-gun French. Over the months I have perfected the art of appearing to understand everything that's said to me by simply mimicking the physical actions and expressions of the speaker. When he nods, I nod. When he smiles, I smile. When he looks astonished, so do I.

I do a lot of looking astonished now, but clearly when I'm running the place this approach to communicating with the locals could be problematic.

Earlier Christiane had been giving me instructions on the behind-the-scenes details of running the restaurant – when the suppliers arrive, what they should be paid, how a coffee machine operates and how, if I buy any lamps for the terrace of more than 24 volts, there'll be a small explosion and the electricity will instantly be cut off.

But I am rapidly being won over by Christiane. She radiates a warmth and tranquillity, which seem to spring from a simple philosophy of life that's based on love, humour and an adoration of good food.

'Where do you get the roses for all the tables?' I ask.

'From the gardens of my friends round here in Laurac,' she replies, as though it was the most obvious thing in the world. I haven't noticed it before, but nearly every morning she's off to collect fresh flowers. I can't believe how much there is to do. I'm also now beginning to understand why she has such a fantastically loyal group of customers, why so many of the visitors return year after year. This should be good news for business but it actually scares the hell out of me. I would be appalled to let her and the restaurant down in the face of such hard-earned devotion.

I'm slightly confused as to why Christiane is still doing lunches at all, when she had explained to me specifically that during the summer she only did one meal a day, in the evening.

'Summer hasn't started yet,' she explains patiently.

Outside it's 35 degrees and for most of the day I've been on the verge of collapse through heat exhaustion. I go for a swim in the wonderful outdoor pool in Vals Les Bains and try to snatch a short siesta. Fail.

At last, a message from Reza. He met up with Ramesh, three hours late, and together the two of them set off into the Indian quarter to the east of the city by the Gare de Lyons, and Reza watched the guy like a hawk as he bought everything for the meal he'd been told to prepare: a traditional Indian chicken dish, lamb *rogan josh* and pureed aubergine and pumpkin.

'It was adequate, not exactly Michelin star, but he's keen and I reckon he's got potential and he'll do, I think,' said Reza. Not exactly a ringing endorsement, but then we don't have much choice.

He arrived back here at Les Fabres just an hour or so ago. I'm really pleased to see him. I'm reassured, of course, but he's also amusing company, and I don't feel quite so alone.

Mind you, he's not in the best of moods after the strike-stricken rail journey, which took eight hours instead of five. It's a moonlit, balmy night and I've taken the trouble to light a few candles on the terrace and open another bottle of Côtes du Rhône to soothe Reza's troubled spirits and welcome him home.

Ramesh is forty-two, he's been cooking Indian cuisine for fifteen years and he is excited about the project. He's available. He speaks good French. It's all going to be great.

'Just a couple of things,' says Reza, downing a large draught of wine. He looks thinner than ever. 'He's married. With two kids.'

I don't know why, but somehow I'd expected he'd be a young, single guy.

The only accommodation we have is the flat where Sal is staying. We can't afford anything else.

'I've suggested one month's trial,' said Reza, his wide eyes now like saucers with worry and fatigue. 'By then we'll have a much better idea of how much money we are likely to take over the summer. If the money's there, we can hire him something bigger, and he can then bring his family down.'

'OK.'

'And another point.'

'Yes.'

'He can't drive.'

Now this is rather more serious. Laurac is a remote village and Christiane has to make endless trips every day to pick up fresh meat and fish, vegetables and fruit and the countless other provisions required from her local suppliers.

(NB: Why doesn't anyone deliver here? Must ask Christiane about this.)

There will be quite serious implications if one of us has to constantly drive Ramesh everywhere he needs to go.

'We'll have to live with that, I guess,' I say.

'And just one other thing . . .'

At this point I notice, through the shadowy flicker of the candle flame, that something strange is happening to the features on Reza's face. The fatigue has suddenly vanished. It looks like he is struggling to suppress some sudden and inexplicable pain.

'Ramesh doesn't speak any English.'

There is a long silence while I take this in.

'No English at all?'

'Not one word.'

Another long pause. Reza's face is now twitching and contorting, sudden, jerky movements accompanied by short, stifled squeaks. Then I slowly realize he is trying desperately to hold back waves of laughter that are rising up uncontrollably from his heaving chest.

'What does he speak?'

'French.'

At this point a small tear rolls down Reza's cheek.

'And Hindi.'

Now the wall of the dam suddenly gives way and Reza's little body starts to be racked by sobs.

'Reza!' I protest. 'I can't believe you find this amusing!'

'I'm so, so sorry,' he says at last, wiping the tears away. 'It's not even remotely funny.' He takes another gulp of wine.

'I thought most Indians spoke at least a little English?'

'They do.'

I reflect on this for a moment as the last of the chirruping tree frogs decide to call it a day and settle down for the night.

'So let me just get this straight,' I say. 'I have no business experience whatsoever and no knowledge of Indian cuisine. I can't speak the language of any of my customers. And you've found me the only Indian chef on the planet that can't speak English.'

'You'd better make the best of it, Nigel,' says Reza, now having fully recovered his composure and wagging a finger at me. 'If you can't make it work with Ramesh, the good ship L'Été Indien is steaming straight towards the biggest iceberg you've ever seen, at about . . . er . . . thirty knots!' (Since when was Reza familiar with nautical words like 'knot'? I'm sure he has a hidden past, and if it's going to be revealed at any stage I wish it were now and not later.)

'Rez, this is a recipe for disaster.'

Just then there was more laughter, from within the house.

'Fantastic scene!' says Charlie. 'What a winner! They'll love it back home. Bit of a struggle with the low light levels from the candles right on the end of the lens – what did you think about the exposure, Clouds, did you check the monitor?'

'Vonderful, vonderful in effery vay!' beams Clouds.

∽ 31 MAY ∽

No opportunity for any self-indulgence today, thank God.

We're on a roller coaster and there's no stopping us.

As usual, Christiane is charging around with the energy of a bull elephant. First we head out in *Vin Blanc* through the vineyards and out on the road to Les Vans to a little roadside workshop that specializes in posters and signage. There are over thirty-five signposts to Le Relais Fleuri on all the roads around Laurac and these will have to be replaced by a new design. Then back down towards La Beaume, to the printers. Reza's found a rather beautiful woodcut print of what looks like the inside of an Indian harem which he thinks, edged in a deep scarlet to match the tableware, will make a striking menu cover, and I agree unhesitatingly. Small battles I will readily concede if it makes my life easier.

I have no idea how we would have managed without Christiane. Everywhere we stop, people seem genuinely delighted to see her and readily offer whatever help they can. At each stop, by way of return for their automatic generosity, she relays all the latest gossip picked up in the restaurant, so that even a short trip can take forty minutes. At the end of each visit, her admiring audience smile and embrace her with the fervour of a crowd celebrating the return of an astronaut from a far-off planet, with everyone all the time checking to make sure she's not left her handbag behind.

Then to Aubenas for a lightning-quick lunch with Celine in the smoky little Café du Marché, just up from her office in the Boulevard Gambetta. She's spending so much time setting up the new office in Montélimar that it's rare to catch her here. I tell her we'll be seeing even less of each other over the next few weeks as the race to get L'Été Indien up and running hots up. She takes my hand in hers and looks deep into my eyes.

'*Je comprends, chéri, c'est la vie.*'

As so often I have no idea what she means by this meaningless blabber. Does she mind me working so hard? Long hours are not exactly standard in a country that rushed to embrace the thirty-five-hour working week.

And does she really have to spend so much time in Montélimar?

I gaze back into her gently smiling, inscrutable eyes.

She's never once offered to come to help at, or even see, L'Été Indien. That's sad.

'Your loan has been approved, *chéri*,' she adds. 'If you still want to take it up, I can arrange for an automatic bank transfer for next week.'

'Thank you.'

'Are you happy?'

'Very.'

Reza has spoken again to Ramesh in Paris. I can hear the oddly stern rise and fall of his Hindi at the other end of the house. Is Hindi easier to learn than French? Should I start now?

We decide the earliest date we can open for business is five weeks away, on Friday, 4th July. We'll work through this weekend and have a post-mortem on Monday, which is when we'll close. This time of year, most restaurants work flat out, lunch and dinner, seven days a week, but Reza says that with just one chef (who I can't communicate with – have I mentioned this?) and a tiny kitchen, he can manage dinners only, six days a week. And that only just. I think this must be a missed opportunity but have no choice but to go along with it.

Call Tom. He's still in France! He's gone off to see an old girlfriend at Rennes.

'But Tom! What about all the documents I need from the flat?'

'Chill out, Dad, I'll be home tomorrow.'

～ 1 JUNE ～

The end of an era.

It's Le Relais Fleuri's final day, after twenty-five years of distinguished service to the Ardèchoise stomach. Christiane invites dozens of friends round for a farewell lunch that I tell her might appear more like a wake; as usual, I underestimate her subtle marketing skills. It's a great opportunity, she comments, to extol the virtues of L'Été Indien and tickle the palates of her guests.

For the last time she lays out the tables, pink under-cloth overlaid with clean, spotless, starched green floral tablecloths. Her old French chef, Bernard, arrives warily to chop up the onions and garlic and prepare the *poussin* for the last time before his retirement begins in just a few hours' time. Even JB makes a rare appearance in the restaurant, helping Christiane lay out the wine coolers and check the ice machine. I sense a bucketful of mixed emotions between the two of them: sadness and relief, nervousness and excitement. I know how they feel.

Of course, the celebratory lunch is a great success. I'd hoped Celine would join us but she is busy with Quentin. Reza dances around, like a manic little pixie, helping Christiane serve the dishes and thereby, I sense, beginning to assert his authority, almost as though the handover was already underway. Sal brings a breath of fresh air, prompting a winking smile from the grey-haired men dotted around the terrace. I hope she's enjoying herself. She has been magnificent, working really hard. Already I feel I can't manage without her.

When the last of the guests has gone, we sit around sipping wine amid the sweet perfume of the honeysuckle brought out by the late afternoon sun, and listen to Reza, who explains how food – both its preparation and consumption – has formed the basis of his whole philosophy for life.

'Food is the ultimate means of human communication,' he says. 'It is the ultimate shared experience. We share the work of its preparation. We share the texture, its sense, its ambience and, of course, its taste. It's the ultimate sensual experience. It's better than sex.'

In the evening, JB disappears to have dinner with his ninety-year-old mother who lives with his brother on a hill overlooking Laurac, just as he has nearly every evening of his married life to Christiane.

Reza, Sal and I climb into the back of Christiane's bizarre new acquisition, an enormous battered old jeep, bought for her, in an uncharacteristically romantic gesture, by JB.

With Reza, Sal and I standing upright in the back of the beast, clinging on to the crossbar for dear life, Christiane roars up the mountain behind Laurac, up past the majestic château of Montréal with its great rectangular tower reaching towards the stars, and into the off-road tracks in the forest behind, with the dying orange glow of the sun's memory being gently washed away by the light dusk mist. There's no mistaking the route of the jeep – its fiery exhaust leaves behind a trail of billowing smoke and ricocheting echoes which must puzzle and alarm the tiny hamlets of hill-folk that lie hidden away from view amidst the dense tree cover. Christiane, totally inexperienced with the tank-like vehicle and unsure about the precise curves and contours of the forest tracks, has the look of a possessed maniac, dwarfed behind the huge steering wheel as she hurls us around.

It is wild and exhilarating, but I sense Christiane would rather have JB by her side. I haven't thought about it before, but surely the arrival of L'Été Indien will give them so much more of a chance to spend time together. Normally JB works all day and Christiane all night. Over the last twenty-five years they must have managed to spend only a score of evenings together – tonight clearly isn't going to be another of them.

Afterwards, at the restaurant, we toast the night away with bucketfuls of *pastis* and ice. Tomorrow, Le Relais Fleuri becomes L'Été Indien . . . *our* L'Été Indien.

～ 2 JUNE ～

The transfer of power was rapid, and slightly bizarre.

Reza and I arrived at the restaurant as usual at about nine o'clock after a tense and expectant drive down from Les Fabres, during which it was clear that for once Reza was as keyed up as me. The restaurant already smelt different. As usual Olivier, Christiane's *plongeur* (who thankfully has agreed to stay on with us), had already watered the sea of potted flowers and dowsed down the floor of the terrace so that the morning air had a damply sweet scent to it. But there was something else.

Christiane was up, working, of course. We hugged each other, laughing with excitement. It seemed such a watershed moment that, for some curious reason, I started to make a speech. Sal began to throw cushions at me. We all then threw cushions at each other. No one quite knew what to say.

'*Votre cauchemar est finis,*' said Reza, at length, in a suddenly remembered but well-rehearsed line, '. . . *et le mien commence!*'

'What does that mean?' asked Charlie.

'Your nightmare is over, mine is just beginning.'

'Fantastic soundbite! Sorry to interrupt.'

It was a bit early for champagne or *pastis,* even for the Tochous, so Christiane disappeared into the scullery and returned a few minutes later with four little cups of steaming black espresso.

Then she said: 'So what would you like *me* to do today?'

We all looked at each other blankly.

It was all strangely mechanical. Reza and Christiane started to make an inventory of the entire place. Every single item of equipment was noted, and the laborious tour took most of the day. From the little cabin of a kitchen to the dark dining area inside with its seven tables and the solitary blinding source of light from the little balcony (so vital for mobile phone users). Then through to the tiny scullery with its ancient coffee machine and two squashed, ceiling-high fridges; from there to the narrow sliver of a bathroom, down the bottle-lined stairs to the cellar, back up to the lovely garden of the terrace and its ten tables, then out through the gate to a small annexe which is across the drive up to the Tochous' garage and opposite the terrace entrance. This is the cold kitchen, which Christiane uses mainly for storage and for washing-up, and where the ice cream is kept in rusty old fridges and the desserts prepared. Olivier will be spending the long evenings here, with any luck, cursing the interminable line of dirty plates that will be flowing like an endless production line from the main restaurant.

'So you are now *milord* of all you see,' Christiane declares, with a brief smile of encouragement and a quick kiss. This is now my feudal domain.

Ramsa, our waitress, and Olivier have been drafted in early to help and they stand around, chatting, until once again I slowly realize they are waiting for me to give them instructions. Mercifully, Sal is on hand and sets about organizing the work party with a quiet efficiency, like a fresh young midshipman knocking into shape a motley crew of landlubbers on a Nelsonian ship-of-the-line. One by one all the tables and chairs are carried up and stacked in neat rows beside the old jeep in the Tochous' garage. I watch them as they work up and down the hill, like a team of soldier ants, applying themselves willingly and with goodwill. The place must be swept, all the artefacts and pictures removed from the walls and shelves, noted and carefully stored, all the pots of flowers, even the big ones, heaved or rolled up, in the growing heat of the morning sun, to the garage above.

By the time Manu arrives for *Ricard moins quart*, L'Été Indien is stripped naked. It looks terrible. Enormous pale squares and rectangles have appeared where the pictures have been hanging, revealing a great dark, depressing stain over all the rest of the walls, a residue from the winter months of the smoky wood-burning stove. But oddest of all is the sheer emptiness of the place, its character and soul blown away in the space of a few short hours.

Manu's brought his washing for *Maman*. He's thirty-six years old and lives with his girlfriend, but still the overworked Christiane seems happy to take it in every week, to be washed and starched and pressed and ironed and returned in perfectly stacked piles, uncomplaining, almost grateful to have the excuse to see her son so regularly. The ritual has an almost medieval feel about it, but nonetheless it seems very French. JB appears from his estate agent's office in Aubenas, for lunch, as he always does, on the dot of twelve thirty, and if the food's not ready, there's trouble. He gives me a cursory nod and one raised eyebrow to acknowledge the morning's work, and then instantly joins his son for *pastis* and an animated, impenetrable discussion on the woes of the world. I watch them as they talk and as Christiane, loyal wife and mother, without a word, formally assembles the plates and cutlery, napkins, basket of bread, wine and glasses. It would never occur to the men to offer to help, nor would it occur to Christiane to ask. This is the way it is and always has been and always will be. They barely acknowledge her presence, let alone speak to her. It's a scene I've witnessed many times, and not just around the lunch table, and I've reasoned with myself and learned to repress the instant reaction of disapproval and annoyance. Who am I to have the arrogance to decide what is right or wrong for a family I really know so little about? Maybe it's what Christiane wants, as well as the men; maybe it makes her happy.

I wonder whether the same scene is being played out in the kitchens and dining rooms of the other houses in our street, our village, all over the Ardèche. Despite the brash modernity of some of its bigger, richer urban centres, just beneath the surface this seems to be still a primitive place and the newcomer who tries to change the course of its ancient rituals had better beware.

And this is the place I've chosen to open up an Indian restaurant.

After lunch, as usual, everyone simply vanishes. Sal, Christiane, and JB disappear upstairs to their separate apartments for a siesta, and Olivier and Ramsa evaporate into the ether. Claudio's gone home and Charlie's already asleep. I suggest to Reza that we should drive up to Marie-Elise's for a swim, but he says he has no swimming costume, so I offer him a pair of mine, but he giggles, waving his hand in the air like the Queen Mother, and says he wouldn't be seen dead in *anything like that*. Instead we pull up chairs and doze in the dark but deliciously cool dining room.

I guess this is going to become a familiar pattern in the days to come.

～ 3 JUNE ～

Ominously, Reza announced after breakfast that he wanted a discussion about money. For the last few years this has undoubtedly been my least favourite subject on the planet. But I nod enthusiastically.

I suggested we take a coffee out on the terrace but although it was still early the heat was already intense, which I adore and Reza hates. Like Nippi, Reza will go to great lengths to avoid direct sunlight, which is curious, because I'd assumed Asian skin would be much more adaptable than mine; so instead we sat in the cool of the kitchen, like two *Pooh Bears*, dunking strawberries into a large jar of delicious honey, made from their own bees by the Carberneros next door. I'm gradually coming to the conclusion that the Carbs are almost self-sufficient. And not just in cement. Maybe it's a sign that after all this time I've finally earned his trust and respect, but Marcel has taken to excitedly ushering me round to the back of his house to witness the birth of new rabbits or chicks. And, like most of our neighbours, he spends hours in his immaculate vegetable plot, which he cares for with the enthusiasm of a man going for gold at the Chelsea Flower Show. No matter how unkempt or chaotic the interiors of their homes may be, round here it seems to be a matter of civic pride that your onions should stand in pristine uniformity like guardsmen outside Buckingham Palace, whilst your courgettes never get to see a single solitary weed in their short but hugely well-nourished existence.

The discussion was short, to the point, and alarming. First, review set-up costs: 20,000 Euros for Christiane Tochou – about £14,000 – for the first four months' rent on L'Été Indien. The rent of the apartment above for Ramesh is 800 Euros a month, just over £2,000, for the same period. We have bought *Vin Blanc* for a further £2,000. We've allowed £3,000 to transform Le Relais Fleuri into L'Été Indien, so most of our £20,000 capital, of which Reza and I have each contributed £10,000, will be swallowed up even before we open.

All other running costs such as staff wages will have to come out of income, Reza declared.

I hadn't really thought this one through.

'What happens if there is no income?' I enquired.

'We close.'

'Yes, yes, of course, but what I mean is how much income do we need each week to keep open?'

Reza said that when we've finalized the menu and know exactly what all the daily running costs are, we'll sit down with a calculator and work out precisely how many meals we'll have to sell each day in order to stay open.

◁ Reza Mahammad of the Star of India in London, agrees the deal. 'I do so love a sense of adventure, darlings!'

△ There's not much option: Le Relais Fleurie it is — despite the kitchen

▷ Handover day. If only our proprietor Christiane knew what she was letting herself in for . . .

△△ The film crew arrives at Les Fabres

△ The full team celebrates something but no one can remember what. Left to right: Manu's girlfriend, Olivia; Charlie; Manu; Celine; me; Sally Ann; Claudio

▷ Celine looking stunning, as usual

△▽ La transformation begins

⟍ Disaster – two weeks to go and the chef pulls out!

⟍▷ Attempts at karma –
ach to his own . . .

△ The desperate search for another chef – Nice is our only hope

△ The wonderful Edward arrives in the nick of time

▷ Reza will see me through the troubles ahead. Note Marie-Elise's paintwork on *Vin Blanc* visibly begins to melt in the astronomical temperatures

△ 'The last time there was an elephant hereabouts was a million years ago.' A PR triumph

◁△ Of course Reza was right in the end; the ambience was magical. We are a success!

◁ Nippi and me back home at Les Fabres – in between rows

▽ Sal tries to reassure me. 'You'll be just fine on your own.'

Hereafter, he announced, this will be known as The Target. If we fail to meet The Target, staff will have to be fired. He would draw up a shortlist of who was most dispensable. How easily could we manage without, say, Ramsa?

'We can't fire Ramsa!' I said. 'She's been working here for years!'

'Nigel,' said Reza, looking me hard in the eye. 'I've said it before, but I'm now getting tired of saying it: this isn't a game.'

I've never employed – and certainly not fired – anyone in my life. Blimey.

REZA: Zut alors! I know he's on cloud nine after taking over the restaurant at last, but it really is time Nigel started taking responsibility for his actions! I keep telling him that I'm not running this place, I'm just helping him do so, I'm a consultant. In a couple of months I must return to the Star. He pleaded with me that if anyone has to do the firing it should be me, on the basis that I'm a restaurateur and have been hiring and firing people for years! Mon dieu! I'm not wearing that! Zee reckons he wants a good guy/bad guy approach to any bad news for the staff, with me as the bad guy on the grounds that I'm commuting to and from London and don't have to live with the consequences. But I'm not bending.

Can't believe anyone in this day and age can wear Second World War swimming trunks like Nigel's. They're like something out of a Carry On film.

～ 4 JUNE ～

The days are melting into one another, slipping by seamlessly, but it's all a bit like the Phoney War, with an air of expectancy which remains frustratingly unfulfilled. Maybe it's because, for the first time, we've settled into a well-worn routine.

Sal is up and working by seven o'clock, washing down the walls, rubbing down the woodwork, to beat the heat of the morning sun. Next Christiane appears, roaring off in the deafening old jeep to the *pâtisserie* for baguettes and warm croissants. The sound of splashing water on the terrace heralds the arrival of Olivier, swabbing down the brick floor, an act rendered completely unnecessary since the closure of Le Relais Fleuri – but that's simply what he always does, and does with such obvious pleasure, that to deny him his safe and secure place in the great ladder of the universe would seem sadistic. JB is miraculously amongst us the moment the smell of coffee percolates up through the ceiling and into the apartment above. He's never late, he's never in a hurry, making no compromises to taking life at his own steady pace, relishing his *petit déjeuner* and morning mail as Christiane fusses around him, before setting off majestically like a ship under full sail to Aubenas, in an almost visible cloud of aftershave.

Always Christiane (and sometimes Ramsa, if she's free of other duties) rolls up her sleeves and pitches in to help Sal with the decorating. Today they started on the white undercoat in the inside dining area beside the kitchen, which in the space of just a few hours has become a brighter, lighter room – almost a different room in a different place.

La transformation has begun.

Each day is the same. Siesta follows lunch, painting, early evening swim and white wine at the topless Marie-Elise's, dinner. Each day has its own familiar rhythm – food, work, food, sleep, work, swim, food – always magnificently orchestrated by the great matriarch Christiane, who, despite the closure of her restaurant, simply cannot stop herself preparing large quantities of food throughout the day. It all gets eaten, of course; mostly by the film crew.

Occasionally friends, or even passers-by who don't realize we're not open for business, appear at the gate of the terrace, and Christiane, delighted with the excuse, will invite them in, sit them down, and whatever the time of day will cook them an enormous meal. Often they'll be there for hours, sometimes even the rest of the day, and almost as soon as they've finished one meal, Christiane is up preparing the next, leaving poor Sal, who adores her food, to continue working away nobly on the walls.

At five o'clock this afternoon, I watch as Christiane waves goodbye to a couple who had arrived at eleven o'clock in the morning.

'This is good for us,' she says, and when I look puzzled, she adds: 'They'll be back when we are open again, for sure.'

'Have they booked?' I enquire hopefully.

'No, *mon chéri*, it's much too early for that!'

'Did you suggest they made a booking?'

'There is no need, they will be back, for sure!'

'But why didn't you ask them to book?' I persist. 'Surely it's better to get people to commit?'

'This is not the way. You shall see.'

I find this odd. Christiane is turning people away all the time, yet not once has she produced the reservation book. But I can't – daren't – overrule her.

I have spent a lot of time in *Vin Blanc*, not least driving Reza miles around to scrutinize all the local markets – Joyeuse yesterday, Largentière today, Les Vans tomorrow, Aubenas on Saturday – in a quest to see how much of the local produce he can utilize for Indian cooking, and in an increasingly forlorn search for a local supplier of spices.

Reza has suggested we act as gastronomic undercover agents in the evenings, and spy out the strength of the opposition by sampling the fare of as many local restaurants as we can afford to visit.

Over the last few weeks, Christiane has often referred to a restaurant in Joyeuse, which, daringly, doesn't serve the traditional Ardèchoise fare.

'It's very unusual, exotic, adventurous, for this place.'

We were intrigued.

'How is it different?'

Christiane's eyes narrowed, as though she were about to divulge some astonishing secret.

'It's called Café Valentino and is run by my friend Carlotta. It's . . . Italian!'

'Italian food?' said Celine, with a sense of awe in her voice, when I asked her if she could join us for a meal there this evening. 'I've never eaten Italian food before!' She sounded genuinely excited, miraculously finding a babysitter for Quentin when so often in the past none had appeared available at short notice.

Exotic and *adventurous* are two words I'd avoid using to describe Café Valentino. It's picturesque enough, nestling beneath the huge walls of weathered stone and hanging wrought-iron balconies weighed down with small blazing explosions of pot-bound colour in the corner of the oldest square in the medieval heart of the town. And Celine was thrilled by the bruschetta and large bowl of tagliatelle and clams we shared . . . perfectly ordinary food amongst the kind of perfectly ordinary pasta-and-pizza menu to be found in the centre of any perfectly ordinary British town.

But it is good to see Celine happy. The few times we've been able to see each other recently have been overshadowed by stress, worry, woes and rather more detailed information about the traumas of the French banking and investment industry than I felt I needed to know. She's taking me to see Avignon at the weekend.

'Avignon is at sea-level, *chéri*. So we won't need to worry about your *testicules*.'

I'm not sure whether to be encouraged or not by our unadventurous experience at Café Valentino – it may indicate that the Ardèchoise are indeed ready for change, for something new.

Or the exact opposite?

∼ 5 JUNE ∼

Money's starting to flow from the restaurant bank account like a daily haemorrhage.

Over the years I've had my share of acute financial problems, and I've managed to contain the worries these prompt by compartmentalizing the subject of money in my mind. I take a deep breath, open the box, worry frantically about its contents for a few hours, then close the lid and forget all about it until another time.

Today the box reveals the alarming pace of recent spending. Reza's buying spree in London: £1,500. Printing of menu and publicity leaflets: £900. Plastic-coated cardboard roadside restaurant signs: £600. New large L'Été Indien signage to attach to existing Le Relais Fleuri signs on walls of restaurant: £500. Anticipated first month's rent and salary bill, including Ramesh the chef: £3,000.

But there's nothing to be done. We can't manage without these things.

This morning Reza started throwing the toys out of his pram on the subject of tablecloths. With Christiane's help, he's found some beautiful mint-green and cream tablecloths from a supplier in Montpellier: £360. On top of that, they'll have to be washed and ironed by Ramsa every morning. Sal suggested that we begin by using white disposable paper tablecloths and then buy the material from Montpellier later, when money starts coming into the till. Reza started waving his arms around like a supercharged windmill, ranting on about how he wasn't prepared to do things by half-measure, and the old chestnut about how he has a reputation to maintain whilst I have nothing to lose, etc. He's still not eating properly and just pecks away at his food like a small bird.

On a brighter note, Reza's been inspired by his trawls through the local shops and markets, although he seems resigned to having to source (a favourite word) his spices from as far away as Nice or Lyons. He's been working on his first draft menu. It's deliberately very simple and specifically designed for a palate that's never tasted spicy food before. But he's being quite secretive about the details, and says he certainly doesn't want anything printed up until it's perfected.

This evening we took Sal, who's almost completed the undercoating, to a restaurant Christiane says is one of the best in the area, the Fleur de Thyme, ten minutes away on the road to Joyeuse. In one respect, Christiane was right, the food was fantastic: after a delicious aperitif of white wine with a tangy local *sirop*, I had (rather guiltily, as always) *foie gras* followed by a beautifully served salmon fillet, whilst the *gourmande* Sally Ann positively drooled over her salad of quail and rich, meaty veal and pork with pasta.

The problem was the service; thirty-two people on six tables were being served by one long-limbed, languid young waiter clearly bored out of his mind. With neither apologies nor explanations for the long delays (it took forty minutes just to take the order), our quite straightforward dinner took over two and a half hours to complete. Later, Christiane said that in France it's very common for people to spend an entire evening enjoying the simplest of meals, but I am uneasy about this and think that maybe we should re-assess our own staffing levels.

So far, the team comprises a *maître d'*, N. Farrell Esq., assisted by Christiane, who will also help prepare the bills and coordinate behind the scenes. Reza will, of course, be hopping around for the first two months but must then return home to the Star, so I'm counting him out. Ramesh in the kitchen will probably need a sous-chef, according to Reza, but nobody's put any thoughts yet into where we find one. The *serveuse* will be the highly efficient Ramsa, and alongside her, to begin with at least, will be the lovely Sal (experienced but unable to speak any French) who says she can stay on for a couple of weeks or so after the opening night but must then return to her job at the BBC.

If we're to last the season I feel we must find more help. Christiane clearly doesn't agree, but once again, no doubt biting her lip at the extra expenditure, she gracefully bows to my will, and says she thinks she knows someone who she'll contact tomorrow.

Sense I will have real trouble sleeping. Reza has decided to have yet another stab at Schubert's 'Impromptu No. 1' on the old piano down below me in the study. For many years he has been struggling to perfect his performance of this piece. I often hear him hammering away on the hopelessly out-of-tune keys. He's been going now for twenty minutes. Last time he was at it for an hour and a half.

I wonder what the French is for *piano tuner*.

~ 6 JUNE ~

Hive of activity in L'Été when we finally get down there. After my dispiriting discussion with Reza, I feel quite uplifted. Ramsa, Sal and Christiane are covering everything in sight, including themselves, in pale lime-green paint. (I've got a feeling Reza's made the right choice of colour, but we need to see the pictures up before I finally concede defeat.) Manu's arrived, and even managed to re-hang a curtain rail before *Ricard moins quart*. Olivier is spring-cleaning the freezers in the outside kitchen. Reza's on the phone to Ramesh in Paris, confirming the arrangements for his arrival at the end of the week after next. Even JB, home early for lunch, is attempting to do something useful. He's rubbing his chin, looking at the little water-feature in the corner of the terrace: it's made up of a series of stone dishes running like a staircase down the wall through which, many years ago, a hidden electric pump circulated water. When it broke down Christiane decided not to have it mended because she said the gentle sound of the waterfall sent diners sitting nearby scurrying off on endless trips to her small, already over-subscribed lavatory by the scullery. I'd like it restored. After ten minutes of apparently intense examination, JB, still rubbing his whiskery face, announced he knew the answer. We need an electrician to mend the pump. Thanks, JB.

Watching them applying themselves to their various tasks so assiduously suddenly gives me confidence. With people of this calibre all around us, and with so much goodwill, how can we fail? As with most aspects of life, there must be two sides to being an employer. We are generating an income with which everyone here will earn his or her own living. This is capitalism at its finest. Initiative, invention and enterprise creating employment, wealth and happiness in a completely new venture.

Bathed in this warm glow of self-satisfaction I've just, unhesitatingly, hired a new member of staff. He's called Erique, a very tall, utterly charming, delicately handsome boy of about twenty years old with a ponytail and the long, finely chiselled fingers of the accomplished pianist

Christiane says he has become. Of course, he's the son of a friend of hers, a similarly beautiful, elegant landscape-photographer called Florence who wants to know all the details about L'Été and offers to do anything she can to help, which is what all of Christiane's friends say. I wonder how many of them mean it.

Erique's a student and is free for three months. He asks, in gratifyingly good English, how much he'll earn as a waiter. I say I hadn't really thought about it, he says he doesn't care anyway, I say how about £300 a week, he says *cool* (now apparently a truly international word), and we shake hands. He'll start on 2 July, which will give him a couple of days to get up to speed before our opening night.

Buoyed up by all this, I leap into *Vin Blanc* with a list of errands and charge around the valley like a whirling dervish: to the printers, to collect three hundred of our new L'Été Indien business cards. They look really quite classy, with Reza's scarlet harem picture on one side and a telephone number and a small map on the back. Then on to Le Clerc supermarket for new mops, Mr Bricolage for more brushes and white spirit, and then on to the pretty pair of blonde girls behind the counter at the tiny Banque Marze in Largentière to pick up a handful of cash (stubbornly resisting the idea of asking for a balance), at each stop scattering the business cards like confetti, to much admiring glances, sometimes gushing compliments and ardent promises of bookings to come a little nearer the time. Everyone, but everyone, says they want to eat at L'Été Indien, but I am not sure how to take this – should I be jumping around with glee, or shaking my head wearily that nobody yet has made a booking, like an old cynic? Maybe theirs is just the polite response any of us would give when presented with such a card.

I still keep forgetting why most of the French do most of their shopping in the early morning. *Vin Blanc* must be one of the few vehicles in the south of France without air-conditioning and it quickly heats up in the sun, so soon it's like a highly mobile tin oven. The few locals that are out and about at this time of day invariably bag all the shady parking places so after even just a few minutes at each stop, lowering the posterior (clad only in thin shorts) back on to the van's old leather seats is rather like sitting down suddenly on hot coals, and I set off like a dingbat, squirming and squealing with the blistering pain, sweating so profusely that I arrive at the next venue not only limping with the effects of a very sore bottom, but looking as though I've just stepped out of a shower. But I'm in such a positive frame of mind that I focus on the act of diving luxuriously into the waters of the topless Marie-Elise's pool – which we'll be doing soon – and telling myself this is simply a great way of losing weight. (NB: Reza should avoid travelling in *Vin Blanc* whenever possible.)

Then I get a call on the mobile from Sal in the restaurant and the mood changes.

'You won't believe what's happened. JB's got back from work early, and he's told me to stop work. He says the weekend has started, and that you are working me too hard, nobody in France works at the weekends, I am forbidden to pick up a brush again until Monday morning!'

'He's joking!'

'I'm afraid not. He's taken the pots of paint up to his apartment. Sort of confiscated them.'

This is not only outrageous, but also bizarre. The Tochous own the premises, it's true, but until September at least we are their tenants and as such should be allowed to decorate as and when we choose. What on earth is JB up to?

When I get back to the restaurant, there's a gloomy-looking Sal washing the brushes. JB is not there but it's clear his edict is quite serious. When I confront Christiane about it she smiles unconvincingly and shrugs her shoulders. JB hath spoken. There is no work to be done this weekend. We must all relax and enjoy ourselves, refresh our tired bodies for the week ahead. That's what weekends are for. This is, after all, the land of the thirty-five-hour week. I'm confused. Is JB genuinely concerned that Sal is overworking, or simply flexing his masculine Gallic arrogance, the alpha-male asserting his authority on the hapless females around him? Or maybe a little bit of both? If we weren't under such pressure and against such a tight deadline, it would be laughable.

'What are you going to do?' asks Sal, her face half-frowning, half-smiling, clearly not wishing to get involved, and only too aware that she, like the rest of us, is a recipient of the Tochous' extraordinarily generous hospitality.

I'm actually furious. But the prospect of a major confrontation over such a trivial matter between JB and me, locking horns likes stags engaged in a life-or-death struggle for supremacy, seems absurd. And without the Tochous' continual help and support, we cannot succeed; so on balance and very reluctantly I decide it's probably best to say nothing.

I drive slowly back up to Les Fabres.

I pass a small pile of stones scattered by the side of the road next to a trough of newly dug earth. It looks a bit like the residue of some pagan ritual. I stop and examine it. It takes me a moment to realize that this is the work of one of the thousands of wild boar which roam the hillside, often emerging only at night in fear of the dreaded humans, always searching for worms.

M'sieur Carbenero, baseball hat on back to front, is busy concreting a new area of his steadily shrinking garden. He gives me a little wave, and I wave back. What a strange country this is.

I walk into the cool of the house and immediately sit down at the piano in the study. It is time for my first stab at Schubert's 'Impromptu No. 1'.

～ 7 JUNE ～

Reza is cock-a-hoop after a major breakthrough on the cooking front.

Having been snookered from doing virtually anything else by JB, Reza, Sal and I have been to the Saturday market in Aubenas – probably the biggest of all the markets in the area, involving the enclosure of dozens of little streets which run down the hill from the château. Because it's the biggest commercial centre in the area, Aubenas has a relatively high percentage of North African Arabs, most presumably originating from the former French colonies like Morocco and Algeria, and this unusual cosmopolitan mix tends to become much more visible on market day when the occupants of virtually every house and apartment in the town explode on to the streets; and it's thanks largely to this section of the community that this morning Reza hit upon a gastronomic equivalent of winning the lottery.

Outside an anonymous-looking little shop just across the square from the exquisite Le Fournil restaurant we came across, on a long row of trestle tables, are some of the most fabulous collections of spices that Reza had seen in his life. He danced and skipped around with sheer exuberance at the discovery, before phoning Ramesh in Paris to tell him the news. Ajowan seeds, ground cumin, rose petal masala, green cardamom pods, ground turmeric root, almost anything Reza could conceivably need. And right here on our own doorstep. It transpires the shop is called Papilla and run by the roly-poly Madame Guio, with whom Reza was soon involved in a long and highly animated conversation, on the face of it quite an achievement since he speaks no French and she not one word of English. Clearly the world of spices has its own universal vocabulary.

Leaving behind a beaming Monsieur Guio, Madame led us into her tiny shop, which is so old-fashioned it looks as though it's come straight from the pages of a Dickens' novel. There are shelves from floor to ceiling weighed down with every size of tin and glass jar imaginable. A mass of vivid and exotic yellows, oranges and purples from the labels of the spices alone combine to form a dazzling kaleidoscope of colour. On the old wooden counter stands a pair of ancient scales with which Madame measures out the spices into old-fashioned paper bags; all this taking place amidst the most piquant and evocative of aromas.

There may be no Indian restaurants in the Ardèche, but there's a large demand here, says Madame Guio, amongst the families of African Arabs or amongst mixed-race couples for the various spices that are so common in Indian food.

Anything Reza wants that Madame Guio doesn't have in the shop, she will find for him. And she'll give us thirty days' credit.

The discovery of Papilla led to a general feeling of well-being amongst the three of us.

So after a long lunch in town, we spend most of the afternoon swimming and sunbathing at Marie-Elise's, although for some inexplicable reason Reza still refuses to join us in the water. He needs to get back to London for a few days and we have decided that next week will be the optimum moment for him to be away; when he's back the decorating should be finished, and the chef will be on his way from Paris.

Marie-Elise arrives from the house, brandishing the inevitable bottle of chilled white wine. It is strange to see her with her clothes on. In her other hand she is carrying what looks like a multicoloured piece of paper cut out into the shape of a car. She gives it to me.

'*Pour* L'Été Indien!'

After much repetition and many misunderstandings, it becomes clear that Marie-Elise is offering to repaint *Vin Blanc* in a psychedelic mass of colour based on a series of floral patterns that will make the old van stand out like a Belisha beacon, poor thing, as it races backwards and forwards on the roads around Laurac.

We are all in instant agreement that this is a wonderful idea to market L'Été Indien at no cost whatsoever. Once again I am overwhelmed by the warmth and generosity of Christiane's circle of friends.

I notice that despite her semi-permanent incarceration with the paintbrushes inside the restaurant, Sally Ann's blonde blob of hair is being deliciously bleached by the sunlight, and that her skin is beginning to turn a rich, honey brown.

I can't believe she doesn't have a boyfriend.

REZA: *For the first time since I embarked on this crazy voyage, I'm beginning to think L'Été Indien could work! I never thought I'd hear myself say that, darlings! I even feel relaxed enough to pop back to the*

Star for a day or two to catch up with things there. The menu's sorted, we have a chef, and the discovery of Papilla is a real relief. Nigel seems to have calmed down a little, thank the Lord! He has a good team behind him to hide his inadequacies and get on with the job whatever he says or does. Sally Ann's a huge help and Nigel has clearly taken a shine to her; she's so much more suitable than that tease Celine, although what she thinks of him I have simply no idea! Honestly! The machinations of romance, doesn't it make you sick?

Most, most important: must remember to pick up a pair of Ben de Lisi swimming trunks in Kensington.

∼ 8 JUNE ∼

For the first time in weeks, Celine and I have spent the whole day together, alone.

'I filled the Deux Chevaux up with petrol,' I say, rather amusingly. 'Jump in and let's get on the road to Avignon!' As so often between us the subtleties of humour fail to cross the Anglo-French border. Celine instead marches me out of the house to the Peugeot sports car and tells me to get in. Of course, she drives fast and furiously, and the sunroof remains stubbornly in place, because, unlike Sal, Celine's skin is pale and freckled and, as for so many people living in the south of France, being in the sun for more than a minute or two is regarded as being *de trop*. The road down to Montélimar is steep, windy and extremely dangerous. Six dead, ninety wounded in the last eight years, proclaim huge signs on the roadside, and every now and then we pass the grotesque, life-sized silhouette of a plastic human being, a jagged shaft of red bursting from its chest; each of these represents the scene of a fatal accident. But to show any fear as Celine drives would be so undignified. She is completely familiar with the road. And I am her very *cool* boyfriend, being pursued by pretty English blondes, and shortly to become extremely rich as well as an English television superstar. (Says Charlie.)

Soon we're thrashing down the Autoroute de Soleil and as Celine takes the opportunity to talk in detail about her life, about the financial pressures of the job, the worry of being the single parent of a demanding little boy, of the lack of time and energy for much of a social life in such an introverted and claustrophobic community, I sense again an underlying current of frustration deep within her, a longing to break free. This is a bird who dreams to fly, to travel, to live and breathe and taste the rest of the world.

I have an idea she may be waiting for me to ask her if we can live together. How can one be sure of these things? When I was her age one simply got married. Now it's all so much more complicated. If I ask her, and she says no, where does that leave our future together? And if she says yes? It's possible, after all; if L'Été Indien's a success, I could have a stable financial future locally, and Celine badly needs a father for Quentin. And life could be simple, and sweet.

But, of course, I'm not going to ask her. It's too soon after my divorce. I don't want to live with anyone, certainly not for a few years. I want to sample the freedom and independence I should have had as a young man. But if I don't ask, what will she think then?

The vast thirteenth-century walls and ramparts of Avignon are on a scale that almost takes the breath away, quite amazing. We park the Peugeot in a huge underground car park deep beneath the medieval city and walk up, emerging, blinking in the sunlight, in the square beside the Palais des Papes and the magnificent cathedral of Notre-Dame des Doms. Seizing my hand, she leads me down towards the most famous bridge in France, Le Pont d'Avignon, explaining, as we walk, that the bridge, built in 1147 and the first to cross the mighty river, was the inspiration of a humble shepherd from the Ardèche. He had a vision from God who instructed him that the bridge must be built, and it must be built at Avignon. When asked by the bishops – who deigned to give him an audience – to prove his proximity to the Lord by picking up a huge stone that lay by the river and hold it above his head, the shepherd promptly did so, whereupon the building of the bridge, against the advice from the best engineers of the land, commenced almost immediately.

Cannily, the French authorities have made it almost impossible to see the bridge until you've paid your five Euros and been allowed through the turnstiles. The bridge itself is a bit dull; it's small, plain, and half of it is missing.

'I think I'm going to ask for *half* my money back!' I say with a chuckle, sadly not shared by Celine.

The little bridge is swarming with tourists, each with a large black recorder, telling them the history of the thing, fixed to their ear rather like a ridiculously oversized mobile phone. We walk to the end and back, which takes about forty-five seconds, with me, as no doubt millions of previous simple-minded tourists before me, humming 'Sur le pont d'Avignon', a tune strangely never far from the lips of many English schoolchildren.

'Why is this song so well known in England?' asks Celine.

'I have absolutely no idea.'

Then she steps forward, gives me a brief kiss on the lips, and runs off through the turnstiles into the crowd beyond.

Avignon is a big place, and in the height of summer it's awash with tens of thousands of tourists. It is a miracle I find Celine again. I chance upon her about forty minutes after she disappeared, in one of the hundreds of little cafés which lie spread out beyond the Palais des Papes.

'Look,' is all she says, holding up the ends of a very long translucent blue scarf that is wrapped around her neck.

Blue always suits her so well.

'Do you like it, *chéri*?'

'Very much indeed.'

It is all I can think of to say.

∼ 9 June ∼

Less than four weeks to go before our opening and once again I've made the mistake of browsing through Sir Terence Conran.

At the back of the book he's detailed the countdown to the opening of his first restaurant in Paris. According to his schedule, by now he should have achieved the following:

- ❏ Primary and secondary phases of IT training for all staff completed
- ❏ The induction manual for the front-of-house staff, covering table plans, table numbering, how the service stations work and other vital information has been prepared
- ❏ The health and safety consultants are briefed and give their recommendations
- ❏ Full press packs and invitations to the opening party are distributed to targeted media
- ❏ Half-price-preview mailings go out to targeted customers
- ❏ Ovens are polished

No doubt Conran's Paris restaurant was on a slightly grander scale than ours, but reading this liturgy of precision and detail, intricate preparation and ruthless efficiency reminds me that in reality we are verging on a state of chaos.

Feel better by suggesting to Christiane that Ramsa could polish our oven.

Sal has now completed the final coat of lime green throughout the inside of L'Été Indien so, with Reza back in London, the two of us decide to enjoy a modest celebration down in Largentière at La Calèche, whose tables spill out of the vaulted cellar of a medieval town house just opposite my little Banque Marze. Sal is convinced they serve the finest pizzas she's ever tasted, alongside the rather more predictable list of duck, steak and *caillette* that seem to dominate the menus of every other restaurant in the area.

We'd been once or twice before, and it was clear that the *patron*, Jean-Pierre – a rakish friend of Christiane's, in his mid-thirties, with dubious-looking teeth and a bright red bandanna constantly strapped to his head, and an undoubted cheeky charm manifested in an uninterrupted flow of smiles and flirting – had taken a shine to Sally Ann. He has introduced her to something called *picon bière*, a thick, local dark beer laced with a potent lemon *sirop*, which she guzzles away at gratefully, ordering another and then one more, whilst the two of them chatter away in that odd hybrid language that so often seems the perfect method of communication between two people who are attracted and yet are unconsciously keen to exclude everyone else. Behind the till inside, Jean-Pierre's petite wife, Chloe, occasionally stretches up on tiptoes and casts a dark-eyed glare of disapproval.

Jean-Pierre is a formidable drinker. Often he simply forgets to stop drinking from the night before, bringing over bottles of whisky or wine to our table and knocking back glass after glass, under the pretext that the guests are buying and it would appear churlish to refuse. Chloe looks on suspiciously but seems unable to intervene. But his eye on control of the pizza oven never wavers.

Do I mind the flirtatious exchanges between Jean-Pierre and Sal? I want her to have a good time, to enjoy herself, to ensure she doesn't regret her sojourn here. Why would I mind her having fun with the guy? And why am I even considering such questions?

~ 10 JUNE ~

Reza looks a different person when I pick him up from Lyons airport.

Pounding up the Autoroute de Soleil in *Vin Blanc* under the relentless midday sun, I was sweating so abundantly I had real difficulty gripping the steering wheel. With temperatures again into the forties, even the French are beginning to complain about the heat. All I could do was keep the throttle hard on the floor; once the old tank reaches terminal velocity it keeps going like a rocket, scattering BMWs and Mercedes, with their immaculate, precious bodywork, in all directions.

I walked through the curtain of cold air inside the fiercely air-conditioned terminal looking like a refugee who had just taken a stroll in a tropical monsoon, but I had reached that point where I couldn't care less, even though everyone else in the entire building appeared as though they'd just stepped out of a very cool *Vogue* fashion shoot.

Thanks to *Vin Blanc*'s science-defying speed, I was a few minutes early for the plane, so went straight to the bar and downed two *seize cents soixante-quatre*, scarcely drawing breath. Then I looked around me. On the other side of the concourse, two heavily armed and very sinister-looking soldiers were striding towards me. I suppose this is a common enough sight these days in airports across the world, but these huge guys were like something out of a Schwarzenegger movie, seven-foot high, shaved, bullet-like heads, enormous sub-machine guns, constantly whispering into radio ear-pieces, eyes like lizards, darting around in search of any sudden or unexpected movement.

They were almost beside me by this time and I have to say their presence considerably unnerved me. What could they want from me? Manu had told me always to pretend I spoke no French at all if stopped by the fearsome *gendarmes*, a task not hard for me to achieve.

The face of the barman, a few feet away, was frozen, statue-like, the blood drained from it. He swallowed, hard, as the shadows of the two giants fell across the bar.

One of the soldiers turned his back on the bar, finger on the trigger of the gun, whilst the other – after a final flick of the eyes around the concourse – leant across to the barman.

'*Deux bières, s'il vous plaît, M'sieur.*'

And there they stood, fingers of one hand grasping the machine-gun and those of the other clasping a beer glass, slurping away at their beers, froth forming on their upper lip, cool as cucumbers.

As so often, I'm aware that however superficially the British way of life seems to be drawing ever closer to our European neighbours', just beneath the surface the gaps yawn wider than ever.

Reza seems rejuvenated by his trip to London. His friends appear to have boosted his confidence in our project and he's suddenly overflowing with optimism and confidence, a kind of vibrant energy that immediately evaporates the moment he steps into the sub-Saharan temperature in *Vin Blanc*. If he'd managed to put on a pound or two over the last few days by beefing up on the familiar comfort-food of the Star, he must have lost it all within a few minutes of our high-speed journey back to Laurac.

Back in the restaurant, though – when he walked in and saw the results of Sal's labours – the excitement seemed to return with a rush. He said he was genuinely thrilled. We spent a happy couple of hours together, selecting which pictures of our extraordinary collection should go where: the strange Indian lady holding the Luger beneath a Union Jack, on the wall opposite the little balcony; the bizarre blue infant Buddha with its bulging frog-like eyes, beside the kitchen door; the white handprints on the Technicolor canvas, above the wood-burning stove; the portrait of Celine lookalike Hedy Lamarr with its real paper camellia popping out above one ear, above the bar.

'So many beautiful things in India,' whispered Christiane, 'and he has to bring me these!'

I stood back and tried to imagine how the scene would confront a customer. The more I considered it, the more I became convinced that Reza had made a bold and clever choice in his interior design, an eclectic selection of images, lights and artefacts that are indeed well offset by his warm, subtle, lime-green walls. The object of this exercise is, above all, to be different – to surprise, intrigue, and yes, to shock our introverted and often complacent French neighbours – and Reza's creation is nothing if not different. And soon, I guess, we must get around to what dear Sir Terence recommended we should have done weeks ago – try to tickle the interest of the local press. Surely, then, the bolder the better.

Later, Reza astonished us all by producing, with a typically theatrical flourish, a tiny pair of blue and yellow psychedelic Lycra swimming trunks he'd had made in London by someone called Ben de Lisi.

'Shall we all go for a dip, darlings?'

REZA: Oh merde (pardon my French). It's not what I would have wanted, not one bit. But on a limited budget, one has to do one's best. I used my ingenuity and the best of my contacts to gather together everything I felt we needed from London to decorate the place. It was all begged, borrowed or stolen, at no cost to our restaurant budget, and beggars can't be choosers. The result is a bit of a bodge and a compromise, and I'm not used to working like this; we are chronically under-funded and under-staffed, but I know that if the others had even suspected my disappointment, it would have been worse still. Zee says I simply must pretend to be thrilled. Not hard for me to do! I simply adore pretending to be thrilled! And I really don't mind. A few days back home at the Star has put all this into sharp perspective. It should be fun, an adventure, and if it all goes pear-shaped, so be it. It's just a little restaurant, for God's sake – not exactly a matter of life or death – and restaurants come and go. So I intend to do my best, enjoy every moment, and try to eat as much as I can.

More importantly, the swimming trunks went down (or rather stayed up) a treat. All I need to do now is learn how to swim.

～ 13 JUNE ～

This morning I had an unexpected call from my mother.

'I'm afraid I've got some bad news for you,' she said.

A few years ago I'd produced the long-running documentary series called *Country House* for the BBC, which followed the day-to-day lives of the then Lord and Lady Tavistock in their magnificent stately home, Woburn Abbey, and 13,000-acre estate in the heart of Bedfordshire. The programmes were shot, intermittently, over a four-year period during which, after a slightly frosty start, I not only came to know the Tavs extremely well, but also eventually formed a firm friendship with them both. About eight months ago, Lord T's father, the thirteenth Duke of Bedford, died rather suddenly in Santa Fe, New Mexico. Robin, Lord T, then became the fourteenth Duke and his wife, Henrietta, the Duchess. Now, explained my mother, Robin too was dead, having suffered a massive stroke. He had the first stroke fifteen years ago, and he had always called the time since then his 'extra years'. But even so his death was a real shock. I would, of course, return for the funeral, whenever the date was fixed.

I took a strong black coffee out on to the terrace and inevitably a wave of memories started flooding back. When the contract with the BBC for the first series had been signed, Robin and Henrietta invited me to have dinner at the Abbey and stay over. I left London late, grabbing my one suit, an old and rather threadbare grey one, and threw a clean shirt, pair of underpants and a toothbrush in a plastic bag.

Woburn Abbey, ancestral seat to the Dukes of Bedford for over four hundred years, is a vast palace of a place. I parked outside the front door and rather nervously pulled the bell. An under-butler mysteriously appeared.

'We normally carry the guests' luggage to the bedroom, Mr Farrell,' he said, rather disdainfully, as though he thought considerably less of me for being untitled, and took the plastic bag from my hand. 'Follow me, please.' We then embarked on a fifteen-mile walk to my suite at the top of the house. It was huge. An entrance lobby, a large bedroom and then a dressing room with large wardrobes and a huge selection of make-up, shampoos and sprays. Off that was an unfeasibly large bathroom, with almost everything to hand one could possibly require – toothbrush, toothpaste, razors, shaving cream, soaps, aftershaves, even Paracetamol. The under-butler was waiting patiently for me to return from my tour, still holding the little plastic bag in front of him.

'We normally unpack the guests' luggage for them, Mr Farrell,' he said.

I thought for a moment of the contents of the bag.

'There's really no need, thank you.'

'Drinks will be served in the living room beside His Lordship's study, seven thirty sharp.'

At the appointed time I was there, sipping a large gin and tonic brought by the butler, nervously fingering my tie. I hadn't really thought about this. Shouldn't I be wearing a dinner jacket?

Then the family all arrived, Robin and Henrietta with their son and heir, Lord Howland, their second son, Robbie, and his American wife, Stephanie.

They were all wearing jeans.

I rather took to them after that.

They showed me the famous Canaletto collection, the largest collection of Venetian Canalettos in the world, the fabulous Reynolds Room, and the wonderful Armada picture of Elizabeth I. Then there was dinner, with the two rather intimidating butlers standing a few feet away throughout, and afterwards coffee and brandy in the magnificent Henry Holland Drawing Room, the finest room of its type in the country. Then Robin and I got stuck into two enormous Havana cigars.

'Would you mind blowing the smoke a little more in the opposite direction, Mr Farrell?' said Henrietta quietly, without looking at me as she worked away at her tapestry. 'At the moment you appear to be blowing it on to the Rembrandt self-portrait just above you on the wall.'

This morning, when I got the news of Robin's sad death, I managed to dig out some decent writing paper and an old fountain pen and, instead of going to the restaurant, sat out under the umbrella on the terrace, sipping gallons more coffee and struggling to find the words to write to Henrietta.

It's totally unexpected, and in very sad circumstances, but for the first time in months, I'm going home.

~ 15 JUNE ~

Information-gathering and gastronomic espionage of our principal competitors is producing dividends.

Last night we visited what's become the most fashionable restaurant in Largentière over the last year, the converted goat's-cheese farm, Madeline, on the hill to the north and looking back over the medieval town. It's been cleverly and sympathetically renovated, and has a new terrace, still smelling of wood-varnish, to utilize that mesmerizing view down the valley and to complement the old beamed interior, which they've brought to life with a series of enormous, blown-up, early twentieth-century photographs. These are of gnarled old goat herds, living in incredibly primitive circumstances, armed with a selection of peculiarly looped tobacco pipes boldly emerging from long grizzly beards, and accompanied by their witch-like womenfolk who are bowed down by wide wooden yokes bearing vast buckets overflowing with goats' milk.

The secret of Madeline's sudden success is sheer simplicity. The food is wonderful, but there's virtually no choice. You select one of just two starters – the first is always based on goat's cheese, the other is also always faithful to the locality, like terrine of *marron*, or chestnut. But for the rest of the meal you get what you are given. There's one main course, always a meat dish; that's followed by a deliciously soft *fromage blanc*, a sour goat's cheese like a yoghurt heaped over by lots of sugar or *sirop* of *marron* or thyme; and then on to the dessert of the day, an elaborate dish of fruit tart or meringue decked out in some dramatic theatrical creation, like caramelized spun-sugar lattice-work. But it's a system that works: it's actually a relief as well as something of a novelty to be told what one is eating.

As a result of such a limited menu, the cost of the ingredients is kept amazingly low. Like most small businesses in rural France, it's a family-run affair, thereby avoiding most employment tax (we've been threatened by 20 per cent). So, as long as you trust the taste and professionalism of the *patron*, it's very good value: cost of the set menu for dinner is only 22 Euros.

For lunch today, we drive out of Largentière to the east, up past the unbelievably grandiose Courts of Justice, like a hugely out-of-place Greek temple built on the disproportionate wealth from the silk worms and the silver mines, and out to Chassiers – there to the little two-roomed restaurant operated by two well-known local gay guys. Henri and Gérard is guarded by a Great Dane the size of a small donkey, and boasts precisely the opposite type of menu to Madeline: a huge, weighty, leather-bound bible made up of page after page of individual dishes, and combinations of rich, meaty food, a massive list for so modest a place. You can spend 40 Euros there without a second thought.

The research sparks a heated debate between Reza and Christiane over prices for L'Été. Our set menu – a selection of three starters, then a choice of a chicken, lamb or prawn main dish, followed by a simple choice of desserts – should, according to Christiane, be at least 30 Euros; Reza is convinced we should start at only 25 Euros to draw people in, then increase the price if things go well. Christiane says this would be suicide; it would seriously antagonize our customers. Reza says we need to accurately cost-out the menu before making a final decision. I watch all this unfold and for once enjoy the spectacle of someone else grappling to make a decision.

Later we deposit *Vin Blanc* at Marie-Elise's for her psychedelic makeover. She'll be returned to us in a couple of days. She's become so much a part of our lives, I feel bereft without her; it's like saying goodbye to a close relative about to enter surgery for a life-threatening operation.

This evening, things deteriorate. I'm stricken by an absurd bout of homesickness.

In the space of just an hour or two, all three of my children have called me at Les Fabres, and the sound of their relentlessly cheerful voices has left me with a sad feeling of loss and guilt. Tom, twenty-two, battling his way through a degree course in French and Linguistics at King's College, London, when we all know he'd much rather be running a beachside bar in the remote Greek island of Amorgos, which we'd fallen in love with after two consecutive summer holidays there. Alexandra, twenty-one, studying English at Exeter, beautiful and happy but overshadowed by concerns for her handsome boyfriend, Jonty, whose father is dying of Motor Neurone Disease. And Georgina, fourteen going on twenty-five, just entering that bewildering emotional journey from schoolgirl to womanhood, hormones fizzing like Roman candles.

Apparently today is Father's Day, but piled on top of all the usual guilt of the divorce comes the knowledge that I've simply not been around at a time they need all the help they can get: I've not seen them for months.

I will do my damnedest to see them next weekend, after the funeral. It's not much. And maybe such a fleeting visit will compound the problem.

Tonight, whilst Reza begins the inevitable slogging away at Schubert on the lower deck of Les Fabres, I wrestle my thoughts back to L'Été Indien, which oddly takes much concentration, and some considerable time.

Just over two weeks to our opening night. According to the Gospel of St Terence, by this stage we should have begun IT and systems training, initiated kitchen and front-of-house induction days, and taped service routes on to the floor.

There must be something else I should be doing which we've forgotten all about?

Robin's funeral is in London at the end of this week on Friday, 20 June. It's the same date as their wedding anniversary. The service is at eleven o'clock at the church of St Clement Danes in the Strand, the same place that he and Henrietta were married exactly forty-two years before.

It's all so sad.

～ 17 JUNE ～

The final piece in our jigsaw, Ramesh the chef, is about to drop into place. We are, at long last, about to be in business.

His imminent arrival the day after tomorrow sends a buzz of excitement through the air, with Reza scurrying around the southern Ardèche like a blue-arsed fly in a last-minute panic search for a karhai, chipyo, vaghar bowls etc., all apparently essential utensils for an Indian kitchen. I am to pick Ramesh up from the Paris TGV at Montélimar and drive him back to Laurac, which could be a fascinating journey, given the state of his

English and my Hindi. It'll also be a busy travelling day for me. In the evening I'm to drive back up to Lyons for the cheap late-night flight to Stansted, and home.

This morning, an extraordinary explosion of metallic floral colour pulls up with a bang on the road outside the restaurant. This turns out to be our beloved and newly christened *Vin Psychedelic* after her dramatic spray-paint makeover, with a beaming Marie-Elise behind the wheel. The van really is a magnificent sight. Reza, Sal and I pull out a loudly protesting Christiane and push her, along with the rest of us, into the back, and off we roar, tooting full-blast, on a high-speed tour of the village, much to the astonishment of the locals, with us lot shouting and whooping like a bunch of teenage girls on an illegal outing from St Trinian's.

As Reza says, in his inimitable restaurant jargon, the dear old van has indeed become the perfect *marketing tool.*

In the evening we bomb up to Vals Les Bains, with its casino and theatre and splendid town square, once so familiar as our regular stomping ground when we had time on our hands, but now rarely enjoyed except as a quick stopover for essential supplies en route to Les Fabres; thence up the narrow, rock-encrusted valley of the Volane river to Antraigues, to sample the brand-new restaurant of an old friend.

Over the last three years, the extraordinarily energetic Belgian Annick, with the help (and cash) of her millionaire ex-husband, Herman, has completed the superhuman task of converting a vast old silk mill into the biggest single complex of luxury holiday apartments in the Ardèche.

From the start, everything about Annick's project seemed fantastically ambitious. From within the bowels of the huge old factory, a whole new world of concrete and steel would emerge – there were to be eighteen en-suite loft apartments equipped with amazingly futuristic furniture, like individual works of modern sculpture, from Milan; a restaurant, a gymnasium, a large pool, saunas, rooms for holistic contemplation and yoga, and an enormous and very lavishly equipped honeymoon suite constructed almost entirely of steel and glass and looking like a billionaire's brothel from a sci-fi movie. The place was even to have its own electricity supply, to be drawn from a renovated dynamo system powered by the flowing waters of the river below. The locals looked on with amusement, shaking their heads wearily, saying that it could never be done.

The centrepiece of this new, living organism was to be the dining room, the size of an aircraft hangar, which Annick had transformed into a pastiche of a Paris Métro station – one life-sized steel-framed train apparently leaving one platform (containing lavatories, showers, washing-up machines) whilst another train (bar, massive and superbly equipped kitchen) was arriving at a second platform. It's like a film set. Including the balconies, which lead out from the main eating area – Annick had them built out over the river on huge steel piles – she can feed two hundred and fifty people without difficulty. The investment must have been colossal.

Now, against all the odds, Annick has realized her dream, and Le Moulinage has opened on schedule, with real paying customers, we were keen to sample the delights of the most talked-about new restaurant south of Lyons.

Annick was pleased to see us, although the strain on the striking features of that bold, defiant face, beneath its mop of bright orange hair, was beginning to emerge. The cavernous restaurant seemed strangely quiet. Annick insisted on champagne and sat us down at one of the dozens of circular glass-topped tables that spin out across the floor from the railway sidings, and slowly explained that she was having trouble with the French.

'The locals came to eat here a lot in the early part of the season, we were busy every night,' she said. 'Then the loft apartments started to fill up with guests from Belgium, where I had advertised extensively, and we've scarcely had any French here since. Is this what you would call *snobs*?'

Yet she sounded cheerful enough.

'And now that the Belgians have arrived in force, being Belgians, they bring all their own food and only ever eat in their apartments. Believe it or not, Le Moulinage is full, it's booked throughout July, not that you'd know it from this,' she said, opening her arms wide and looking around. Her laughter seemed genuine enough. 'It's no problem. The French will return when the Belgians leave in September. Now, you must try my food, I want an honest opinion.'

I like her style.

Reza chose whole baked sea bass in a bag, stuffed with herbs, Sal had pappardelle with spicy sausage meat and mixed wild mushrooms, and I plumped for the roasted salmon wrapped in herbs and newspaper. It seemed a bizarre selection. We all swapped dishes and the unanimous verdict was that the French were being stubborn and daft. The food was delicious.

Was Annick's experience an ominous sign for the future of L'Été? I sensed it was a question forming in all our minds, even Annick's, but thankfully nobody had the insensitivity to articulate it.

It was, after all, a bit late to change tack now.

'I'm relieved you like the food,' said Annick. 'I fired the chef last week.'

There was a stunned silence around the table.

'He just wasn't able to cope.'

'So who's been doing the cooking?'

'Fredo, my barman. He's never cooked in his life.'

Annick disappeared into the kitchen, and re-emerged a few moments later carrying a dog-eared recipe book.

'Don't tell anyone, but Fredo found this in an old second-hand bookstore in Aubenas. It's wonderful. The recipes are really imaginative, simple to source and amazingly easy to cook. Everyone adores them. We're working our way through the book, trying new food each night. We've reached page 37,' she said, smiling with obvious pride. This woman has the ingenuity, resources and determination to survive a nuclear explosion. 'It's written by a young chef nobody has ever heard of. Life's unfair, isn't it? With a book like this, the guy should be famous and rich.'

I held out my hand and Annick gave me the book.

'It's by someone called Jamie Oliver,' I said. 'Back home in England, Annick, he's doing just *fine*.'

⁓ 18 JUNE ⁓

The bombshell went off this morning just as we were settling down with the glasses and bottle for *Ricard moins quart*.

Like so many truly devastating explosions, it came from a completely unexpected source, and went off without any warning whatsoever.

The phone rang and as usual Christiane answered it, handing over the receiver to Reza with the words: 'It's Ramesh.'

It was immediately obvious something was wrong. Reza started shooting off questions in Hindi, walking out on the terrace and slamming the door sharply behind him. Through the windows we could see Reza's face, muscles working, shocked and animated, as he paced up and down, constantly pushing his fingers up through his tousled hair.

The conversation lasted an eternity. Sal and I looked at each other, unable to speak.

Eventually Reza stopped talking and shoved the aerial hard back down into the receiver. Unaware that we were observing him, he continued to pace up and down, apparently talking to himself, maybe working out how to break the news to us.

He needn't have bothered.

'He's not coming,' I said.

Reza looked at the ground.

'Not at all?'

'Not at all. He's changed his mind. Something about his family being unhappy.' We all looked blankly at each other, again in silence. There seemed nothing much to add. Christiane in particular looked really shocked, the blood had drained from her face. 'He might have given us some warning.'

The implications are too appalling to contemplate. Everyone in the southern Ardèche knows that the famous Le Relais Fleuri re-opens as L'Été Indien at 7 p.m. on Friday, 4 July. The staff have been hired. The invitations have been printed. The mayor of Laurac has agreed to be present.

It's a public relations disaster. And I have to fly to London tomorrow.

'I'll find someone else,' said Reza, at last.

'Reza, we open in two weeks.'

'I'll find someone, believe me.'

'Find them? And get them here? And train them up, all ready for 4 July?'

'Well, maybe not by 4 July.'

So there it is. The words have been said. We're going to have to postpone the opening. And already we are almost halfway through the season.

Christiane left the room.

'Absolutely bloody fantastic!' said Charlie.

'For God's sake, Charlie!'

This was all too much.

Claudio was already re-running the footage on the little video monitor strapped to his chest. They were hunched over it, *laughing*.

'That's definitely an end-of-episode cliff-hanger!' said Charlie, jumping up and down and whooping like a child.

'Vonderful! Vait till they see dis back in London!' said Clouds.

Reza's spent most of the day on the phone. I feel helpless; there is simply nothing I can do. Except drink *pastis*, which Sal and I decide to do. Copiously.

Sal, bless her, is being relentlessly optimistic. A short delay won't make a huge difference. We have the loyalty of Christiane's small army of friends and customers. We will still be the talking point of the *vivarais*. Reza knows what he is doing; it'll all be fine.

I'm writing this at 2 a.m., with a heavy head as well as a heavy heart. Sleep seems out of the question, to be replaced no doubt by long hours of agonizing and frustration, the same thoughts, as they tend to do in the early hours, spinning round and round, tumbling over and over. I guess Reza has done what he can, thrown out the net far and wide. Long ago exhausted, he has mercifully abandoned Schubert and retreated to his room below, with the promise that at least half a dozen *'reliable contacts'* in the industry will be phoning first thing in the morning.

I search Sir Terence's book for advice on what the hell to do when your chef walks out on you two weeks before opening night. Oddly can find none.

REZA: On the phone tonight Zee's tone has an annoying I told you so quality about it: 'this was a disaster waiting to happen'. I too am not remotely surprised, this is absolutely typical of the business, and it's only Nigel's complete ignorance of what he's doing that's resulted in him blaming me totally – and this, despite the fact that one of his most irritating phrases – 'We're flying by the seat of our pants, Reza old bean, so let's enjoy it!' – is never far from his lips. I'm so angry at the way everyone assumes that the responsibility for finding a chef is mine alone, and I'm so angry with myself for allowing this to happen. Of course, this is an ill-conceived project, but I rather liked the barminess of it all, and went along with it because I like the guy and genuinely want to help him out. But, darlings, I simply don't do miracles. Frankly, I don't think we stand a hope in hell of finding a good Indian chef at such short notice. But I'm going to try in Nice, where apparently it's nicer. Zee has a good contact there, who says he may be able to help. The clothes shops are simply to die for anyway, so all may not yet be lost.

∼ 19 JUNE ∼

I'm sitting on the plane.

A brilliant white moon is casting a thin, pale glow on the surface of the wispy cloud all around. As always, the plane's almost full, but nearly everyone seems dead, slumped in sleep. At the back, two bright-orange-clad flight attendants are moving around silently in the shadows, giggling conspiratorially, hands guiltily over their mouths.

In a way it's a relief to leave Laurac and all its problems behind.

For most of my life I've been terrified of flying. Not just the fear of crashing, but a loathing of the sheer claustrophobia of it all, the paralysing lack of control. (Does this mean I always have to be in control of my life in general, and if so, is this a weakness?) It reached a point a few years ago when I started to find excuses for turning down journalistic or broadcasting work abroad if I discovered that it might involve climbing into a plane.

Reluctantly, I decided I had no option but to confront the fear. My hands shaking, I signed up to a one-day 'fear of flying' course run by two British Airways pilots at a Heathrow hotel. The morning would involve lectures by engineers and technicians on how it is physically impossible for an aircraft to simply drop out of the sky. Later, the psychologists would take over, giving advice on how to cope with stress, irrational fear, panic. At the end of the day we were all to take a deep breath, get on a Boeing 737 waiting specifically for us on the tarmac, and take to the skies for a short flight.

As the dreaded day drew closer, I became more and more nervous. After a sleepless night, I drove to Heathrow as slowly as I could, hands trembling on the steering wheel, dripping with sweat.

I parked outside the hotel. Maybe I should quit now, just turn around and drive back home, no one would be the wiser. Then I grew angry. It was a Sunday; everyone else was enjoying a day of rest, why should I put myself through this? I should be at home with my family, carving the roast joint, drinking too much red wine.

With feet of concrete, I dragged myself out of the car, and into the lobby of the hotel. It was packed. Fighting back the urge to flee to the lavatory and throw up, I looked around me. Everyone else seemed amazingly calm and relaxed, sipping coffee and smiling at each other's little witticisms. We assembled in the lecture hall, and the senior pilot stood to address us.

'Of course, you are all dreading the day ahead,' he began, coolly. He'd clearly done this once or twice before. 'And what, I wonder, will be the worst moment of this dreadful day?' He looked around theatrically, clearly not expecting any response. We were in the hands of a well-rehearsed, polished, master performer. I was transfixed.

'You may be thinking that the worst moment of the day will be climbing aboard the 737? Or maybe as the wheels take off from the runway? Or reaching 40,000 feet? Or the touch-down?'

Again he paused for effect.

'Well, I have to tell you, ladies and gentlemen, that the worst moment of the day . . . is behind you.'

Another pause.

'Walking into this room is the hardest thing you will have to do today. If you have the courage to be here at all, you will find the fear of everything else will be dwarfed by comparison.'

It was brilliant psychology, and it worked brilliantly. Of the two hundred and twenty-six people in the room that day, two hundred and twenty-five walked on to the 737 for the flight around southern England. There may have been a round of applause when we touched down forty-five minutes later, but for most of us the monster had been lanced.

Without that day, my life over the last few years would have been completely different. I've now flown backwards and forwards to Lyons or Nîmes on so many cheap flights I've actually started to enjoy it, and even reassure fellow passengers, nervous when we hit turbulence (trying hard not to sound smug or patronizing, you understand, but normally failing), that, really, there is no need for concern. Just breathe deeply.

Reza is going to Nice tomorrow. There's been no tradition of Indian cuisine in Nice but, like Paris and Lyons, over the last few years one or two Indian restaurants have started to appear there, and are surprisingly popular. More are opening by the month. Reza has found a contact there who says he is sure he can find a chef, although I'll believe it when I see it.

I'm not looking forward to tomorrow. Has anyone ever looked forward to a funeral?

∼ *20 June* ∼

Instructions were quite clear: no black.

It is piercingly hot in London, too, and only when I arrive here do I discover in the English press that the heatwave that is intensifying right across Europe is already beginning to claim lives in the south of France.

The service, with shafts of sunlight beaming through the Gothic windows of St Clement Danes Church in the Strand, is simple and moving, as I knew it would be.

Henrietta, dressed in dark blue, would have planned every last detail of her husband's funeral just as she had told me she has already done for her own. Every hymn to be sung, every prayer to be said was laid down years in advance. Henrietta has even had her own coffin made to her specific design.

This matter of fact approach, such an implicit acceptance and acknowledgement of the inevitable role death has to play in life, I find both humbling and inspirational. Of course, it puts the daily trivialities of the living into harsh perspective and sobers and calms the furrowed brow, which is why I emerge blinking in the sunshine, strangely elated, as I always have from so many funerals before.

The immediate members of the family are heading straight back to Woburn, so, unusually, there's no wake, although I do catch the eye of Andrew Russell, who upon the death of his father becomes the fifteenth Duke of Bedford. He thanks me for coming, and asks how the restaurant idea is going in France.

'You don't know the names of any good Indian chefs, do you, Andrew? Or should I say *Your Grace*?'

His reaction to the concept of our Indian restaurant is very gratifying, and typical of everyone I talk to over here: they're intrigued, enthusiastic, amused. After the service I call round to my old office in Soho Square. At least four old mates say they are going to fly out one weekend, stay at Les Fabres and eat their way through as much food as they can at L'Été Indien. I say: 'Sure, I'll believe it when it happens.' Whereupon they all pull out their diaries and we make a date for early September. I'm unbelievably grateful for the moral support. Then some bright spark suggests we go and have lunch at the Red Fort Indian restaurant just round the corner in Dean Street. This turns out to be a deeply depressing experience. Décor: smart and simple modern furniture, soft pastel colours, clever lighting gives an atmosphere of cool spaciousness. Food: sophisticated menu, beautifully produced. Exquisite. I had a wonderful *bhaap gosht*, Jules a magnificent *murgh mirchi ka salaan* and Lindsey a lovely *tandoori pasliaan*, and all for £14 a head. Service: unobtrusive, impeccable.

Verdict: I'm never, *ever,* going there again.

Afterwards I go for a walk along Oxford Street, across Tottenham Court Road, and into Bloomsbury, partly just relishing what has become the strangeness of London, partly because I want to be alone, and partly because I'm drawn there. Much of it is still owned by the Russells of Woburn; it was the fourth Duke of Bedford who developed the whole area in the seventeenth century, including Covent Garden, which the eleventh Duke sold in 1917, investing the entire proceeds into Russian War Bonds a few weeks before the Revolution, and lost the lot. The streets and squares are all named after the family: Russell Square, Bedford Place, Howland Street, Woburn Place.

By an odd coincidence I find myself in Tavistock Square, which is where I lived in a hall of residence as a very green young medical student. I come from a family of medics, so when I left school it seemed perfectly natural to decide to become a doctor. I applied to St Bart's and – after being relentlessly quizzed by a panel of interviewers about my prowess and potential on the rugby field – to my amazement got accepted. Unfortunately I rather abused the privilege. I was only seventeen and, living in the heart of one of the most exciting cities in the world, I was astonished and delighted to learn that one didn't get caned if one skipped lectures. I spent most days asleep, in the cinema or theatre, or partying. The first year passed me by in a haze. The end of year exams were a farce. My physics professor was the distinguished Polish-born Nobel Prize winner, Sir Joseph Rotblat, who worked on the Manhattan team in Mexico during the Second World War, developing the world's first atomic bomb, and then spent most of his life afterwards working tirelessly for the case against nuclear proliferation. The only one of his questions I could even vaguely attempt to answer was along these lines: Explain what happens to the physiology of the pilot of a fighter jet undergoing fast and tight turns and manoeuvres during an air battle. I'd read *Reach For The Sky*, the biography of the legendary Douglas Bader, only a few weeks before, and remembered that whilst for most pilots the effects of centrifugal force meant that in tight turns blood was forced down into their legs so they were in constant danger of passing out, for the legless Bader this simply didn't apply, and he was much the better pilot for it. Faced with a three-hour exam ahead of me, I stretched this story out so that it almost became a potted history of the Second World War, with the Nazi jackboot striding victoriously across Europe *despite the unbelievable courage and heroism of the Polish pilots flying with the RAF.* Sadly my strategy failed to impress the good professor, who merely put a question mark at the end of my fifteen-page essay, and, for probably the first and last time in his career, awarded this student zero marks for the exam.

Sadly, I fared little better in the biochemistry. We were each asked to conduct a particularly revolting experiment on a live locust in the exam; it had to be pinned down on a board so that we could dissect its stomach and extract its intestines, which then had to be dunked in some chemical in a small glass dish to test their active enzyme levels. Predictably, I had no idea how one properly pins down any live creature, let alone a small squirming locust clearly very eager indeed to stay alive. Fighting back my growing nausea, I engaged the locust in mortal combat until I managed to hold it down long enough to get a section of intestine out of its gut, whereupon, with a mighty contortion, the beast wrenched itself free of the pins, and flew off. Much to the consternation of the lecturer in charge and all the other students, we all watched, transfixed, as the poor thing crawled across the ceiling, clearly in its final death throes, the pins sagging from its wings and its intestines hanging out like washing on a line, blood splashing down indiscriminately on the examination papers below.

Later I was summoned to the Dean's office.

'My colleagues and I have held a meeting about you, Mr Farrell,' he said, sternly. 'We decided unanimously that I should put the following question to you.'

'Go ahead, sir!' I responded chirpily, blissfully unaware of my impending fate.

'The question is as follows: *Have you ever considered any other career apart from medicine?*'

The next minute I was out of the door, and unemployed. I collected my bags from Connaught Hall, here in Tavistock Square, and set off to begin a new life. That was the last time I was here. Over thirty years ago.

The remainder of my tertiary education was firmly based in the University of Life: I worked as a labourer on building sites and motorway projects, as a chauffeur, in bars, and even – in the unfulfilled hope of ensnaring some millionaire widow – as a freelance domestic cleaner. Then I got a job on my local newspaper as a cub reporter, and discovered an enduring and true love: journalism, which I have pursued with vigour and huge satisfaction in print, on radio and television. And in a way, opening a restaurant is part of the same story. Good journalism is about *the experience* of people, things and events. It's been a dream for years to open a restaurant. Now I want to try it. I want to see what it's really like. And if I can earn a living from it, great.

I go back to my tiny flat in Farnham. It's part of a nine-apartment block built in the early eighties, overlooked by the regional headquarters of the Inland Revenue, whose employees, rather unnervingly, look straight into my living room. There always seem to be more of them hovering about when I'm late with my tax bill. Which is most of the time. And which is probably why I so adore the terrace at Les Fabres, which isn't looked over by any tax inspectors at all, at least to my knowledge. Most of my fellow flat-dwellers are elderly gentlewomen who have a very possessive nature about our *enclave*. There's a row of neatly numbered parking bays in the courtyard, and woe betide anyone who parks in the incorrect place. The day I moved in I put my car carefully in my bay, but we had to park the van with my furniture in it in one of my neighbours' parking bays. In less than a minute its owner had hurried out, complaining bitterly.

I tried to explain that I would be unloading only for a short time, to no avail. The van had to be moved and moved now. In the end I relented. 'OK. I give in. We'll move the van now so you can put your car in your bay.'

'Car? What car? I don't own a car.'

It's strange to be back in my dusty little home. The perspectives all seem to have changed; I feel rather like a child who has been away for a long time and returns, much taller, to rooms that suddenly seem much smaller.

Marie-Christine, from number seven, knocks on the door and pops her head around.

'I've still got your azalea plant, I've been watering it every day and it's fine.'

'Thanks.'

'How much longer are you likely to be away for?'

'I'm afraid, Marie-Christine, I have absolutely no idea.'

The words have a horrible ring of truth about them.

This evening I take Tom, Alex and Georgie round the corner to my local, the Nelson's Arms, for dinner. They are amazingly understanding, very sympathetic.

'Don't worry about a thing,' says Tom. 'It's cool. We just want you to be happy.'

Later, after a couple of glasses of wine, Alex asks me how I'm getting on with Celine.

'We had a wonderful day together in Avignon. Fantastic city.'

'Dad, how's it really going?'

The subject of Celine has become an awkward one between us. I'm well aware that my elder daughter probably disapproves of the match, not least because Celine is closer to her age than to mine, but so far she's been tactful enough not to say so directly.

'Why don't you all come out to L'Été Indien and see for yourself?'

Much to my delight, there is real enthusiasm for this idea, although I've no idea if I'll be able to pay for their air tickets.

Just before going to bed I have a call from Sally Ann at L'Été Indien.

'Just as well you're not here now. The Tochous are very unhappy; they're very upset about the way things are working out. Christiane's been crying for much of the day.'

I'm shocked to hear this. Apparently Christiane, seemingly always so cheerful and optimistic about everything, is appalled that Ramesh has pulled out and has become convinced we are heading for disaster, and taking with us the Tochous' standing and reputation within their own community. And it seems JB, again in a very French macho kind of way, feels angry on his wife's behalf.

'And since it's your name on the contract, it's you, not Reza, who's the villain of the piece, I'm afraid,' said Sal.

I feel wretched. The Tochous have become firm friends, and as such I feel a strong moral, let alone legal, obligation to them; that they now feel I've betrayed their trust is hard to take.

'So sorry you've had to carry this on your own, Sal,' I say.

'Don't worry, Freckles, you owe me. And maybe it's better you aren't here. Maybe it will help clear the air now that the tears have flowed.'

I have reached an all-time low. And I'm powerless to do anything about it.

It's tempting just to stay here. At home.

∼ 22 JUNE ∼

I remember that when Richard Nixon resigned the Presidency of the United States of America after the Watergate Scandal, he went on television and said: 'Only when a man has experienced the depths of the deepest valley can he appreciate the heights of the tallest of mountains.' Or was it the other way round?

Anyway, it's one of those meaningless quotes which I have a curious *penchant* for recalling extremely well. It's rather like the only Shakespearean quote I can ever remember, from *Julius Caesar*: 'There is a tide in the affairs of men, which, taken at the flood, leads on to fortune.' Completely pointless, but sounds impressive, and can be used in almost every conceivable situation.

But now I can see that Richard Nixon has been cruelly misjudged by history. Far from being a crook, he was really a great philosopher, for it's become obvious to me that his famous phrase has a deep and resonant meaningfulness. Without wishing to overstate the case, we may be witnessing a miracle unfolding, and it's wonderful.

I was on the train back to Stansted Airport when the phone rang. Reza thinks he's found a chef in Nice, so I've changed my flight and I'm travelling straight there to meet him.

With the help of a friend who has an apartment in the city and knows the place extremely well, Reza has spent the last few days trawling every Indian restaurant and the entire Indian community. Miraculously, he has found a chef who is actually from Sri Lanka, bizarrely called Edward, who has been unable to find work as a chef, and instead has been employed as a waiter in a well-known Indian restaurant in the *vieille ville* in the east of the city, called Delhi Belli, which fortuitously closes for the whole of August. Edward thinks he might be able to persuade his employer to let him go early, so he could conceivably join us next Friday.

This means we could open only one week behind our original schedule, on 13 July.

'Does he speak English?' asks Charlie.

Mercifully, he does. I don't give a damn what his cooking is like, Edward's hired already.

∼ 23 JUNE ∼

Nice is an unexpected delight. It has real class, a kind of faded aristocratic splendour. No wonder Picasso and Toulouse Lautrec fell for its charms.

Reza and his friend Monty picked me up from the airport and we drove into town along the famous palm-lined Promenade des Anglais, racing the gangs of beautifully bronzed roller-bladers who seem to spend all day streaking at astonishingly high speeds up and down the promenade.

Monty has a large, one-bedroom apartment in an ochre-coloured nineteenth-century block overlooking the magnificent Place Masséna, with the long white spumes of its fountains reaching out across the blazing greens and oranges of the tropical garden, the white Italianate clock tower of the Hôtel de Ville, and the lush green of the Provençal hills beyond. It's one of the best locations in one of the finest cities in Europe and it cost him £80,000 a year ago, £40,000 less than my dusty little flat in Farnham. To my knowledge it is not overlooked by the offices of the French Inland Revenue, nor indeed by any offices at all.

The place is just magnificent. I could spend the rest of my life here.

Reza and Monty had visited over a dozen restaurants in their attempt to press-gang a chef into service in Laurac, half of them Indian, and were on the point of giving up in despair.

Reza had actually called me and told me he was really thinking we had reached the end of the road. I told him that this was not an option; not least, at the back of my mind, was the image of the tears rolling down Christiane's face.

'What the bloody hell do you suggest then?' It was the first time that I'd ever heard Reza swear. He was clearly nearing the end of his tether.

'There's no point in bloody asking me, you're the bloody expert.'

Then, as if by divine intervention, they had a lucky break. Monty works in the travel business and has a large number of contacts in the Nice hotel and restaurant scene. Someone mentioned Edward. And Edward needs a lucky break of his own. Furthermore, Edward has a wife and young children and seems keen to move out of the city and into the country. He likes the sound of Christiane. He likes the sound of Laurac. He likes the sound of L'Été Indien. I like the sound of him.

We meet tomorrow.

REZA: *I confessed to Zee on the phone last night that to be really honest, this was the only point so far that I really felt like quitting. Nigel has simply no idea whatever of how incredibly lucky we really have been. Most of the Indian restaurants here are actively looking for staff themselves. Encouragingly (on the one hand) there's been an explosion of interest in ethnic food in this most cosmopolitan of places and it's suddenly become chic amongst the French to be seen trifling with Thai, Chinese, Turkish, Moroccan and Indian food. Zee says she's read somewhere that this willingness of the French to want to experiment gastronomically is in the process of permeating northwards. But as a result (on the other hand) capable chefs are like gold dust.*

I'm so exhausted and relieved we've found Edward that Monty and I went for some much-needed retail therapy on the Rue de France, which is simply heavenly. I've bought a pair of angelic tanned-leather sandals with gorgeous little silver bells on each thong. Charlie says I'll have to stand very still when being interviewed.

~ 24 JUNE ~

Edward is pefect.

We meet him after he's finished his lunch shift, amongst the debris of the daily flower, fruit and vegetable market in the Cours Saleya, also in the old town, which we find by Monty negotiating us through a bewildering network of wafer-narrow, sunless streets, beneath a ceiling of a densely packed patchwork of red-tiled roofs. An odious, sickly sweet scent of squashed Mediterranean lilies, mimosa and rotting pineapples (according to Monty) hangs in the air.

Edward's a tall, roly-poly Sri Lankan with a flashing white smile and a passion for cricket, which instantly endears him to me. Reza says his cooking is *not exactly Michelin style,* but this is a turn of phrase I've heard before, and perhaps it's just Reza hedging his bets. Besides, I know by now that Reza's very hard to please. Hiring an Indian chef for the famous Star of India in the Old Brompton Road, SW5, is one thing; hiring an Indian chef for a small village in the south of France where nobody has ever tasted a curry is quite another.

Edward will come up-country at the end of next week and, if he's happy with what he finds, he'll stay. The thirteenth of July – three weeks away – is now definitely our preferred opening date. And if, after a month or two, the sound of ringing tills is echoing in our ears, he'll rent a flat in Laurac and move up the family; a better incentive is hard to imagine.

Reza spent another afternoon in the Rue de France, hopping like a jackdaw from shop to shop, darting in and snatching up anything that catches the light. His wardrobe is enormous. There are mountains of clothes deposited everywhere he stops to draw breath, Les Fabres, L'Été Indien, a friend's house in Largentière, the back of the van. He'll have to charter a Jumbo to get it all home. But he's happy, and if he's happy, so am I.

Sally Ann arrives in *Vin P* to take us back to Laurac. She's not at all surprised Reza has found a chef.

'That's what he said he would do, and that's what he's done. He's a professional. You're lucky to have him.'

I say nothing.

Then she blasts me an extraordinary broadside for constantly underestimating the people I work with.

'Sometimes you're like a bull in a china shop, Freckles. You have an idea set in concrete right at the front of the brain. That is all you can see, it blocks out everything else; the wider view, the horizon, the sky, just disappear from your radar screen. Everything and everybody is subjugated towards the single aim of achieving your vision. You are blind to the perspective of others. They're merely your foot soldiers, bullied into submission by your unbending will. You cannot, will not, understand if they fail to deliver. And, if deliver they do, you don't for a moment consider

– or even have the courtesy to enquire – what they've been through to achieve what is ultimately your dream. Freckles, you're an absolute tyrant.'

I look at Sal in disbelief. She must be joking.

'Sal – you must be joking.'

'You are a living definition of the words *control freak*.'

'Thank you very much.'

'Don't be so po-faced,' she says, slapping me on the back, laughing. 'Come on, let's go for a swim.'

'Fantastic!' says Charlie. 'Brilliant sequence. Well said, Sal. Someone had to tell him. I've been telling him that for years. And Nice is so bloody *photogenic*.'

It's dark by the time we park and hobble across the stone beach directly opposite the legendary Negresco Hotel, with its still-sweating porters and doormen ridiculously overdressed like flunkies at a pre-revolutionary court at Versailles. There are scores of people on the brightly lit beach, noisy and drunk. This moment feels like a real watershed. We can do it; *together* we really can do it. We bury a bag with our wallets and passports deep into the sand. Then, holding each other against the pain of the pebbles, and giggling, Sal and I slip into the warm, luxurious waters of the Baie des Anges, the lights of Cap Ferrat twinkling, expensively, in the distance.

REZA: This is just hysterical! It may have been a long and stony road, but at last one senses that whilst, as Judy Garland might have said, it may not be the beginning of the end, it certainly seems to be the end of the beginning. Golly! Not only do we seem to have found our chef; something else has changed. It's weird. It's unexpected. And it's very unsettling. Nigel appears to have undergone some kind of metamorphosis. He actually said to me: 'Reza, you're amazing. Without you I would be nothing!' and he gave me a hug, the darling! What can he be thinking? Was he drunk? Or do I have grounds to be suspicious of an ulterior motive? Time will tell. So, things are really looking up. We have a restaurant, a chef, a menu and a maître d' *who's started to resemble a human being. And Nice is just spiritual, in the retail sense.*

～ 25 JUNE ～

We've been putting it off for weeks, but today, in our new spirit of optimism and goodwill, it seemed the right time to go in search of the one critical statistic which will determine our entire future.

In the cool damp air of the terrace, the earthy aroma of Olivier's freshly watered pots mixing with the steam of our espressos, Christiane, Reza and I sit around a small altar of paperwork piled high in the centre of the table and, armed with the restaurant's ancient calculator, set down to work.

Forget our start-up costs. List instead: rent, wages, taxes, gas, electricity, water, petrol, food, alcohol, the detailed breakdown of weekly running costs on one side of the equation. On the other, 25 Euros a head. Dinners only, six days a week, Mondays off.

Once agreed, all the figures are fed one by one into the calculator. The machine pauses, digests, and then two glowing red digits appear: a two and a seven.

For a moment we look at each other in silence, minds racing. Good or bad? Achievable or not? And why on earth have we not been through this exercise weeks ago?

In order for L'Été Indien to stay in business, we must sell an average of twenty-seven set meals a day.

I smile. Reza frowns.

'That's not so bad,' I say, at length.

'Every day. Every week, Nigel,' Reza says, wide eyes fixed on me, lips pursed. 'Not twenty-six or twenty-five, that won't do. Twenty-seven, every single time, or there's real pain.'

I contemplate what he's said for a moment.

'Could we manage without Ramsa, in an emergency?'

'We must have Ramsa,' says Christiane, definitively. 'We need her, she needs us.'

'No subsidies, Nigel, no more money. Twenty-seven. Or bust.'

'I think I've got the message, Rez.'

In a sense, I console myself, this is a purely academic argument. We're on an unstoppable wave and, of course, there's no going back.

～ 28 JUNE ～

Celine calls me. From Spain!

I'm not happy. My girlfriend's in Barcelona, and it's the first I know of it.

'Why didn't you tell me?'

'I did, *chéri*. Your memory's not so good.'

Now my brain may have been a bit overloaded of late, and the Farrell memory's not exactly famous for its super-human capacity, but this cannot be true. Even I would recall if my lover had announced she was disappearing to another country for nearly a week. Is she consciously lying? And if so, why?

Spend four hours removing all the price labels and washing every single glass and dish Reza brought over from London, also all Christiane's plates and cutlery. Spend a good deal of time cursing.

'Don't be so grumpy, Freckles,' says Sal. 'We're nearly there.'

～ 29 JUNE ～

We open exactly two weeks today and Reza's hopping about in a total tizzy. And he's unusually aggressive, as though searching for a battle to win. He's decided we are not paying enough attention to detail. And in this he seems to have a great deal in common with Sir T.

To some extent the customer is a captive audience, with time to notice the finer points of presentation and an expectation, until

*proved otherwise, that everything will be perfect. This sense of
expectation is, however, quite fragile ... the right details may not be
immediately apparent, but they carry on working at an almost
subconscious level to perpetuate a happy mood of contentment and
anticipation.*

The first disagreement is over music. Reza says we need soft music *to
enhance the feeling of well-being* and that in the Star this is created by a light
classical soundtrack that's so low as to be almost indiscernible. Customers
say they love the ambience but often can't specify precisely why. Christiane
and I are adamant that any kind of music in L'Été Indien would be tacky.

'I'm not talking about sitar music,' said Reza, offended.

'We're not talking about music at all.'

Rest of the World, one; Reza, nil.

The subject of bread prompts a complete realignment of allies, although
the strategy, in a military sense, remains consistent. This time it's Christiane
who is out-manoeuvred.

'The French always, always, always expect bread at a meal.'

'This is an Indian restaurant. No bread.'

One-all.

The future of the little water fountain beneath the grapevine on the wall
of the terrace by the entrance causes a similar division. Christiane is
absolutely serious about this: experience shows that the trickling sound
of the water descending the stone saucers will cause a permanent queue
outside our tiny, inadequate *toilette*, which in turn will cause a major
blockage for the waiters moving between the terrace and the kitchen, and
for any customers arriving at or leaving the inside dining room.

Reza and I argue that despite this, the sound of the water – particularly
in the absence of music – must add a certain charm to the place. We vote
to get the pump repaired; Christiane, as always, graciously demurs.

ROTW, one; Reza, two. A victory, then, of sorts. And it is important that
Reza is happy.

I am preoccupied by Celine. The trip to Barcelona must have been planned long ago. She has been sponsored by her company in Aubenas to attend a convention of insurance and mortgage brokers as a reward for dramatically increasing turnover of the business, and she's one of a number of people to receive 'business man/woman of the year' awards. Tickets must have been bought, reservations made, Quentin booked to stay with the ex, or the parents.

So why didn't she tell me?

After much searching and anguished cogitation, there are only three conceivable explanations:

1) The Jealousy Factor. Celine is still in love with me, but feels neglected and ignored by my obsession with the restaurant, and maybe even bored out of her brains. She intends to provoke me into drastic remedial action by a vivid illustration of her capability to have a good time without me, as and when she wants. *'It's wild here,'* is how she had phrased it on the phone. A beautiful single girl surrounded by hundreds of unattached men on a four-day convention miles from home! Oh please! So you don't need to be Sherlock Holmes to get the message: buck up, Farrell, or lose me, I can't hang around for ever. Verdict: A real possibility because it's a card Celine has played very effectively before.

2) The Memory Factor. Celine is still in love with me, but simply forgot to tell me about the trip. Or she did remember to tell me. And I forgot. Either way, it's a mistake to read too much into it. Get a life. Verdict: Most acceptable explanation, but sadly almost inconceivable.

3) The Factor I've Put Last On The List Because It's Too Painful To Contemplate. Celine is no longer in love with me. She's fallen in love with someone else. But instead of telling me this, she's decided to cheat on me. Does this make it more exciting (see Explanation No. 1)? Can she really be enjoying a wonderful holiday sharing a love-nest with a rich, impossibly handsome lover in one of the most vibrant cities in the world? (Obviously he has to be rich and impossibly handsome to compete with me.) Verdict: Presumably, sadly, a real possibility.

My usual response to an emotional crisis is to make a joke. I explain the situation to Sal, who nods sympathetically but understandably hesitates to offer an opinion.

I say to Sal: 'When Celine gets back – in the words of my dear mother – we need to Sit Down, and have a Serious Talk, although why one can't have a Serious Talk standing up, I've never quite understood.'

Of course, I make light of this because I went to boarding school and, like so many British males of my generation, I'm emotionally constipated. Isn't that it? Expressing love, pain, anger, hurt, desire or loss can only ever be achieved publicly through humour. It's something Celine will never understand, because French men can't be like this. French men relish the expression of love. I know this, because Christiane tells me so. Even JB was like that, long ago.

I really do not want to lose Celine.

∼ 30 JUNE ∼

The momentum gathers pace.

The wine list is agreed. For weeks Reza had grandiose plans to research intimately all the major vineyards in the area, and I envisaged filling a charabanc with friends and going on the wine-tasting binge of all time, but we've run out of time, and have unexcitingly but pragmatically (i.e. lazily) decided just to stick with Christiane's cellar and established suppliers, a selection of wines from Louis Latour, Domaine de Bournet and Domaine du Colombier. Reza says that most of the local Côtes du Rhône goes well with Indian, and that Indians never drink wine with their food anyway. Christiane's pulled off another miracle and tracked down some Cobra beer in Nîmes. She's brought back a dozen 'sample' bottles, which N. Farrell (resident dipsomaniac) and R. Mahammad (teetotaller) demolish in about ten minutes flat.

Reza's still lording it over us by pulling rank with his *experienced restaurateur* card. Actually, I think he's been sneaking a look at my Conran book. He's now become paranoid about theft and fraud. I say that, as usual, he's being ridiculously melodramatic. He says that in a recent survey of the American prison population, the most common former occupation quoted by the inmates was 'cook'. I say that this is a slur on Edward, and he says it's not just the staff, it's the customers, too – as an example, he quotes a scam perfected by an impoverished David Niven and a pal in pre-war New York which still graphically illustrates the vulnerability of an industry that relies totally on the goodwill of its customers. The starving Niv enters restaurant, sits at a table for two, and orders an enormous five-course meal. Pal follows, pretends not to know Niv, asks if the other seat at his table is free, sits, orders a coffee, reads newspaper. When the engorged Niv completes his final brandy, he asks the waitress for the bill, and pal says, can I have my bill, too? When both bills are placed on the table, Niv staggers out, clutching not his, but the pal's bill for just one coffee, which he pays at the till by the front door, before leaving at high speed. Pal waits for a few minutes, then picks up what is, of course, Niv's bill, demands to know why he's been given the wrong check from embarrassed waitress, threatens a scene, finally exits amongst a plethora of apologies, having also paid for just one coffee. This scene is then repeated at next restaurant, with roles reversed. Niv claimed to be able to live like a king for about six months in New York on just a few pence a day.

I can't wait to give it a go.

Reza decrees we must have a staff-training day before we open for business. Security, health and safety, fire drills must all be explained, memorized, and rehearsed. Sal and I nod sagely and say we think this is a sensible and very responsible idea. Personally, I think it will almost certainly end up looking like a scene from *Dad's Army*.

There then follows a row. It begins when Reza says he's had bad experiences with credit card fraud. He quizzes Christiane about the details of the French *Carte Bleu* credit system we'll be using, and Christiane suddenly says, out of the blue, that we won't be using any system, because

Nigel hasn't registered himself as the new proprietor of L'Été Indien at the Aubenas Chamber of Commerce, and, as such, the business is forbidden to trade.

Reza goes ballistic. For a moment I think he's going to walk out. Maybe he changes his mind because there's really nowhere to walk out to, and anyway he can't drive. But he does have a point. I have completely forgotten to get my documents in order. Most of them are still sitting in a cupboard in the Farnham flat. I can't believe I didn't remember to pick them up when I went back for the funeral.

'I'm really sorry, Rez. I'll phone Tom right away. We'll get everything required in the next couple of days and we'll be registered by the end of the week.'

'Nigel.'

I recognize this instantly as an indication of the severity of Reza's anger. He says my name quietly, through gritted teeth, and then pauses for the maximum dramatic effect.

'Nigel. Don't you understand how serious this is? We are a business. We may be able to negotiate thirty days' credit with some suppliers, thanks only to Christiane's goodwill. But sooner or later, any business has to start paying bills.' I sense he's enjoying this. Can this be possible? 'Any day now, you, the moral and legal proprietor of this highly regarded establishment –' *Oh for God's sake, Reza!* '– will be asked to sign a cheque, or run a card through the credit machine. And you won't be able to. You'll have to say, I'm sorry, old chap, I can't pay you now, it's because I have left my birth certificate in my flat in Farnham, which is a small market town in the south of England.'

'I have my birth certificate with me.'

'Birth certificate, house deeds, whatever. This is all too, too absurd,' says Reza, looking skywards for a moment, then gliding out of the room like the Queen Mother.

'Fantastic!' says Charlie. 'What a star!'

Tom says: 'Chill out, Dad. Don't get stressed with me. I'll send everything you need tomorrow. What does it really matter anyway? We're all on this planet for a relatively insignificant period of time. Put all this in the context of not just our own galaxy, but the universe as a whole.'

This makes me feel a whole lot better.

~ *1 JULY* ~

Edward arrives tomorrow.

The air is heavy with expectancy, yet the scenes are all too familiar. Christiane and Ramsa are cleaning the kitchen – yet again. Olivier is scrubbing out the outside kitchen – yet again. Sal, bless her (are we really not paying her?), is working her way through an enormous pile of washing and ironing the new table linen. JB has given Reza a lift into Aubenas to buy clothes he *desperately needs* before the restaurant opens. I am worrying about Celine.

I am working on a new theory.

Celine maintains that's she's not a materialist, that the accumulation of wealth can never be morally justified as an end in itself, and that all that really matters in this turbulent world is love. The man she gives her heart to, she proclaimed to me once, could be penniless so long as he could fly with her, carry her off to fulfil her dream of reaching for the stars. But can this really be the same Celine who spends a huge proportion of her income on clothes, runs a high-octane, brand-new convertible sports car, and who longs for a life cruising the world on a teak-decked yacht, with frequent stops at California to catch up with all the latest news from Hollywood? Is this the same Celine who wants the best money can buy for her boy, and who must be searching, albeit unconsciously, for a provider not only of security and finance, but also of a brother or preferably sister that she once confided to me she wants badly for the beloved Quentin?

Maybe none of my three previous explanations are correct. Maybe Celine is simply sitting on the fence, biding her time, waiting to see if L'Été

Indien is a critical – and more importantly, a financial – success.

She doesn't have long to wait now.

REZA: I can't think straight, I'm so angry. This is an absolutely critical moment in the run-up to our opening, yet Nigel's mind is just not on the ball. Zee simply can't believe how inefficient he is being, how irresponsibly he is behaving. His ridiculous laxity over the Chamber of Commerce issue is threatening the entire project. Does he know how unhappy he is making Christiane? She is a meticulous woman, who likes and expects things to be done meticulously. Does he know how unhappy he is making me? JB thinks he's behaving pathetically. Manu's cross, too, but won't say anything. Nigel's distracted, of course. His nauseating infatuation with the girl Celine is beginning to affect us all. Can't he see what a fool he is making of himself? He's in danger of making a fool of us all. The trouble is compounded by the fact that he cannot, will not, take anything I say remotely seriously. I could kill him.

As well as some divine shirts, I've found this amazing tooth-whitening paste in Aubenas. You put it in a sort of plastic gumshield, which you fit to your teeth overnight. Charlie says it's a brilliant idea; teeth are really noticeable on television.

~ 2 JULY ~

Everyone's on edge.

Edward assured us he'd be setting off first thing from Nice, driven by his brother-in-law, and should be arriving at Laurac by ten thirty at the latest.

By eleven thirty there's no sign of him. We call his mobile, but there's no response. Already thin, dark lines of concern are beginning to etch themselves on Christiane's features. We cannot, surely, be about to go through this all over again?

Eager to escape the tension of the restaurant, Sal and I go for a walk up to the main part of the village. Jacques, standing as ever like a sentry on duty behind the counter of the only bar in town, opposite the church, has spotted us walking up the street and already has our *morescs* poured and ready.

'How goes it, you Red Indians?' he asks, grinning. 'You really going to open down there on the thirteenth? Or maybe there's another delay?'

'Jacques. *Ecoutez*. We are not *Red Indians*,' I say, taking a deep draught of the sweet *pastis* drink. I need it. I can feel it instantly warming the belly and relaxing the nerves. 'Our restaurant is based on the food they eat in the country of India. *Inde!* Between Pakistan and Bangladesh.'

'Thank goodness you've no major marketing problems here, Freckles,' says Sal.

When we turn the corner of the Rue d'Externat on our way back down the hill, I notice there is a *gendarme* standing outside the restaurant. I stop abruptly. Over the years, I have developed an unhealthy respect for the French police, and not just the gun-toting, beer-swilling types seen so often at airports these days.

So it was with a certain degree of nervousness that I stood now, looking at the tall *gendarme* engaged in an animated interrogation of Christiane at the gate to the terrace of the restaurant. I know that in France the boundary between civil and criminal law is not nearly as clear-cut as in England. An armed policeman is as likely to visit you to investigate the non-payment of local taxes as a revenue officer. So why is he here? Is there a problem over the delay in my registration at the Chamber of Commerce? Or concerns over Edward's work permit?

Sal and I loiter, kicking stones across the road to each other, trying not to look guilty. Eventually the policeman replaces his notebook in his top pocket, lights a *Gauloise* and saunters off down the hill towards the large blue van parked at the end of the street.

We walk slowly down the hill and nervously enter the restaurant, like a pair of fugitives.

'What was all that about?' I enquire.

Christiane looks puzzled.

'The policeman.'

'Oh Pierre!' says she, smiling. 'He just wanted to know if he could bring his child along when he comes to eat here. We ought to consider a children's menu or else we might be losing business.'

Edward and his brother-in-law arrive just after lunch, to be greeted by large, communal sighs of relief. He is carrying a suitcase; a good sign, because it must mean he intends to stay. Reza shows them around and Edward nods a good deal, occasionally flashing his glowing smile. It is an anxious few moments while he and his brother-in-law carry out a detailed examination of our minuscule kitchen; Edward produces a tape measure, and the two men start chattering away noisily in what I assume is Tamil. Reza and I wait outside and await the verdict.

'I'm a big man,' says Edward gravely upon emerging. 'And this is not a big kitchen.'

We all look at each other rather awkwardly for a moment.

'But maybe, in time, if business is good, more and more of the cooking could be done in the outside kitchen.'

This is a really sensible idea, which strangely none of us has even considered before. The outside kitchen is actually quite sizeable.

I am beginning, to use a phrase of my grandfather's, *to admire the cut of Edward's jib*. A problem solver, not a problem finder.

He's happy with the accommodation – Sal has moved out of our flat and into the spare room in the Tochous' apartment below – and, even more significantly, he's fallen head over heels in love with Laurac. He really does seem to be considering a long-term future here with his family.

'It's a very, very *jolly* place,' he says, beaming. 'Much like you, Reza, you are a very *jolly* boy!'

This is a bit cheeky. I am aware that Reza has a very formal relationship with the staff back at the Star of India and can see that he is slightly peeved by Edward's words. *Très amusant.*

Later we have champagne to celebrate Edward's arrival. Amongst all the smiles and mutual congratulations, I notice a tear in the corner of

Christiane's eye. This time, thank God, I assume it has nothing to do with worry, fear or sadness.

~ 3 JULY ~

It's as though L'Été Indien has suddenly come alive.

The atmosphere of the place has changed completely. Edward has got straight down to work, and the restaurant echoes to the sound of his uninterrupted labours. There's a constant clinking-clanking of pots and pans, ladles, spoons, whisks; the ceaseless murmur of voices as Edward and Reza explore recipes, exchange and compare techniques, or as Christiane is told to add this or that to the list of new requirements. And as the hours go by, the unmistakable aroma of spices begins to permeate every corner of every room in the building.

And it smells good.

We've decided to organize a tasting before the opening night, with a selection of friends who will be invited to give a brutally honest assessment of the new menu. It's also been agreed that Edward should have an assistant chef. He knows a young Sri Lankan boy from Nice called Jamal who he seems sure would be happy to join us, certainly for a few weeks. Apparently he's a very *jolly* boy.

Just as I am starting to enjoy the fact that, for the first time in months, everything in the garden seems warm and rosy, I receive a completely unexpected telephone call from England.

It's Nippi.

He's flying over to Lyons tomorrow afternoon – can I pick him up from the airport?

Why on earth is he coming over? And why now?

I know Nippi well enough to be sure that he never does anything that hasn't been carefully worked out in advance. So there must be some kind of a plan afoot.

I'm poleaxed.

'Good stuff,' says Charlie. 'Nippi's really good value, he looks great on screen. You should never have got rid of him in the first place.'

~ 4 JULY ~

Celine is back but I've been able to have only a brief conversation with her on the phone. This has merely added to, rather than resolved, my utter confusion. For someone with a pretty shaky knowledge of the English language, Celine's use of superlatives is impressive.

It had been *without doubt* the best few days of her life. Barcelona is *magnificent, spiritual, uplifting*. The convention was *wonderful*. She had met so many *sensational* people. They had partied every evening dancing the night away – with champagne, *bien sûr*. It had *opened her eyes to the real world*. And most enigmatically of all: *it was such a shame that I hadn't been there to share the experience with her.*

I suggest that perhaps we could meet today, maybe she could come over to the restaurant? Not possible, after four such *memorable* days away, there is a mountain of work to catch up on, and Quentin to collect. She will call me when she is free.

I'm exasperated by the girl. It's a blessing, in a way, that I have other things on my mind.

I feel completely wrong-footed by Nippi. There's a game being played out here, but irritatingly I haven't a clue what it is.

Of course, he knows all about L'Été Indien and Reza. But I rather had the sense that, having decided that investing his own money in an Indian restaurant out here was too much of a gamble, he'd rather turned his back on France. He'd not suggested using our house at Les Fabres for a summer holiday this year; in fact, he seemed rather disillusioned about the whole idea, so why would he suddenly want to come out here now, at very short notice, and without his family, just over a week before the official opening of the restaurant?

Mercifully, it's been cloudy most of today so *Vin P* wasn't quite the boiler room it's been of late, so with all the windows open there were only a few moans about the lack of air-conditioning. Nippi made up for this by deriding the van's new colour scheme. It was colourful, he admitted, but meaningless rubbish, bearing no relation to anything remotely Indian, which is probably true.

'But don't you think it's better than driving a dreary white van around?'

'Nigel, listen to me, it's such a blank canvas! Think what you could have done with it!'

We could have argued like this for most of the two-hour journey back down the A7 and all the way to Laurac, as we had done on so many other occasions, but I decided it was time to change tack.

'So what's all this about, Nippi? Are we here for work, or play?'

'Oh, a bit of this and that.' Nippi has honed to perfection the art of the utterly ambiguous answer. 'We'll talk about it later.'

To give him his due, Nippi was generous in his praise about what we had done to L'Été Indien. Reza was up a ladder fixing the fairy lights to the main beam on the terrace when we arrived. The two men shook hands awkwardly.

'Love the turban!' said Reza, wickedly. 'Give us a twirl.'

'You mean you've never seen a turban before?'

'Looks marvellous!'

Nippi lowered his voice and said: 'Where did you find him?'

'He fell out of a tree.'

Christiane greeted him like a long-lost son, and I introduced him to Sal and Edward. Big smiles all round. He seemed genuinely pleased to be here, and liked the redecoration. No sour grapes or recriminations. Apparently.

Once unpacked up at Les Fabres, the mood changed.

I poured us both a G&T and waited for Nippi to begin.

'Nigel, I understand you have borrowed money to fund your investment in the restaurant. Against this house. Our house.'

I wondered for a moment how he had established this. From Manu? Maybe he had simply worked it out for himself; Nippi had helped me financially over the costs involved in the original renovation of our house here, so there were no secrets between us. I guess it didn't really matter.

'Nippi, I have explored every other possible way to borrow or earn the money I needed to pay for my half of the setting-up costs for L'Été Indien. There was no other way. And as soon as the restaurant is up and running, it will not only start to pay for itself, but we'll be able to re-coup our initial investment.'

'So you don't deny it?'

'Of course not.'

'Don't you think it would have been courteous to have at least informed me you were intending to borrow money on a house we jointly own?'

He had a point. I'd hoped he wouldn't find out.

'Nippi, there's no risk involved.'

The grilling continued. Had I had the house valued? Yes, Manu believes we would get £120,000 for it. Was this a written valuation? No. Did he come and measure the place up? No, not exactly. Has a survey been done? No. If the restaurant fails, can I repay the loan without selling the house? Probably not.

Put like that, it sounds a bit grim.

'So it's perfectly possible we might have to sell the house because of your financial incompetence? And you didn't even bother to run it past me first?'

Was Nippi making too much of a meal of all this?

'The restaurant won't fail, Nippi, and I can repay my loan, and the house will not have to be sold.'

'And if it does fail?'

'It won't.'

Can't sleep. It's an unfamiliar experience. I've been so physically tired of late that I haven't had a bad night for weeks. This will be a bad night. There's an owl very close by, its persistent hoots echoing across the valley. It's unbearably hot. Legions of tiny bedbugs, too minute to even see, let alone exterminate, are pricking my sticky, sweat-drenched skin. The sheets should have been washed. I've neglected the house. It's filthy. I've neglected everything, save L'Été Indien; my children, Celine, my life.

If the restaurant fails, we shall have to sell the house. I shall have to return to England.

And what would happen if Nippi simply refused to sell the house?

This will be a bad night.

～ 5 JULY ～

I thought I knew Nippi well. I thought I knew him so well I could almost predict his every move.

One day, some years ago, Nippi asked me if I'd like to join him and his family at the Sikh temple where he worships in Hounslow. I was flattered to be asked and, of course, agreed. Nippi explained that any man setting foot in the temple must have his head covered, and he offered to buy and fit me out with a turban. It was bright purple, and, without a hair in sight, I looked absolutely bizarre in it. Furthermore, in order to hold it rigidly in place, he pulled the turban extremely tightly around both ears so that I couldn't hear a word that anybody said and spent much of the day observing events unfolding before me as though everything was happening underwater.

The temple is large and modern. It bears little resemblance to any church I've ever entered. You remove your shoes as you enter. Services last the entire weekend. Prayers are said continually in a huge room on the first floor. The men are segregated on one side, the women on the other, and friends and families just drift in and out as they please. I was introduced to many of Nippi's friends, including an old man who said he had no family and came here on Saturday morning and left on Sunday evening. It makes up his entire social life. There's a charitable community kitchen run by volunteers serving food around the clock and anybody, of any religion or denomination, can come in and have a free meal, providing, of course, they wear something on their head. While we were eating, a couple of slightly tipsy old drunks came in off the street for what looked like their regular Sunday Indian feast. It's an extraordinary, exuberant, all-embracing place, full of life and music and light.

I thought then, and still do now, that since I had been invited to such a splendid occasion, I must have passed some kind of a test in Nippi's eyes, and that whatever rows, disputes, disagreements we may have in the future, we would remain blood brothers.

It turns out I don't really know him at all.

As I tossed and turned through the airless early hours of the morning, the thoughts spinning inside my sleepless mind gradually became more tortured. L'Été Indien is doomed. We are under-financed and inexperienced, toiling to succeed in an enterprise that is chronically under-researched. There's no business plan. There are no reserves of cash to see us through the early days, no contingencies whatsoever. Not even the genius that is Sir Terence Conran could salvage the good ship L'Été Indien as it steams full ahead, brass bands playing, into the iceberg that Reza and everyone else – save the novice captain and his motley crew – had seen miles away.

And there, from the safety of the distant shore, is a gloating Nippi, rubbing his hands with glee as the inevitable collision unfolds before his eyes. 'Nigel, Nigel, Nigel! If only you had listened to me! Why didn't you listen to my words of warning, Nigel!' And, of course, he would be delighted as we start to sink, and he would shake his head in despair at the sheer caprice and foolhardiness of others. The malice of the man! The manipulation! His sheer arrogance!

Failure, humiliation and bankruptcy inevitably beckon.

But it wasn't like that at all.

It must have been at about 4 a.m. that I was finally able to escape the agonizing images, and slipped into a light, fitful sleep. After I was awoken a few hours later, feeling groggy, by the sounds of Nippi stretching his turban, we drove down to Vals together for warm croissants and espresso. There is no food at all in the house.

Afterwards we walk in the shade of the plane trees in the square. There was a big music festival in town last night, and the debris is scattered all around, with teams of workmen dismantling the scaffolded stage and banks of lights. It is too early for the boule players but further down, by the casino and the children's merry-go-round, we stroll past the sprinklers spraying water in great rainbow arcs across the immaculately maintained lawns, and smart municipal gardeners raking and weeding the flowerbeds, as they do every morning.

'Nigel, I've been thinking about our conversation last night,' says Nippi. It is the first time today the subject has been raised. As I have discovered so often in the past, Nippi and I have an odd capacity to ignore completely a recent row, even a fiercely fought one, and proceed with life as though nothing untoward had ever happened.

'I've decided that you need help,' he continues, at length.

The words *patronizing old git* float briefly to mind, but under the circumstances I feel it wiser to keep silent.

'You have got yourself in a mess, and now you definitely need help.'

'Nippi, the money is safe. I assure you there really is no risk.'

'You need help. And I intend to give it.'

'Really?'

'The best way to ensure the house is safe from the bailiffs is for your restaurant to succeed. It is therefore in my interests to do what I can to help in that aim. Plus, the weather is wonderful here now, and the place looks a picture. The village post office back home can tick over for a few days without me. So I'll stay for a bit. Enjoy myself. And help you out.'

Now this complete about-turn in mood and approach really is unexpected. For Nippi to have the grace and breadth of mind to wish us good luck with an enterprise he thought too dangerous to invest in himself is one thing. For him to actively offer his services to help us succeed, and thereby maybe prove himself wrong, is extremely uncharacteristic.

Is there a catch to all this, an ulterior motive? I can't see one. Perhaps I really had misjudged the man.

'What do you have in mind, Nippi?'

'Nothing too strenuous, of course. What are you doing to market and advertise L'Été Indien?'

'Not much money left over for that.'

'Money's not necessarily what you need. Believe me, I've done this kind of thing before. Leave it with me.'

And he's been as good as his word. I've been busy most of the day with Reza and Sal in the restaurant, but when I caught up with Nippi for a drink up at Pierre's this evening, he produced a piece of paper with a flourish, and proudly waved it beneath my nose. There's a long list of names and telephone numbers scribbled on it. Nippi's made contact with all the local tourist information centres, who have agreed to take our flyers; both local newspapers; a radio station in Montélimar; and the regional TV news film crew based in Aubenas. And, everyone he's spoken to speaks English.

I am impressed.

'The local media are all mildly interested in covering the opening, although naturally they'd much rather sell us advertising space. But being the first Indian restaurant here, we should get at least some editorial coverage. But we need a publicity gimmick.'

I've discovered over the years that whilst Nippi is a great one for *stating the bleedin' obvious*, he's maybe not so strong on ideas, or action. But once again I was about to be proved quite wrong.

Circuses are still big business in rural France. I had noticed, throughout the spring and early summer, scores of small family-run circuses coming and going through the main market towns of the area, just as they must have done in Britain a century ago. Sometimes they stay over for just one night, often parading bedraggled groups of camels or llamas through the streets to advertise the shows, or tethering them in the squares or on prominent street corners in a way that would outrage animal rights' groups in Britain.

And today and tomorrow, according to Nippi's diligent research, there's a circus just down the road at Joyeuse.

'Why don't we see if we can borrow an elephant for a few hours?'

'Sorry, did you say an elephant?'

'Yes, he damn well did,' says Charlie. 'Fantastic idea!'

'Shut up, Charlie!'

'Yes, why not, an elephant,' says Nippi. 'And parade it around the towns, advertising L'Été Indien? It would be wonderful!'

Now call me an old cynic, but I find it extremely unlikely that one could just pitch up at a French circus out of the blue and borrow an elephant, even if it is only for a few hours. But I was loath to dampen Nippi's evident ardour and enthusiasm for the idea.

'It's a thought,' say I, giving Nippi an encouraging smile. 'When were you thinking of going along to enquire?'

'Me?' asks Nippi sharply. 'It's no good me going along, you know I can't speak any French.'

'Then who?'

'You, of course.'

Not everything's changed, then.

So tomorrow I will rise early, drive to the circus in Joyeuse in *Vin P* before the heat of the morning sun hits hard, and see if I can persuade someone there – in my faltering French – to lend me an elephant.

Just for a few hours.

REZA: Hell, just how wrong can you be about someone? I've met Nippi at last! I've heard so much about him, he's not at all as I imagined. Over the months Nigel has painted quite a dark picture of Nippi, but he's utterly charming, he has great presence, he's immaculately turned out, with perfect manners. I don't understand Nigel's suspicions about him; he's offering to help. Just having him around adds class and style and interest. Zee says the elephant idea is simply inspired, the man should get a medal. I must just keep him out of the kitchen; Edward and Jamal are behind schedule. God knows how the tasting will go. Sacré blu! I'm leaving it all very much up to Edward. He'll still be here long after

I've gone. It's a good test of his ability, but a high-risk strategy, of course. I'm very nervous.

I'm taking my long green frock coat with the silver buttons to be dry-cleaned and ironed at Le Pressing. Charlie says it'll look gorgeous beside the grey skin of an elephant.

～ 6 JULY ～

Armed with a French dictionary, an intermittent tremble of the upper lip, and a vanload of misgivings about the sanity of my mission, I arrived at *Cirque Mondiale*, which is holed up in an empty field just outside Joyeuse.

The first problem I had was locating any humans.

But for the dozens of animals lazily grazing, or staring blankly at me through their cages as I stepped over the guy-ropes and began my search of the rather small Big Top, the place seemed deserted. There were indeed camels and llamas, alongside rather less exotic miniature ponies, donkeys, and half a dozen mangy-looking ostrich. There were tigers, but only a pair, and one thin lioness, sporting a large sore patch, which she was licking incessantly, in a rather delicate area of her anatomy.

Eventually I spotted a small, dark woman, in the shade of a caravan, in the process of apparently washing her armpits. I asked to speak to the *propriétaire* and she pointed, waving a soapy hand, in the direction of the largest caravan in the group.

I knocked on the door, and waited. The ostriches, motionless, were looking at me intently like I was an intruder and probably a real threat, and as though, if they had half a chance, they would gladly peck me to death, probably eyes first. The other animals ignored me.

At length a man with enormous hands and a barrel of a stomach straining to escape the captivity of a tight, sweaty T-shirt appeared, seized my fingers in a crushing handshake, and asked me about my business. I tried as best I could to explain my need for the temporary loan of an elephant. He nodded seriously, as I stumbled through my explanation, with an inscrutable expression on his face, almost as though he received this kind of request several times a day.

'I would love to help you, *mon ami*, but we don't have elephants here.'

'No elephants?'

'Would a camel be any help?'

'Is it Indian?'

'I'm afraid not.'

'The lioness?'

'African, I'm afraid.'

We weren't making much progress.

'I could let you have a pair of Japanese pot-bellied pigs, if you're desperate?'

'No, thanks.'

I was just about to pull stumps on the whole idea when the man, as if seized by divine intervention, bade me follow as he suddenly set off at a fast pace down the steps of the caravan and across towards the Big Top, muttering: 'Maybe I have something which could be of help, *mon ami*.'

Casually chewing on the leaves of a large gorse bush behind the circus ticket office was an emaciated, pale-skinned creature, with large protruding brown eyes and hideously visible ribs, that looked like a small, desperately undernourished cow with possibly just a few hours to live.

'This,' said *mon propriétaire* proudly, spreading the fingers of his huge hands out wide. 'This is . . . a humped Zebu.'

'Humped Zebu?'

'It's from India!'

The Zebu looked at me, pitifully. I looked back. I had no wish to be discourteous to the man, who was, after all, trying his best under difficult circumstances, but there was no way even Nippi would regard dragging this poor specimen through the streets of Largentière or Aubenas as anything other than a public relations disaster for a new restaurant.

'I think, probably, it is an elephant we need, M'sieur. But thank you for your kindness.'

'I know a man who has an elephant a few hours' drive from here. I will gladly furnish you with his telephone number.'

'*Merci beaucoup, M'sieur! Bonne chance avec la cirque!*'

'*Bon chance avec le restaurant!*'

I've just come off the phone. It's sorted. For a few hundred Euros, in used notes, 'Baby' the elephant is at our disposal. And for once we are all in agreement that this is an investment we can't afford to ignore.

We've booked Baby and his keeper, Rodriquez, for next Thursday. They are based somewhere near Montpélier, but whether it's a zoo or not, I'm not sure. They travel in an enormous juggernaut, so I have to find somewhere big enough locally to park it.

Nippi looks like the cat that got the cream.

'Nigel! Perhaps now you see what can be achieved . . .' he says, nodding wisely, '. . . with just a little imagination?'

~ 7 July ~

With the arrival of Jamal, our young Sri Lankan sous-chef from Nice, our team is virtually complete and in place.

Reza has decided it's time for our first staff meeting.

He's organized a big chart detailing the countdown to our opening night, which on Christiane's advice we have put back two days. We've now realized that 14 July is, of course, Bastille Day, one of the biggest public holidays of the year, when the French tend to stay at home to party with friends and family rather than go out to a restaurant. She says it would be crazy to open the previous night, although we might still organize some kind of celebration then, so we now officially open for business on Tuesday, 15 July.

It's the first time we've all assembled in one room together, and I survey the team with a mixture of pride and amusement. Reza, the slightly absent-minded, constantly giggling bundle of nerves, maybe the Corporal Jones to my bumbling, grumpy Captain Mainwaring. The unflappable Christiane, filling the room like a Spanish galleon under full sail – perhaps our Sergeant Wilson. The lovely, diligent Sally Ann, with the laugh that can shatter a champagne glass at ten metres. Big Edward and little Jamal (apparently a famous spin-bowler in Sri Lanka), endlessly discussing the finer points of cricket while working away like demons, now inextricably bonded twenty-four hours a day, not only in our little kitchen, but also sharing, uncomplainingly, the small flat above. Our beautiful, dark-skinned waitress Ramsa, with those big startled eyes, not understanding a single word I say, in either English or French. And the prickly chinned, always humming, youthful Olivier, condemned to a life-sentence washing up in the outside kitchen. The only missing person is the tall, willowy Greek God Erique, our supplementary waiter, who will start only a day or two before we open.

We gather around Reza's chart as he talks us through the schedule for the next few critical days. This should look like one of those tense RAF briefings before a particularly dangerous bombing mission over occupied France, but in fact it's more like a scene from a *Carry On* movie. Everyone is straining to keep a straight face. But it is important.

Tomorrow: *Le tasting*. Edward to decide precise menu, Reza to oversee. Our guests: Christiane, JB, Manu, Nippi, Celine (she said she'll *try* to make it – no chance yet, then, for that *sit down* talk), and a couple of neighbours from Les Fabres.

Marketing: Nippi to begin distributing publicity flyers in hotels and tourist offices in all major towns.

Wednesday: Prepare for Baby's arrival. Sally Ann to brief Christiane's friend Marie-Elise on making up a publicity blanket for elephant's back; Reza to organize Indian costumes for us all to wear (fortunately he has cases of the stuff); Nigel to organize permissions from the *mairie* in Joyeuse for Baby to parade through the streets. Everyone else will follow, giving away flyers to onlookers. Nippi to alert local media. Edward, Reza and

Jamal to assess verdict on *le tasting* and adjust recipes and menus as required.

Thursday: Final menu to printers. Edward and Jamal to practise preparing food; Nigel, Sally Ann, Ramsa and Christiane to sample all the dishes and so familiarize themselves with exactly what's on offer to customers. All save Edward and Jamal to work with Baby in Joyeuse. Christiane to investigate if the mayor of Laurac is free to come to some kind of party on Sunday night. Final preparations for opening night on Tuesday.

At this point in the proceedings the little yellow Le Poste van pulls up with a toot outside. My documents – the deeds of ownership of our house at Les Fabres along with the EDF and SAUF invoices – have arrived from the Farnham flat at last.

There's no time to be lost. Collecting up all the other paperwork I've put on one side for my official registration as the new *propriétaire* of L'Été Indien, I take my leave of the assembled company and head up to Aubenas and the Chamber of Commerce.

Now I've developed an ambivalence towards French bureaucracy. Superficially, much of it seems absurd and ridiculous. For example, in my rather more affluent days, we invited Manu and his girlfriend, Olivia, only seventeen at the time, to London for a long weekend by way of showing our gratitude for all Manu's hard work at the house at Les Fabres. We booked them on the early flight from Nîmes, but having checked in, they were stopped by the *douane* at passport control on the grounds that Olivia was still technically a minor. Since she wasn't travelling with a member of her family, it was against the law for her to leave the country – despite the fact that with her fabulous figure she looked at least twenty-five and had shared Manu's flat with him for nearly a year. The only way that they could leave the country legally as a couple together was by obtaining a letter from the mayor of Aubenas, Olivia's home town, certifying that he had spoken to the girl's parents and could vouch for their consent to the trip. It took all day to arrange, and they finally left Nîmes on the late-night flight, fourteen hours after first arriving there.

At first sight, a loopy law, but after consideration, maybe in reality not such a crazy one. I bet there are fewer child abductions in France than in the UK.

The saga that was about to unfold between the Chamber of Commerce and N. Farrell Esq., however, has no such noble logic.

First stop, to the *mairie* in Laurac for a signed and stamped letter from *Monsieur le Maire Champetier* stating that I had taken over running the business from Christiane. Armed with this, I made the forty-five-minute drive in a truly sweltering *Vin P* to the Chamber of Commerce. After a short wait, a petite, perfectly dressed and manicured lady called Madame Souberon agreed to see me and together we went through the documents. Inevitably there was one missing: a customs certificate from the *douane* office in Aubenas authorizing the change in liquor licence.

So it was back into the town centre, to the little office just down from the huge Le Poste, where I was politely informed that the certificate could only be issued on receipt of a letter from the mayor of Laurac authorizing it. So it was another forty-five minute drive back to Monsieur Champetier who I just managed to catch before he disappeared for lunch. The letter was issued. Then back to the *douane* office, which was, of course, closed for lunch. By the time I got back to the Chamber of Commerce with the appropriate customs form, it was four o'clock.

The charming Madame Souberon and I went through the documents, and all was now indeed in order. Huge sighs of relief. She produced a large green form, which she then, meticulously, began to fill in.

After about half an hour's work, she stopped and looked at me.

'Are you single, married or divorced, M'sieur?'

'Divorced.'

'Divorced!'

She looked surprised.

'Can I see your papers of divorce?'

I tried to explain that I wasn't in the habit of travelling the world with my divorce papers. They are, inevitably, somewhere in the Farnham flat.

'*Tant pis, M'sieur!* Without the divorce papers I cannot complete the form.'

Christiane has assured me all along that the registration process was very straightforward, a mere formality. Had I know it was going to turn into this bureaucratic nightmare, I'd have got going with the wretched thing weeks ago.

As I stumbled out into the shimmering heat of the afternoon, the full implications of Madame Souberon's words began to form clearly in my mind. Without the divorce papers, there would be no official registration. Without that, I am apparently forbidden to trade under French law and I cannot issue cheques, or use a business credit card. I can't access cash, or pay any of our suppliers; I am utterly and completely financially impotent.

And we open on Tuesday of next week.

I frantically make dozens of calls in an effort to locate Tom. He must find the divorce papers and express-post them to me today.

I feel an almost overwhelming sense of panic.

∼ 8 JULY ∼

All day Edward and Jamal have been toiling away in the heat of the kitchen, in preparation for tonight's critical tasting.

After breakfast on the terrace at Les Fabres, Nippi and I had a big argument about this. Down below us M'sieur Carbenero is busy erecting a new concrete post for a bird table. God knows what he must make of us.

Unsure whether Nippi does this kind of thing just for the fun of riling me, or whether he really does intend – at least to start with – to be helpful and constructive.

'You know you've left this tasting far too late, Nigel.'

'Why?'

'If you really do need to radically rethink the menu, you don't have the time to do it.'

It's not so much what is said, which is often quite close to the truth; it's the way that Nippi says it, as though I was slightly *educationally challenged*.

'Nigel, listen to me. This is a serious commercial undertaking. You're treating it as though it was a game.'

Then he gave me a long rambling lecture on good business practice, every now and then patting me on the shoulder to emphasize a point or to make sure I was paying attention.

'Nigel. Take a good note of what I am saying. I know you very well. It would be such a pity if you fell flat on your face.'

'Nippi, would you bloody well stop tapping me on the shoulder!'

'Nice one, boys,' says Charlie. 'Nippi, you should have come over before. Good stuff!'

For once we don't talk on the drive down to Laurac. I'm consumed with that old image: of a Nippi, in truth, relishing the prospect of our imminent failure. But this simply can't be true. Over the last few days Nippi has worked really hard, distributing over a thousand publicity flyers – would he really do that if he secretly wanted L'Été Indien to be a disaster?

Bad news. I've been to the *mairie* at Joyeuse to inform them that we intend to bring Baby there on Thursday, market day, for publicity pictures. The mayor nearly had a fit. Thousands of shoppers and stall-holders pack into the narrow streets of this old town on a Thursday, and the prospect of an elephant let loose, maybe even going on the rampage, is too much for him to take. Another time is possible, but Baby is most definitely banned on Thursday. It's too late to change the day of Baby's visit so the obvious next town on our hit list is Largentière, but I'm reluctant to contact the *mairie* here in case, once again, we are turned down. I've decided we'll all just pitch up and see what happens. The image of the *gendarmerie* arresting a group of English and French restaurant workers, dressed in Indian clothing, along with a baby elephant, could make a great story for the local newspapers.

More bad news: the post-mortem on *le tasting* reveals that the boys in the kitchen still have a lot of work to do. Reza gave Edward rather too free a hand. It was a fun evening, though, and I did my best to lighten the mood and be as amusing as possible, as clearly any good *maître d'* would. I think I'm slipping into the role rather well. Charlie and Claudio have done a superb job with the lighting, the place looks pretty as a picture, especially after dark. One or two passers-by stopped to enquire about the opening, which is encouraging, although no one actually made a booking.

Since our guests were indeed brutally honest, there are lessons to be learned. Manu said the *rogan josh* was reasonably tasty, but the *chi nilgrie* was much too dry. Celine (looking cute in a red pinafore dress and multicoloured T-shirt) is a vegetarian, but thought the *prawn nariyal jhinga* is *the nicest food she's tasted in her entire life*. She's in a very flippant mood tonight and is slightly drunk. I'm sure she feels guilty about Barcelona. Unbelievably, it's the first time she's seen the restaurant in its new colours and layout. I didn't really have time to talk to her and anyway she had to leave early to relieve Quentin's babysitter. She probably wants to avoid any serious talking involving *sitting down*.

Eric the taxman, and Christine, our neighbours from Les Fabres, found everything too hot, even though the curries were the mildest Reza says he's ever prepared. We're now thinking of introducing a two-tier system on the order slips: *mild* and *even less mild* (if that's possible). JB said it was all *d'une beauté sublime*, but maybe he was just being polite, and anyway he'll eat anything. Nippi, predictably, thought the food was very poor. The *rogan josh* and the *chi nilgrie* tasted bland, and exactly the same.

Reza's panicked at their reaction, and wants to bring over his head chef from the Star of India as soon as possible to rectify matters. I urge him not to over-react, nor alarm Edward and Jamal, for fear of damaging morale. We still have time to get things right.

Reza's also in a state over the looming crisis over bookings, and for once I'm in complete agreement.

We don't have any. And we open in a week.

REZA: I've talked everything through with Zee, and tried to be cool and analytical about it all. Edward's cooking is undoubtedly a worry, but with some help and guidance, he should in time make the grade; it's the creation of a menu, its balance and texture, that is the delicate part of the process, so difficult to get right. Once the template is in place, though, its constant replication is relatively straightforward. If we can just get that menu sorted, Edward will run with it, reliably and smoothly.

But to be honest, it's Nigel I'm more worried about. The man's in real danger of becoming an embarrassment. As maître d' *he is the 'face' of L'Été Indien and frankly the image he's projected tonight is one of a bumbling, hapless guy who doesn't really have any idea of what he's doing. In front of friends, it's amusing; in front of paying customers, he could be a disaster. He's so HAM. His French seems to be getting worse by the day, although this could be nerves. I'm perfectly happy to accept his inexperience, but he should go about his business quietly, observing, checking, learning – not charging about in front of a bemused, captive audience like a bear roaring with a sore head. I have tried, diplomatically, to point this out. His reaction was: 'We're supposed to be having fun, Reza; if it's not fun we might just as well pack up and go home.' I mean, really!*

I've suggested Christiane should play a bigger role front-of-house but Nigel will have none of it. I have a real fear of us all appearing unprofessional. On the plus side, the teeth-whitener is working a treat.

～ 9 JULY ～

Reza is over-reacting.

Brinda, his head chef from the Star, was ordered to jump on the first available flight over, and has spent the latter part of the day in heated conversations with Reza, Edward and Jamal, amid much banging and crashing of pots and pans, in the kitchen. It must be like a sauna in there – I had no idea it was physically possible to fit four human beings in so small a space, and once again the temperatures outside are over forty degrees. Occasionally, I've heard raised voices. 'On no account are you to use artificial colouring ever again in this establishment, Edward!' was one phrase that permeated through to the terrace, along with, oddly, 'the greatest googlie I've ever seen bowled' and 'the third leg umpire had overruled the no-ball', although in the main I have just left them to it.

The lack of bookings, to my mind, is a much greater cause for concern, although I've not let Reza know I'm rattled. Despite all the interest, despite all the visits and calls by friends of the Tochous, despite even the casual interest of passers-by, we've not had one single booking. My only consolation here is the enigmatic Christiane, who's not remotely concerned; she keeps giving me reassuring kisses on the cheek, muttering, 'They will come, you will see, they will come, trust me, *mon chéri*.' And there's not a lot I can do about it.

No express-post delivery. Tom promised he sent off the divorce papers yesterday, adding helpfully: 'If they don't arrive in time, Dad, maybe that's a sign things were just not meant to be.' If I don't get them in the next day or two, debates about fine-tuning the menu or why we have no bookings yet will become utterly academic.

～ *10 July* ～

One of the most bizarre days of my life.

It started with a 7 a.m. telephone call from Rodriquez. The lorry containing Baby won't fit under the railway bridge that spans the only road leading into Largentière from the south. There were no other practical routes to enter the town. Did I have any suggestions?

This was a blow. Largentière, with its medieval cobbled streets, picturesque bridges and backdrop of the fabulous château at Montréal, would have provided the perfect photo opportunity for Baby. We were banned from going to Joyeuse. What were the options?

'You must make a quick decision, *mon ami*, Baby is getting restless.'

'You had better bring him straight to Laurac.'

The problem with Laurac is that it's just a quiet, moribund, sleepy little place with one small bar, half a dozen mostly empty shops that are closed most of the day, and a church that only ever comes to life on a Sunday morning. Nobody would notice even if Baby really did go on the rampage.

Rodriguez had parked his huge juggernaut, coincidentally, in a large parking area outside Marie-Elise's house; she had emerged, fully clothed for once, and was helping hose down Baby as I arrived. He's a small elephant as elephants go, but I realized the moment I saw him that our gamble on spending precious Euros on this most unusual of publicity gimmicks was likely to pay dividends. He is really cute, and already a gaggle of locals had gathered around him, mesmerized by his every movement. He sways constantly, the trunk incessantly reaching out and searching the air in great circles.

When he was dried off, we put Marie-Elise's purple blanket, bearing the immortal words 'L'ÉTÉ INDIEN, LAURAC, 04.75.36.85.03', on Baby's back, and as Rodriguez, armed with a short stick with a nasty-looking spike on the end of it, and his protégé set off for the centre of the village, followed by a growing band of curious onlookers, I drove back to the restaurant to organize the rest of the gang.

Reza's Indian costumes are splendid. I wear cream leggings (which take about forty minutes to get into), a black knee-length shirt and black embroidered cloak. Nippi looks quite majestic in a traditional orange turban, a true Maharajah. Reza has a green suit with large silver buttons – straight off the cover of *Sgt Pepper's* – and Sal's beautifully tanned face positively glows above an all-white trouser suit. There is a costume for everyone – Christiane, her daughter, Isobel, and Ramsa complete with bindis; even Manu wears a Jodhpuri. Only the three chefs are banned from the party, locked away in the steamy confines of the kitchen all day, although Brinda pokes his bearded, turbaned face briefly around the door, unable to believe his eyes.

Armed with hundreds of publicity flyers, we walk up the Rue d'Externat and turn the corner into the main street. The scene before us is extraordinary. Baby and Rodriguez are already there, standing patiently outside Pierre's bar. They are surrounded by a sea of people. The traffic really has stopped. People are crammed around windows, hanging off the balconies. There are two local TV news crews, alongside photographers and journalists from the local press. It is a truly miraculous sight.

'Nippi, you are a genius!' I say. And I mean it.

'Nigel, listen to me. That elephant's not Indian, it's African. Look at its ears!'

It hardly matters. Baby starts to walk casually across the road, up towards the church, and the amorphous mass of people move as one with him, shouting, pointing, laughing, taking endless photos. Even the staff of Le Poste desert their posts and are waving from the steps. An old man beside me mutters: 'The last time an elephant was seen in Laurac was just after the Ice Age.'

Charlie's camera is just rolling the whole time. He and Claudio are on the other side of the road, but I can see Charlie's face through the throng. He is ecstatic.

Baby moves forward and his gently roaming trunk locates the first in the row of Laurac's neatly planted and meticulously maintained lime trees. Instantly he starts tearing down the branches and stuffs them in his mouth. Rodriguez tries to pull him away, but the leaves are clearly tasty, and with alarming power the trunk continues to tear away at the tree. Someone screams, and the crowd moves back, warily. I hope *Monsieur le Maire* isn't at hand.

'He needs distracting,' says Reza, who darts up to the elephant and, after a brief word with Rodriguez, and much to everyone's astonishment, clambers up on to Baby's back, feeding the rampant trunk sweets from his pocket as he does so. It is quite obvious that Reza knows exactly what he is doing. It turns out that he learned how to ride an elephant during his schooldays in India.

Reza takes Baby up to the huge doors of the church, scattering rose petals for the photographers and camera crews. It is a surreal sight. The rest of us are all amongst the crowd, giving out the flyers as fast as we can to rows of outstretched hands, and since we have now agreed to throw an impromptu party at L'Été Indien on Sunday evening, the night before Bastille Day, we start dishing out invitations to all and sundry. Heaven knows how many will turn out.

With Reza now on his mobile phone ('You'll never believe what I'm doing, Zee darling, I'm in the south of France riding on an elephant ...') Rodriguez decides Baby needs to answer the call of nature, and leads him into a narrow street around the corner of the church, out of sight of the crowd. On a given command, Baby produces an enormous pile of dung, which he unceremoniously deposits a few inches from the front door of a tiny end-of-terrace house, and it stands there, steaming away like a dark, brooding volcano. The owner of the house could be in for an interesting surprise.

Afterwards we take Baby down to L'Été Indien, where the chefs are released from their captivity in the kitchen for a few minutes to join us outside the gate to the terrace for more press photos.

It's an absolute triumph.

When the party was dispersed, and Baby and Rodriguez were back on the road to Montpélier, reality returned with a bump. I looked around for the Fed. Ex. envelope Tom had assured me he's sent from England. Nothing.

There's a pile of bills that Christiane says must be paid if we are not to seriously upset our suppliers, our opening night is five days away, and soon the rent and wages will be due; yet it seems that as far as the French state is concerned, officially our business simply doesn't exist.

How on earth have I got myself in such a mess?

∼ 11 JULY ∼

You may find the most wonderful location in the world for your restaurant, you can design the interior and equip the kitchen to perfection, and then employ the most attentive of staff, but if the food is atrocious, the entire exercise is meaningless. Paying for a meal that one has not enjoyed is an experience most people are reluctant to repeat.

So says the wise Sir T. He has a point; maybe Reza is right to fuss so.

So today there should have been white smoke emerging from a chimney in the roof of L'Été Indien, like the one on the Vatican when a new Pope is appointed. At last, from the sweaty bowels of the kitchen, Reza and the chefs have reached a consensus: the menu has been finally agreed:

ENTRÉES

BAINGAN-E-BAHAR

Aubergine cuite au four, farcie de coriandre et de paneer (fromage
Indien fait maison), recouvert de tomates hachées sautées aux
feuilles de curry et aux graines de moutarde. Servi avec une
sauce d'ail.

Baked aubergine steaks stuffed with cottage cheese and sesame seeds,
topped with diced tomatoes, tempered with curry leaves and mustard
seeds. Served with a garlic dip.

MURGH TIKKA

Morceaux de poulet marinés dans l'ail, des piments verts et des
graines de sesame, avec un soupçon de muscade, grillés au four.

Oven-cooked diced chicken flavoured with garlic, green peppers,
sesame seeds and nutmeg.

MEEN SHIKAMPURAI

Petits pâtes de poisson parfumés au gingembre, à la ciboulette, à la
coriandre et la ciboule. Servi avec une sauce au yaourt et à la tomate.

Small fish pieces cooked with ginger, chives, coriander and onions.
Served with a yoghurt and tomato dip.

* * * *

Tous les plats sont accompagnés
All dishes are accompanied by the following:

SAAG PANEER

Épinards cuits avec du fromage Indien fait maison (paneer), sautés
à l'ail et au cumin, et légèrement parfumés au curcuma et au sel.

Spinach and grated home-made cottage cheese with garlic, cumin
seeds and Indian spices.

KAJU POSHO THORAN

Haricots verts et noix de cajou sautés aux graines de moutarde,
aux noix de coco rapée et aux feuilles de curry.
*Green beans and cashew nuts tempered and braised with mustard
seeds and coconut.*

LIMU CHAWAL

Riz basmati parfumé au citron
Steamed lemon rice

PLATS

Au choix:

MURGH KOFTA LUCKNOWI

Boulettes veloutées de poulet haché, farcies aux raisins secs et cuits
doucement dans une sauce au yaourt et à l'oignon, parfumée à la
cardamome et au macis (écorge de la noix de muscade).
*Chicken morsels cooked with raisins and Indian spices, marinated in
an onion and yoghurt sauce.*

ACHARI HANDI

Morceaux d'agneau doucement mijotés parfumés avec un mélange de 5
épices Indiennes (graines d'oignons, cumin, fenouil, graines de moutarde
noire et fenugrec) avec de l'ail rôti et des petits champignons de Paris.
*Diced lamb cooked in an assortment of Indian spices and served with
chopped garlic and mushrooms.*

DUM KA JHINGA

Cassoulette de gambas légèrement épicée cuite dans une sauce
crémeuse avec des légumes.
Lightly spiced prawns cooked in a creamy sauce with vegetables.

DESSERTS

Au choix:

DUM MALAI CHIKKI

Crème brûlée parfumée à la cardamome et au noix de muscade.
Caramelized steamed milk pudding scented with cardamom and nutmeg.

BHAPA DAHI

Yaourt aux noix de coco avec des raisins sec.
Coconut yoghurt with raisins and nuts.

PHALON KI BAHAR

Mangues et lycees avec une crème de safran.
Mangoes and lychees served with saffron cream.

The menu covers were here weeks ago, and now the inner page detailing the food and drink on offer (to be attached to the covers by gold tassels; very tasteful) is ready to be printed up. Sal drove up to the printers to get this done, but – embarrassingly – was told that nothing else would be printed until we have paid our first bill in full. I have told Sal not to mention this to anyone, particularly Christiane.

It was, therefore, with a certain degree of relief that I witnessed a van pulling up outside the restaurant this afternoon, and a large white envelope bearing the wonderful words Fed. Ex. in big blue and orange letters was deposited. Inside were the divorce papers, stamped by the Aldershot County Court, in the county of Hampshire, August 2001.

I never thought I'd be so pleased to see them.

Wildly waving the document, like Chamberlain on his misguidedly triumphant return from meeting Hitler at Munich, I announce to a relieved Reza that the last piece of paperwork required for my registration is now here, and set off like a bullet from a gun in *Vin P* to the Aubenas *Chambre de Commerce*.

The demure Madame Souberon seems strangely pleased to see me. She sits me down in her office, and even offers me coffee. I hand her my divorce papers. She smiles.

'So all is now in place, M'sieur Farrell. At last. Congratulations!'

She takes out a delicate pair of reading spectacles, and examines the document. She leafs through the pages. Then she removes the spectacles.

'But M'sieur Farrell. This is no good. I cannot accept this!'

'No good?'

'It's in English!'

Now I like to think of myself as a cove not easily rattled, someone who can keep their head while all around others are losing theirs. But at this point in my meeting with the utterly charming Madame Souberon I feel as though, at any moment, steam is about to emerge from my ears.

Does she really believe that the clerks of the Aldershot County Court, in the county of Hampshire, issue bilingual divorce papers in English and French, just in case the recipient may decide one day to open an Indian restaurant in the Ardèche?

'Of course it's in English.'

'But M'sieur! I must have this in French. Two copies. And to be acceptable to the Chamber of Commerce, the translation must be authenticated. By a *notaire*.'

I stagger out into the sunlight. It's Friday afternoon. Our party is on Sunday; we open for business on Tuesday. I am technically penniless.

I call Marie, my solicitor in Lyons. If I bike up the papers by courier, can she have them translated and signed off in time for them to be returned here by the end of the working day? She is sympathetic. But it's not physically possible.

'Then what am I to do?' If the ground opens up in front of me, and reveals a boiling reservoir of bubbling molten lava, I will gladly plunge into it.

'Have you explained to them the seriousness of your situation?'

I go back into the hated reception area of the *Chambre de Commerce*, and ask again to see Madame Souberon. I will throw myself at her mercy. I will go on my knees.

She listens quietly to what I have to say. Without the registration, I can't trade. L'Été Indien is due to open in a few days. Suppliers need paying. We are already behind schedule, the summer is slipping away. Disaster looms.

Madame Souberon pauses for a moment after I finish. Then she looks at the ceiling. Then back to me.

'M'sieur Farrell, why did you not say all this before? We could have avoided much pain and unhappiness.'

'Yes?'

'What do you English take us for? Devils and demons? You are an entrepreneur, setting up a new business in the Ardèche, creating wealth and employment.'

'Yes.'

'And, of course, here at the *Chambre de Commerce* we are keen to encourage such initiative and enterprise.'

'Yes?'

She pulls out the registration form from her drawer, slowly puts on her spectacles, and scribbles something. Then she stands up, and shakes me by the hand.

'Congratulations, M'sieur Farrell. You are now registered. As of this moment, you may legally begin to trade.'

'How's that?'

'I have simply changed your marital designation,' she said, with a charming smile. 'Instead of ticking the box marked "divorced", I have ticked the box marked "single".'

∽ 12 July ∽

Christiane came roaring in from the jeep, waving a copy of *La Dauphine*, the major local newspaper in the Ardèche.

We've got half a page. They've used the picture of Baby and the rest of us standing outside the restaurant, alongside a long article giving all the background to L'Été Indien. Nippi is looking pleased as punch. We're all looking pleased as punch. It's the kind of publicity one dreams of.

'Has anyone made a booking yet?' I enquire casually, not wishing for a moment to sound a killjoy.

We all look at Christiane.

I know the answer before she even begins to speak. The phone hasn't rung all morning.

Sal and I set off in the searing heat with a vanload of roadside L'Été Indien signs. It's a laborious task. They must all be wired on top of every Le Relais Fleuri sign on every approach road to Laurac.

It's another cloudless sky. The air is dry and dusty. The sun beats down remorselessly.

'Sal, are people really going to want hot, spicy food in this kind of climate?'

'They do in India.'

When we reach La Beaume we allow ourselves a lunchtime beer by the river and half an hour in the shade. It's tempting to leap into the water.

'Nije, I can stay another three weeks. Then I must go back to London. I've got some work.'

Her words come as a shock. Sally Ann has become part of the fabric of the place. She has worked away, tirelessly, all day, every day, often without thanks and certainly – to date – without payment.

'As soon as the money starts to come in, I can pay you.'

'It's not the money.'

It's not just her work I shall miss. Sal's the best company, a real tonic, bright and witty, as well as being one of life's natural optimists. Had I really imagined she would stay here all summer? Of course she wants to go home.

We got back exhausted, backs broken, soaked with sweat, but everything done. I looked at Christiane. She hesitated for a moment, and then slowly shook her head.

'I've found an Indian dancer who can come along and perform at the party tomorrow night,' she said, no doubt by way of a diversionary tactic.

'That's good. But Christiane, why don't we have any bookings?'

'It will happen. Trust me.'

This time I flipped.

'We've had the most fantastic publicity. Everyone is talking about L'Été Indien. We are the most exciting thing that's happened around here since the Hundred Years War.'

'The Hundred Years War?'

'And not one booking. We open in three days. And not one of your friends, not one of your family, not any of the thousands of people you know so well in this place has made a booking. Not a single one. Not one bloody reservation. Why?'

Christiane looked surprised, and hurt. She smiled helplessly.

'New tape please, Clouds,' says Charlie.

Then, suddenly, I had a possible explanation. Maybe she has deliberately avoided taking bookings. She has, after all, been the silent witness to everything that has happened over the last six weeks, the uncertainty, worries, fears, misjudgements, errors, rows. Nothing will have escaped Christiane's notice. And she has simply lost confidence in us. She thinks we are incompetent. She'll believe we'll open next Tuesday only when it happens. She is shielding herself from public humiliation.

Part of me can only sympathize.

～ 13 JULY ～

There's consternation in the kitchen.

Sir Terence would have had a fit. All of us, individually, have been merrily dishing out invitations to tonight's party, and now no one has the slightest idea how many people to cater for. Reza says this is my fault. It's hard to know how I could have been expected to keep track.

So Brinda and Edward have no choice but to prepare a vast quantity of food. Reza says this is an appallingly inefficient way to run a kitchen, but leaving people hungry would be a marketing disaster.

Everyone's on edge.

Normally the rest of us are strictly banned from the domain of the chefs, but today the press-gangs are out in force, there's been a Three Line Whip – Christiane, Manu, Sal, Ramsa, Olivier, even a grumbling JB and the newly arrived Greek God Erique have been enlisted to assist the four toiling pairs of hands in the kitchen. Every corner of the restaurant is humming. It's curiously satisfying work, and seems to meet some basic, atavistic need, like hunting or fishing. Humans have been doing exactly this, together, since the start of time, and will do so until its end. There's a growing mountain of chicken and lamb *koftas* in the middle of the room, alongside huge cauldrons of thick creamy coconut and cardamom sauce, tubs of yoghurt and milk, heaps of beans, aubergines, coconuts, potatoes, chickpeas, and cashew nuts. We could be eating the stuff for months.

Then, some real drama. The phone rings. We have our first booking! A table for four, Tuesday night! It breaks the tension. I do the rumba around the restaurant. Everyone smiles. Including Charlie.

Well, it's not quite twenty-seven, but it's a start.

When all the prep work and *mis-en-place* is done, Sal and I slip away into the late afternoon sun for a quick swim in the river. She does something she's never done before: she asks me about Celine.

I decide to be honest.

I am confused. I have hardly seen Celine; I haven't spoken to her properly for weeks. Real communication between us is difficult, sometimes impossible. I have no idea what's going through her mind or if we have any kind of a future together.

'Are you serious about her?'

'Sometimes I'm not sure,' I said. 'It was just fun to start with. Now a chasm has appeared between us. How can you be serious about such an unknown quantity?'

'Do you think she's serious about you?'

'I just don't know.'

'Find out.'

'How?'

Sal's suggestion is very simple.

Tonight I'm going to invite Celine to England for a weekend as soon as the restaurant is safely up and running. To meet my children, my family.

If she turns me down, I'll know.

Celine should have been at L'Été when we returned, she said she would leave work early for once and come over to Laurac to help with the party. Of course, she's not there. She calls me at about seven o'clock to say she's on her way. I tell her not to hurry, the work's done. This is not a good omen.

But some better news from Christiane. Eight more bookings, six for Tuesday, two for Saturday: our total so far for the week ahead now stands at twelve. Suddenly Christiane's reservations book doesn't look quite so naked.

Our guests are to be greeted by a glass of a traditional Indian aperitif of rose syrup, milk, gelatine and cardamom. We all try some. It would taste better with a little alcohol.

'It would taste better with alcohol,' said Sal, loudly.

'Why are you shouting?'

'I'm nervous!'

'There's not supposed to be any alcohol,' says Reza impatiently. 'Indians don't drink alcohol with their food.'

A sinister air of tension has returned. We still have absolutely no idea how many people will turn out. We all change into our Indian costumes.

Christiane asks about the rose syrup, examines it suspiciously, and takes a sip.

'There's no alcohol in it!'

Our first guests are Monsieur Champetier, *Monsieur le Maire*, his wife and a couple of friends. I'd always thought mayors in France loved formality and would turn out at the drop of a hat in smart suit boasting the traditional tricolour sash across a proud breast, probably humming the 'Marseillaise', but Manu says they only doll up like this to marry people. Disappointingly, Monsieur Champetier is in jeans and an open shirt straining around the predictable, middle-aged male paunch. Still, at least he's here.

I offer him a glass of the rose syrup.

'*Pas d'alcool, M'sieur, je suis désolé. Mais c'est une boisson traditionale Indienne!*'

'*Santé!*'

Monsieur le Maire takes a large gulp from the glass. Then he suddenly turns very pale, his cheeks blow up, and his eyes start revolving rapidly. He slowly turns away from the group, and noisily ejects the syrup from his mouth in a large, milky spray into a pot of slightly surprised-looked geraniums.

There is a stunned silence, followed by a brief outburst of rapid, animated discussion in French, which goes right over my head, while the mayor recovers his composure. Manu turns to me and says: 'I'm afraid *Monsieur le Maire* is allergic to milk.'

Things are not getting off to a great start.

Next Nippi arrives, again looking splendid and positively regal in a black turban, and black and silver striped and braided Dhoti Kurta and long white shawl. More familiar faces follow: Marcel and Elise Carbenero, our neighbours from Les Fabres; our builder Monsieur Golette; Christine and Eric, from Vassellent; and eventually Celine, looking even slimmer and more lissom than ever, in a tight black shirt and trousers, and almost translucent pink tabard. We greet each other warmly. Then comes the Indian dancer Christiane had somehow tracked down from a village near Nîmes, accompanied by some bemused-looking musicians. Suddenly the place is starting to buzz.

By the time Reza and I have made short speeches of thanks, and the dancing is underway, L'Été Indien is packed to the rafters. There is hardly room to stand. There are even people spilling out on to the street. We have reached a wonderful, fantastic, exhilarating watershed.

'Reza,' I whisper excitedly, hardly able to speak it out loud lest I am speaking too soon. 'Rez, it's working!'

'Of course it is,' says Reza coolly, with a disparaging glance, and starts to urge guests towards the food tables with calm and polite efficiency. It is almost as though he has become a different person. Gone is the nervous, giggling flapper. Reza is in his natural environment, this has been his world for over twenty years; the consummate professional, gliding about effortlessly amongst the guests, constantly scrutinizing and rearranging the dishes, smiling, chatting, topping up drinks, the perfect host. It's wonderful to have him here; a privilege, and I make a mental note to tell him this later.

It's all happening so fast, I'm having trouble taking it all in. There must be two hundred people here; they're trailing out, way down the street. The food is a hit, a palpable hit; we really are in danger of running out. I cruise around the groups of guests with Manu, and there's compliment after compliment: they love the stuff. We're too busy to celebrate; that'll have to wait.

We are a success!

How can I be so sure? One look at Christiane's face on the other side of the room, and there's no doubt in my mind. She is radiant. In one hand there's a pen, in the other, our reservations book. She holds it up to show me. There's a mass of scribbled names and numbers, spread right across our first week.

We are a success!

But most intriguing of all is Nippi's reaction to what is unfolding. He's strutting around like a peacock and looks magnificent (Reza's right, his presence here adds a real pazazz) but what I notice now, for the first time since he's been here, is that he has more of a proprietorial air than that of a guest. He too is moving from group to group, asking about the food, shaking people by the hand, eagerly accepting their appreciation and congratulations. It's almost as if he can smell the scent of success, and wants to ensure that he is part of it. Can this really be the same Nippi who had poured scorn on the whole idea right at the start? Who constantly told me that the Ardèchoise were simply not ready for Indian cuisine? Who had refused to gamble a single cent of his own money in the project?

'Nigel, listen to me. Look at the reaction of these people. Can't you see what's happening here? Look at the faces! What are they saying about the food? Nigel, you don't even need to speak French to know what they think ... *superb*! ... *merveilleux*! ... *fantastique*! We've struck gold!' Then he adds a phrase that I think will stay in my mind for quite a while: '*We are going to make a fortune!*'

But now isn't the time. I'll file that phrase away for another day.

But, of course, it is a success, a huge success. I say the words out loud.

They sound just great.

Just as the thought is at last starting to sink into my overworked, befuddled brain, amidst the waves of chatter, music, laughter and, yes, happiness, I find myself standing next to Celine.

I should have seen it coming. But I didn't.

Of course, it was the wrong place and the wrong time. Maybe that's why it all seemed to be over with so quickly.

I told Celine that I intended, just as soon as I could, to book tickets for us both to go to London to see my family. She responded without a moment's hesitation.

'I can't do that.'

'Why not?'

Then, in her slow, faltering English, it all came out, and every word was perfectly as predicted:

Language problems, the great cultural divide (isn't that what makes it interesting and fun? It was to start with). My future is so uncertain (I looked around at the sea of laughing faces and empty plates; it's a lot more certain now than it was an hour or two ago. So she's not a gold-digger after all). And then the inevitable Big One: she needs a vigorous father for

Quentin (i.e. not a grandfather); she is just too young for me (I'm too old); and then: 'Nigel, *chéri*, I am not the girl for you.'

At which point she leant forwards, hugged me, lightly kissed my cheek and left.

At moments of unexpected shock, when I drive around a corner at high speed, suddenly to be confronted by an unmapped crossroads, I cast around wildly for thoughts, any thoughts, to fill the sudden void.

All I could think of now was: what *brilliant* timing.

Prompted by a series of huge explosions, people were streaming out on to the road outside, like a great river of humanity. It was exactly midnight, the start of Bastille Day, and the sky above Laurac was being sliced into multicoloured sections and circles by fusillades and broadsides of fireworks, throwing the church and the little rows of medieval terraced houses around it, on top of the hill, into sudden, sharp relief.

We are almost fully booked for the next few days. The sky's on fire with a spirit of celebration and liberation, of colour, excitement and optimism for the future.

It's the end of a perfect evening.

And all recorded for posterity by Charlie. Every detail.

～ 14 JULY ～

I am now a restaurateur.

Being a restaurateur speaks to those instincts that give us, to use a well-worn phrase, the 'feel-good factor'. It's about providing a total experience, the abstract aesthetics of hospitality, comfort, sustenance, conviviality, companionship and entertainment. But, above all, being a restaurateur demands passion.

Sir Terence, bless him, clearly has passion. Reza Mahammad has passion; now I too have passion. L'Été Indien is a success, just as Reza and Christiane always said it would be. I will clear my debts, we can even pay Sally Ann; and we can now enjoy the luxury of expanding our horizons. Maybe we should start introducing lunches. Maybe we can keep open through the winter. Maybe, who knows, we should begin to consider opening another Indian restaurant? Isn't that what Sir T. would be thinking right now?

Passion, then quiet satisfaction, and now a chance to relax for a few hours. For the first time in days we have an opportunity to recover, draw breath and re-assess ourselves and the days ahead.

Earlier I had awoken, though, to multiple and multicoloured images of Celine. The explosion of beautiful hair. The high, freckled forehead. The huge eyes. The cheeky, all-encompassing laugh. The sheer zest for life. Her scent. The gentle touch.

Was there somebody else? I hope not. Wouldn't she have said?

It's an ugly way of looking at it, but the painful truth, which I must confront, is this: I have been well and truly *dumped*. And it does hurt. It hurts in a strange and unfamiliar way, because I have just realized that I have never been dumped before. Is this divine retribution for my other, failed relationships? There must be something good to come out of this, please. Maybe it's therapeutic for the soul to be dumped. For the long term. Maybe it should be a pre-requisite for everyone to be dumped at least once in his or her life.

Should I contact Celine? Try to persuade her to change her mind? Is that what I really want? And should I tell the others what has happened?

Eventually I come to the conclusion that maybe it's best that I do nothing for a few days, and instead throw myself into the (hopefully) distracting passion of being a restaurateur.

Christiane insists on champagne first thing, so we sit around, amongst a legion of empty wine bottles (amazingly Olivier did all the clearing up last night, single-handed, long after we had collapsed back at Les Fabres; what a team we have become!) and enjoy a late, leisurely breakfast, savouring the highlights of the previous evening, and re-living them over and over again. The chefs get off to a late start, but even in the kitchen there's an air of unpressured jollity. Brinda will stay with us for the opening night tomorrow, and then – assuming all goes well – return to London on Wednesday. He's been a joy to work with, we shall miss him.

Nippi goes home today. He says his job is done, there is nothing further for him to do here, and in a way, he, too, has played an invaluable role. We are, after all, good friends. It's been fun just having him there. Well, that *was* what I was in the process of thinking right up to the point when Nippi and I had what is probably our biggest argument to date.

We left the rest of the team at the restaurant, to tinker with tomorrow's menu, wash and iron the linen, and just enjoy a little of the Bastille Day holiday. Up at Les Fabres, Nippi started to pack.

Then he said, in that curiously meaningless yet foreboding way of his: 'Nigel, listen to me. I have been thinking.'

Just then I remembered the phrase from last night: *We are going to make a fortune.*

I waited for him to explain.

Sometimes it's hard to know exactly what Nippi has in mind – after all, English is his second language – but my reading of what followed is this: Nippi regards himself as an astute businessman, and he sees in what we've created at L'Été Indien a great business opportunity. Together we should seize the initiative. Together we should begin plans immediately to expand. And he will help us, guide us and make sure we convert the seed of a potentially great idea into a large and hugely profitable tree. And how do we finance this expansion? Nippi will invest in us, of course; he will become a partner. And thereby, to use a phrase, make a fortune.

The logic of this, if one is completely dispassionate, makes sense. If we need a financial injection, does it really matter where the money comes from? Why shouldn't Nippi help us?

But I am a man of passion, and I can't help finding Nippi's suggestion slightly ungentlemanly.

'Let me get this right, Nippi. You refused to join me originally in this venture, you've sat back and watched as Reza and I have taken all the risk, and now that you have seen it's a success – and only now – you want to join in!'

'Listen to me. I didn't join you originally because of the way you were going about it. But the principle of the idea was always a sound one. In fact, when I first thought of this idea—'

'This was not your idea!'

'It *was* my idea!'

We went on like this for several minutes, like a couple of six-year-olds posturing for fisticuffs; then, when I tell Nippi that he had just been too much of a coward to take the risk, he went really ballistic, shouting that it was he who had taken all the risk because I had borrowed against the house, against his investment, without even consulting him. Things became really heated. I don't think for a moment that Nippi remotely understands my resentment towards his arrogant stance. He regards me as over-emotional, irrational and irritatingly inexperienced. Emotions and business simply should not be combined, he told me patronizingly, then – having just nearly bellowed the roof down – had the nerve to start telling me to calm down.

But then, in typical fashion, it was suddenly over. Don't I think arguments are a pointless waste of time and effort? Yes, Nippi. Shouldn't grown men know better? Indeed, Nippi. Nigel, isn't the sensible thing just to wait for a few weeks before making any decisions and see if the success of the restaurant can really be sustained? Maybe it's just a novelty? Good idea, Nippi. Having bought and renovated the house here together, I'm becoming convinced Nippi believes he has a moral right to a share in the restaurant, which grew out of it. Does he have a point? Or is this just an attempt at cynical exploitation?

He seemed insistent that I should not mention any of this to Reza yet, and I'm certainly happy to go along with that. So after a few straightforward goodbyes, it was back on the road to Lyons airport. I used the time to try to prevent him becoming too animated about the potential of joining our project. Apart from my own, yes, *emotional* reaction, and real misgivings, heaven knows what Reza would really think.

Unusually, I waited and watched the plane take off, relishing the inactivity. As it slowly lifted, the intense sun dancing off the glass of the windows, and disappeared into the shimmering, cloudless sky, I wondered when I would see Nippi again.

REZA: Mon dieu! A huge sigh of relief. The party was sublime, wonderful. The chefs are on course at last, the food is really beginning to work out according to my master plan and, for the first time perhaps, I can take a step back and start to let the powerhouse of the kitchen run by itself. But I watched Nigel carefully last night and far from calming down he seems to be becoming more manic than ever. Early in the evening he drove me nearly INSANE, jumping up and down as though he'd got a ferret in his trousers – he should be carrying hazard warning lights. The real danger of someone thinking they're in charge when it's obvious to everyone they're not, is not just appalling public relations; it simply increases everyone else's workload ten times. As Zee always points out, drawing on her experiences as Brown Owl, 'That's why on the battlefield it's sometimes necessary to order a marksman to take our general out'. The trouble is that there's no marksman to hand around here. Maybe I should slip a tranquillizer into his pastis tomorrow evening.

∽ 15 JULY ∽

A sobering start to what is probably the most significant day in the restaurant's history.

The euphoria is over. The place has been swept, candlesticks replenished, tables polished and tablecloths ironed; the chefs have been up since dawn, dripping brows, pots bubbling away for hours on the stoves. And everything is cloaked in that familiar sweet, spicy aroma that must by now have started to infuse the very woodwork of the place.

In just a few hours the ultimate test begins. No more tastings, no more parties, no more overblown compliments about free food – these will be real paying customers with real wallets, wanting and expecting the best. There is a growing knot of nerves gnawing away at the base of my stomach. Hold your breath, but the food seems almost right. Tonight the emphasis is on service. We haven't rehearsed enough; we haven't really rehearsed at all.

The logistics of maintaining the beast, day in, day out, must also now be considered. We have a brief meeting about transport. It's clear that if L'Été Indien is to run at anything like near capacity, we're going to need more than just *Vin P* to ferry in daily provisions. The Deux Chevaux, bless her, is on her last legs. There's Christiane's jeep, which is a scene-stealer to look at and very handy if you're the props buyer for a Hollywood movie, but in fact it's quite useless as a restaurant runabout. You can't safely leave anything in it – there isn't a roof. Also, Reza has no driving licence. Manu suggests we could buy him a *motobicyclette* with a big pannier, which would not only give the restaurant an extra pair of wheels but would also lend Reza a measure of independence. Under French law, all he needs to drive it on the roads is insurance, and a quick call to Christiane's insurance company in Joyeuse can fix that.

Manu and Reza set off to Aubenas together, giggling, and return a couple of hours later with a real beauty, very stylish, very Reza: it's a classic little blue 1959 *Velo Solex Motobécane*, in extremely good condition which – because inevitably Manu knows the shop-owner – they've picked up for a mere 200 Euros.

I don't know why I'm surprised, but Reza's absolutely thrilled with the bike. He's thrown himself into driving it round and round the little streets of Laurac like Evil Knievel. When I first met him, he struck me as being precious; but it seems nothing could be further from the truth. He threw himself on to the back of a restlessly aggressive Baby, the elephant, like a diminutive but very hyperactive Harrison Ford. Now he keeps pleading with the chefs to send him off on more errands.

We're ready for business hours early, of course. It's only 5 p.m. and I'm already in costume. I am terribly nervous. We have twenty-five reservations. Christiane and Sal (probably in a desperate attempt to distract me) offer to pretend to be customers. I show them to their table, I take their orders; I make a mess of it. The carbon paper on the order pad doesn't seem to work. I get the 'spicy star rating' the wrong way around. Then I step into the kitchen when Edward has expressly forbidden us from doing so, and now, in a bate, he's pulled a table across the door as a barricade and is refusing to talk to me. His nerves must be as frayed as mine. I can't even find the gin and tonic.

I can't believe how many crises appear from nowhere. There's consternation that the blender's broken, it appears to have just given up the ghost and died. It's a pretty vital link in the production of our prestigious cold fruit soup (everything local and seasonal, melon, strawberries, raspberries). We're offering it as one of our star desserts. I panic, although I hide this convincingly from the others. The bloody blender's brand new, isn't it? Opening night and on top of everything else I have to work out how to say 'Sorry, cold fruit soup's off' in French. Then someone spots that the blender's plug has come partially adrift of its socket, and we're suddenly back in business.

I check out the wines on our list. There's only two bottles of the Domaine de Bournet Cabernet Sauvignon 1997, which is top of our list. Why wasn't this checked before? It's Reza's fault, he's in charge of bloody victualling, I can't be responsible for bloody everything. Then Sal finds a few more boxes of the stuff in the cellar. But there's not enough Louis Latour Chardonnay Vin de Pays des Coteaux de l'Ardèche. Christiane dashes off to buy more, we shout her back. Edward's just started work with the mortar and pestle, mashing up the lime for the aperitif we're to serve, along with sugar syrup and vodka, to every customer – but there's only a drop of vodka left in the bottle. Christiane thinks she can find more in time, and she roars away in the jeep, leaving a terrace billowing with grey, poisonous exhaust fumes. Sal's shouting somewhere. The phone keeps ringing. We're way past our target of twenty-seven covers. More like thirty-seven. No time to celebrate.

By the time our first guests arrive, I'm already exhausted. They are a young couple, plus child, and I greet them – I trust not too obsequiously – but feeling both Basil Fawlty-like and almost paralysed with terror at the same time. I smile a good deal. They smile a good deal back, although whether from mere good manners or because they find the situation hugely amusing, I have no way of knowing. I don't understand a single word they say. There's no Christiane to help me out. What would they like to eat? For some reason, I feel compelled to know this information immediately, almost as they are sitting down. Red or white wine?

'For God's sake, Nigel, calm down,' hisses Reza, pulling me, subtly but firmly, away from the table. 'Give them a few moments. They've come here for a good evening out, to sample the ambience of the place, to enjoy the company. Stop trying to bloody force-feed them. Let them savour the experience. Go out the back and have a bloody drink.'

Of course, I know Reza is right. Maybe it's just the culmination of weeks of stress; maybe just because I have never done anything remotely like this in my entire life. I take a large slug of *pastis* and watch Reza and Sally Ann in operation with complete admiration. Somehow it doesn't seem to matter at all that they can speak virtually no French. More guests are arriving. They are quietly, politely greeted by the girls; names checked, jackets and bags efficiently taken; effortlessly led through the terrace, to be shepherded to their table. And now Christiane is back after her last-minute but successful mission to restock the depleted cellars. You would never know she was flustered. She's like a queen, smiling, embracing and waving at friendly and strange faces alike: she seems to know everyone. At this moment, suddenly, I know beyond any doubt that I could not have managed this without any of them.

And L'Été Indien does look idyllic. Now the light is dropping, the hundreds of candles Reza has had placed on every available surface – on each of the tables, on the walls beside the pot-plants, in the red, blue and yellow cups hanging by fishing line from beneath the lush grapevine at the entrance (some of them so high only Erique can reach to light them) and in the selection of eclectic wrought-iron and boxed wooden Indian candlesticks he brought over from London – all combine with Charlie and Claudio's lights to produce a wonderful communal glow which spills into the massed dazzle of coloured fairy lights and lanterns Reza has hung from every beam. It looks an absolute picture.

I am being summoned by our very first guest and his wife.

'*C'est bon, le manger, M'sieur?*'

'*Oui, oui, mais du pain, s'il vous plaît!*'

'*Je suis désolé, M'sieur.*' Oh dear, Christiane was right. '*Pas de pain!*'

'*Pas de pain? Ce n'est pas possible! C'est incroyable!*'

Sadly, Christiane was absolutely correct on another key point: there is now a growing gaggle of people, with tense, slightly contorted faces, huddled in the narrow corridor outside the *toilette*.

'Go and turn the bloody pump off the fountain,' mutters Reza as he squeezes past me.

On the road outside, I can see faces in the darkness.

'*Avez vous faire un reservation?*'

Every seat in L'Été Indien is now either taken or booked. We are so busy that anyone who hasn't made a reservation I must reluctantly turn away, although not without animated attempts – usually, I have to say, successfully completed – to sign them up another night. Or should I try to hang on to them and their goodwill by persuading them to stay for a drink? Not everyone who made a reservation appears to have turned up, and I'm haunted by some words of Sir T's:

A full reservation book is no guarantee of success. The bane of the restaurateur's life is the 'no shows'. Sometimes customers will book several restaurants in advance and then decide which one to go to on the night . . . for a small business with fifty covers or fewer, holding a table all evening for diners who do not turn up can make the difference between success and failure . . . a few no shows can cripple a family restaurant and threaten closure.

Just something else I must keep a weather eye on.

My brain is hurting.

I have another *pastis* and contemplate the scene unfolding before me. All the months of dreams, planning, worry, great hopes, dashed hopes, the fateful meeting with Reza, the almost coincidental discovery of the Tochous and Le Relais Fleuri; the six frantic weeks of preparation, redecorating, re-equipping, finding and training the staff, advertising, the triumph of Baby and the ultimate riot of the opening party; it's all come to this, the first working Indian restaurant in the Ardèche, breaking such new ground, making real money, employing real people.

Yet no amount of rehearsals could have prepared me for what I am supposed to be doing in reality. The restaurant may be buzzing, but for me the words 'fish', 'water' and 'out of' come to mind, and not necessarily in that order. I can't get to grips with the *pacing* of the evening. Reza and Sally Ann, on the other hand, seem to know instinctively when to act, when to move forward – and when to hold off.

And there's so much interminable standing around.

My mistakes, too, come thick and fast. I drop a plate. A cork gets stuck in the neck of a wine bottle. After carting endless trays of dirty, piled-high plates and glasses to join the growing mountain of washing-up in the outside kitchen, my back goes, a twinge at first, then a real pain at the base of the spine. I try some emergency stretching exercises beside Olivier, loading up the machine, but Sal says I'm in the way and should bugger off.

By eleven o'clock, I'm ready to drop. I'm also, much to my surprise, bored and fractious. The place is still half full. They've all finished their meals, but they don't seem to want to go home. We've blown out most of the candles in the restaurant except those close by their tables. They're not even ordering more drinks. Unlike in England, a table of four or even six people can apparently survive an entire evening on a single bottle of wine. We've not sold any Calvados or Cognac at all.

It's one thirty, and only the diary is keeping me sane.

～ *16 July* ～

Awake with a seismic headache.

I was at L'Été Indien, tallying up the cheques and cash, until two thirty in the morning. The chefs had crashed out upstairs. I'd sent Ramsa and Erique home. We've done splendidly on the financial front, of course, and everyone – particularly Christiane – was relieved and delighted, so dealing with the mountains of lolly should have been a sheer pleasure. It was not. Twice I nodded off to sleep. I couldn't have cared less about the money. I wanted to die. Poor Sal had to drive Rez and me back home to Les Fabres. Her stamina is astonishing.

It's only D-Day Minus One but an awful, terrible, totally unexpected question is already filling my mind as I slowly open my eyes. It is late, eleven o'clock, but then, not late at all. This isn't just a new career; it's a new way of life. I must learn to adjust. Two thirty to bed, eleven o'clock to rise. Normal.

The question: is this really the life for me?

I need to get to the bank. We've run out of so many provisions. Incredibly, the chefs already need more meat from Le Clerc's. There are tons more vegetables, fruit, vodka, candles, washing-up cubes, bottled water, urgently required. Even the salt and pepper supplies are exhausted. Why isn't any of this stuff delivered, I ask Christiane? I know what she will say before she says it: because it never has been.

This must be like the life of an actor in the theatre.

All day one waits, killing time in all kinds of mental and physical preparation for tonight's show; cleaning, driving, buying, phoning, cooking. And then, just as it seems everyone else in the world is coming home and closing down for the day, exhausted after their labours, the important part of my day is just getting underway, the show's about to open.

This evening at L'Été Indien is an almost identical replay of last night and, of course, one can only be gratified for that. It *is* wonderful.

The real fun begins when you open your doors to paying customers. Neither does it stop at the opening night. Day after day, night after night, week after week, an amazingly complicated ballet of events takes place . . . at every single stage there is a potential for something to go wrong . . . the rewards, however, are great. I can honestly say there can be few pleasures to equal the thrill of walking into one's own restaurant and experiencing that amazing buzz of people having a good time.

And Sir T's right: it is a thrill. But.

Can I really do this every day of my life?

On our opening night I was kept alight by adrenalin. And the nerves are still there tonight. But so is the creeping, insidious feeling of boredom. I just want to sit them down, for God's sake, feed and water them, and get them up and out on the street as soon as physically possible so I can go home and get back to my real life.

Why do people take so long to eat something? The ambience of L'Été Indien may be novel and utterly charming for them, but I've been living with it for weeks. Every time I want to rush in and clear the plates, Reza has to forcibly hold me back. 'Don't you want these people to come back to the restaurant?' he says, with growing annoyance. 'And not only do we need people to come back time and time again, we need them to spread the news. There's nothing, *nothing* more important than word of mouth. Are you really intent on commercial suicide?'

Perhaps as the days go by I will learn to settle down. But perhaps not. Unfortunately, this is a feeling I've now started to recognize from my past. You work at something until your back breaks, and then, when you finally achieve it, your first instinct is to move on.

And maybe that explains quite a lot about my life.

REZA: With great kindness, Zee's just reminded me that eighty per cent of restaurants close within two years. Nigel needs to keep that at the front of his mind. It would be too easy to be damning on him, but he does have so much to learn. He's done the difficult bit, he's climbed every mountain, he's forded every stream, and now he has two important lessons to learn: how to enjoy his success (and that takes a certain maturity, too); and how to run the business day to day. He has created a fantastic opportunity but he cannot afford to take his eye off the ball for a moment. He must fine-tune the operation, build on that first success, improve its productivity and thereby its profitability. He's been talking, ridiculously, about spending money on 'team-building' exercises, like paint-balling, or recreating jungle expeditions, but that – worryingly – could be because he's bored. And he hasn't much time: my job here is nearly over. He must be able to run this place on his own. My thoughts are turning back to London, to my friends, to the Star.

And besides, the 'new look' will be coming into Harvey Nicks menswear in the next few weeks.

~ 18 JULY ~

The days pass slowly, each so much like the last.

When we're not motoring around the Ardèche like blue-arsed flies picking up endless lists of supplies, Sal and I swim a good deal, so we're fit and tanned; afterwards we've taken to sitting in the shade beside Marie-Elise's pool, or at the bar in La Beaume, reading to each other. Michael Frayn's book *Spies* was a revelation; Ernest Hemingway's *The Sun Also Rises* was harder work, but it has made me want to jump in the van and drive down to Spain. In fact I'd quite like to jump in the van and drive anywhere, anywhere other than Laurac. It's fun sharing these stories with Sally Ann. It is not, however, what I came to France for.

I arrive at the restaurant each evening as late as possible, which is very unprofessional. To help kill the time in between serving our customers, who I suspect I'm gradually coming to resent, I drink *pastis*, much too much – also very unprofessional. The trouble is that it's always there. The rich spicy smells from the kitchen, which seemed so original and refreshing just a few weeks ago, are now so familiar they have started to irritate. From time to time, I walk around the block.

This has given me plenty of opportunity – probably too much – to consider the subject of Celine, and now the dust has settled (she's not called me, nor I her) I begin to look back over our relationship with the growing bitterness of one who has indeed been well and truly dumped, and keen to re-write history. This is probably a self-survival technique designed by nature to enable people unlucky enough to be in my position to *move on*. Sally Ann agrees, but says the process has kicked in unusually early in my case; it often doesn't begin for months, which casts doubts over the original validity of our relationship.

And it's true, looking back, that Celine and I must have appeared a most unlikely liaison. She has youth and is a locally famed beauty; she is sexy and stimulating. I am middle-aged, broke, with a family and a past in what is perceived, at this end of Europe, at least, as a dim and distant land. But at least we each brought to the table something lacking in the other. Of course, she made me feel twenty years younger. She found me amusing. I'd like to think I'm well read and well travelled, and maybe I was able to offer her a different perspective on the world.

But now I suspect (naturally with hindsight) that I was probably more of a temporary boyfriend than a potential long-term partner. A slightly unusual older man, former television producer, who could have whisked her away to exciting and exotic locations – but in the end, never did. I guess my daughter Alexandra was right: it was doomed. Now I curse myself for not seeing this so much earlier, for wasting so much time.

And there's precious little about anything in the restaurant to cheer me up. What makes the daily evening stint at L'Été Indien so much more of an ordeal is that my French seems to have actually started to deteriorate. I still can't understand a word most people speak. But at least I've now come up with an ingenious way of expressing myself, which also hugely helps to relieve the tedium.

I've remembered from some distant French lesson a fantastically useful fact: every English word ending in the letters 'tion' – with just three *exceptions* – is exactly the same in French. This has, in a very minor kind of way, given me a new lease of life.

Whingeing male customer: *M'sieur, j'ai un problèm avec mon poisson!*

NF: *Pardon, je n'ai pas un 'explanation'. Nous sommes encore en 'evolution'. En 'reflection', c'est un pauvre 'situation'. Le resultat sera une 'revelation', je crois. Si non, vous pouvez faire un 'castration'.*

WC: *Vous parlez bien français!*

NF: *Merci, et sans 'procrastination'!*

Attractive female customer: *M'sieur, le restaurant est très bon, vous habitez près d'ici?*

NF: *Mais oui, Mademoiselle. J'ai une 'habitation', à côte du restaurant. Et tu as très 'attraction', tu as une 'revelation', veux-tu visite mon 'location' après? Si non, cela sera un 'devastation'.*

And it does help to pass the time faster.

～ 20 JULY ～

I am just beginning to sink into the serious and lonely despair of routine – albeit potentially profitable – when everything starts to change.

Reza had set off early on the *motobicyclette*, to the market at Les Vans, for potatoes, onions, melons, and a selection of fruit that's turned out to be so popular with the punters – tiny, wild, unbelievably sweet strawberries collected from beside the roads, bilberries, enormous peaches and nectarines, bursting – to my tough, insensitive English tongue – with extraordinary, unforgettable taste.

We certainly expected him back for *Ricard moins quart* before the shops all closed down in deference and supplication – or *supplication* – beneath the fearsome heat of the midday sun.

We definitely expected him back by mid-afternoon.

When he wasn't back by early evening, we started to realize that something must have gone horribly wrong.

And it has.

Eventually we receive a call from the accident and emergency unit at the main general hospital in Aubenas. Reza has come off his beloved *moto-bicyclette*. No bones are broken, but he had skidded on a tight corner approaching one of the bridges on the way back from Les Vans and crashed off the bike. On first sight, his hands – which he'd held out instinctively to soften the blow of his fall – are badly grazed by the gravel on the road. He is in great pain. And he certainly won't be working in L'Été Indien tonight.

Will I be able to manage without him?

They wanted to keep him in overnight but Reza was having none of it.

When we picked him up, both hands heavily bandaged, he was clearly in agony. But once again I am struck by his unexpected physical durability and courage.

And humour.

'Darlings, I can't tell you how glamorous I looked in casualty, blood all over my arms, just like a Hollywood war hero, my sunglasses perched on the top of my head!' If Claudio hadn't got there just in time to take some shots and immortalize the moment, we'd never have heard the last of it.

Armed with bucketfuls of painkillers, we dropped him off at Les Fabres and headed down to Laurac.

It's true, it's only when they've gone that you really start to miss someone. Since we'd opened our doors for business, Reza has been almost inconspicuous in his quiet efficiency, the unseen pilot at the front of the plane; seamlessly moving from room to room, table to table, the perfect host, sorting out problems with a whisper, lightening the mood, buoying up the staff, checking and tasting everything before it leaves the kitchen. He is the transparent glue that holds all the different sections of our operation together. Although I'd always thought of him as a drama queen, creating more crises than he solved, most of his dizziness is purely for dramatic effect. When no one is taking any notice of him, Reza just gets on quietly with the job.

And now he's not here.

As a result, there was little opportunity to be bored tonight, especially since Christiane had managed to pack in no less than fifty guests. There were a couple who got noisily drunk (for a change – I've not seen anyone even tipsy since we opened) and there were complaints from tables nearby.

'*Pardon*,' says I. '*Ils ont un celebration.*'

Charlie was trying to take some pictures on the terrace, when a couple jumped up and the man put a hand over his lens. There was a short *altercation*.

'*Je ne sais pas un problem,*' I say, grabbing Charlie's camera with a flourish. '*Je prends sans contraption en effet, il serait un liberation.*'

'What's going on?' says Charlie.

'They are having an affair,' I whisper.

'Pardon?'

'Don't film them, they're not here.'

We ran out of prawns. The coffee machine started making dangerous gurgling noises and had to be switched off. Then the most colossal thunderstorm broke just above L'Été Indien. The terrace was ankle-deep in water within seconds. So we have now proved, scientifically, that it is physically impossible to squeeze fifty human beings into the restaurant inner dining area. Everyone seemed surprisingly good-humoured about the downpour, and to my surprise and delight it sent most guests on their way rather earlier than usual.

It's been a long day. Earlier I had become exasperated by yet another legal document Christiane said I should have signed, to do with the lease of the restaurant.

'It is just a signature, it won't take long, *chéri*,' she said.

I signed, as required. But that was far from the end of it. Christiane and I then had to print our names individually at the bottom of every single page. After that I had to copy out, *in long hand*, *word for word*, three large paragraphs of French legal gobbledegook that were printed within the document. It felt rather as though I was being punished at school for larking about in front of the French teacher. It took forty-five minutes to complete, and was an utterly pointless waste of time. When I asked Christiane why such a ludicrous transcription was necessary, she merely shook her head and said she had no idea; that is the way things are done in France, *chéri*.

One of the unexpected parts of this job is that I am spending more and more time each day on meaningless administrative paperwork. It's driving me crazy. This is not why I wanted to open a restaurant. No wonder foreign companies seem reluctant to invest in the French economy (obviously it's not just the effect of the thirty-five-hour working week).

'You should stop moaning about it, *chéri*,' Christiane said. 'It is the way, *c'est la vie*; it is something that just has to be done. Either be quiet or do something about it.'

'Like what?'

'Stand for mayor!'

It took me a moment or two to realize it, but this is an inspired idea.

Just for fun, I walked up to the *mairie* in Laurac to find out a few details. One must be a French citizen, they said in the mayor's secretary's office, to stand for mayor. Well, then maybe I shall change my nationality, and become one! There was then a short debate about whether mayoral candidates actually had to be *born* in France. Someone pointed out that even if this was so now, there was new legislation coming from Brussels under the Human Rights Act that would deem this irrelevant by the time the next mayoral elections come round. As well as making a dramatic statement on an anti-bureaucratic ticket, standing to be the next mayor of Laurac could be hugely entertaining. Reza and Nippi could be my campaign managers. Of course, I'd need to brush up on the old lingo a bit. The only seriously worrying aspect of the idea is if I actually *won* the popular vote, and became mayor. Manu says that a high percentage of the local young people would relish the opportunity to cock a snook at the old guard, the old reactionary establishment, and vote for a maverick like me.

Well, it's certainly something to ponder over during the long winter evenings that lie ahead.

Reza is fast asleep when I return to Les Fabres at just before 3 a.m. I pour a large glass of Scotch whisky – now up there along with the Marmite and Tetley tea as one of the few English commodities I can't live without – then take a shower and hand-wash my rain-soaked Indian costume. Half an hour in the morning sunshine on the terrace and it'll be dry.

The routine of the restaurant, like a drug, is slowly changing my body. I'm not remotely tired. My mind is still humming. It's also spookily quiet. The one consolation of Reza injuring his hands is that, mercifully, for a few days at least, the house will not be echoing to any Schubert whatever.

I'm praying that he'll feel better tomorrow.

~ 22 July ~

Last night's monsoon has provided at least some temporary relief from the onslaught of the relentless heatwave. It's cleared the air, which is sweet and deliciously damp. The view from the terrace has miraculously returned to green. Christiane says thousands of old people are being found dead in their beds as a result of the heat. It's causing a nightmare for the farmers; the grape harvest is going to be weeks early.

I give a cheery wave at Marcel Carbenero, who seems to be in the process of creating a second large set of concrete steps from his patio down to the garden.

He points up to the sky and rolls his eyes. '*Le ciel…c'est plein de plusiers plus de pluie!*'

'*Ça fait,*' I say to him, '*un bon alliteration!*'

He looks at me oddly.

My prayers have not been answered. Poor Reza apparently had a terrible night. Even the strong painkillers proved ineffectual and he slept fitfully for only an hour or two. He's stopped eating completely. His trousers will soon be round his ankles and now it'll hurt his hands too much to pull them up. Actually, there's nothing funny about this at all. Christiane took him back to the hospital for even stronger painkillers, and he spent most of the rest of the day feeling light-headed and hallucinating. There are dozens of fig trees around the restaurant – recently the huge fruit have become so heavy they've dropped to the ground, creating what at first sight looks like pools of dry blood all along the pavement – and Reza says he saw Baby the elephant trying to climb on top of one of them. I said I thought Baby would be more inclined to eat the tree than try to climb it.

Reza insisted on joining us at the restaurant this evening. There's really not a lot he can do. He's very miserable and sorry for himself, moping about, clearly still in great pain. I think he feels bored and lonely at Les Fabres.

Again, it's been a very feverishly busy night.

For once, Charlie and Claudio aren't filming.

'How much footage can you shoot of happy French people eating your Indian nosh?' Charlie says, offering the assembled company a yawn the size of a hippopotamus's. He's bored. 'Seen one, seen them all.'

Charlie and Claudio have their story. It's time to pack their bags. Claudio has a new job, quite perfect for him, although just a *little* different from what he's been used to here. He's going to Iraq, to shoot a programme on the aftermath of the war. He's really excited. He can't wait to go. I ask him if I can come with him.

Charlie returns to Soho. For the editing. My God! I don't even want to think about it. I've remembered a second Shakespearean quote: 'What's done is done and cannot be undone.' Sal says, theatrically, it's from *the Scottish play.*

I can't really believe the boys are leaving. No more re-takes; no more arguments about what was shot, and what wasn't; what should be in the programmes, and what shouldn't. I just hope they are happy with what they've got. I don't really care, but I shall miss them. As Charlie keeps reminding me, they've become part of the furniture.

At least they've agreed to leave the lights in the restaurant. For the time being.

I'm beginning to feel a little isolated and lonely.

~ 23 July ~

What can be worse, what can be more frustrating in life, than being unable to enjoy the fruits of one's labours?

Again, I should have expected it, should have seen it coming. I'm just hopeless when it comes to looking ahead more than one step at a time.

Reza's gone home.

I thought at worst he'd be unable to work for a few days; but what's happened is a real bombshell. Sal took him back to the hospital in Aubenas to have his poor wounds re-dressed.

I'm amazed. Doesn't France boast of having the finest health service in the world?

His hands have become infected, and despite the fact that he's been put on really strong antibiotics, Reza has decided to go back to London as soon as possible.

Sal packed his bags for him. He bade a wan and weary farewell to the restaurant, and got the next plane back from Lyons.

I feel bereft, yet I suppose I shouldn't really blame him. He could be in pain, unable to work, for weeks. He wants to be in his own home. He's unhappy with the treatment he's received here (why on earth didn't they put him on antibiotics to start with?) and anyway he can't communicate with the medical staff. And his job at L'Été Indien, he says, is done. He makes a rather unconvincing attempt to reassure me: Christiane will be by my side. He is always at the end of a telephone. Don't worry.

I had expected him to be here for another month at least. I don't feel reassured at all. It's going to be purgatory without him.

The house at Les Fabres feels more enormous than ever, and empty. No Reza, no Nippi, no Charlie. I have a deep sentimental attachment to the place but tonight, oddly, I long to be anywhere than here.

It's been another draining evening at L'Été Indien. Nearly fifty covers. The tin's bulging with cash and cheques. They're beginning to greet me at Banque Marze like an old chum.

Surely never can a man have become so unhappy by banking so much money in so short a space of time.

REZA: Plus plus commiserations, Nigel. But you're fine; you're okay without me. I've literally given my blood to this place. L'Été Indien is here to stay. It's been an extraordinary experience. But my job is over, my wardrobe is exhausted. Let's savour the moment with one glass of rosé. There are few enough triumphs in life.

This one has been unforgettable.

Salut!

～ 24 JULY ～

Slowly the little empire that I have so carefully, so lovingly chiselled away to construct here in the rock face of the Ardèche is beginning to crumble all around me, before my very eyes.

Having Sunny Sal over the last six weeks in the restaurant has been a joy. She stayed much longer than she'd ever intended. The diligence and *application* of her work has been exemplary and extraordinary – she's frequently worked a sixteen-hour, or sometimes even an eighteen-hour, day. On a personal level, too, she is quite irreplaceable. She's become a true and steadfast friend. Even now, after the blow of Reza's sudden departure, she's offered nothing but support and encouragement.

'You know, Freckles, like so many people, you've become terribly good at underestimating your own capability. You'll be fine. It's happened, you've proved them all wrong.'

I'd sort of forgotten (or maybe wanted to forget) that she, too, must go home. This afternoon she announced that she's booked a Eurostar ticket to return to London next Monday. The BBC beckons. I could tell by the look in her eye there was no point whatsoever in trying to persuade her otherwise. Thanks to my *beloved* restaurant, I can't even take Sal out for a final, farewell dinner.

And now a new idea has kicked, struggled and forced its way to the surface.

It was Sal who first put the question. I never thought I'd seriously consider this: but maybe Nippi and I should sell Les Fabres?

I love it, and I love the role it has played so dominantly over the last couple of years in my life.

But it is (if I dare for a moment – and I know it's very uncharacteristic – to be ruthlessly pragmatic) extremely . . . well, what's the word . . . *impractical.*

As Sal is so keen to point out, that long winding drive up from the valley, through the *marron* forests – which seemed so compellingly charming and utterly delightful when we first bought the place – starts to lose its appeal when one is biting one's lip hard to just keep awake every night at 2 a.m. after an exhausting day's work. And can I really face the prospect of another long, freezing winter rattling around these vast, unheated rooms? The house has risen relatively well in value; Nippi, I'm sure, would be happy to sell. He's taken precious little interest in the place and hasn't contributed anything towards the running costs.

A small flat just round the corner from the restaurant in lovely Largentière would be ideal.

I can't believe Sally Ann is leaving on Monday.

~ *28 JULY* ~

It was like a scene from *Brief Encounter*; only the Rachmaninov was missing.

We've had a wonderful final few days together. We've snatched a few hours here and there for Sal to enjoy some sightseeing; it's a bit of a reward, something we've not had the chance to do before. Lunch at the lovely hilltop restaurant, Le Tour de Brison, the highest restaurant in the whole area, with just extraordinary views looking down over the impenetrable lush-green forests that encircle, in what seems like some kind of honour

– like a wreath – the footstones of the fairy-tale château of Montréal. To Banne, another unforgettably picturesque medieval village, where Marie-Elise is staging an exhibition of her sculptures, curiously endearing little human and animal figures, intriguingly constructed out of discarded household refuse, like old bicycle wheels, flowerpots and garden tools. It's great in France, where art is held in such respect; if you are an artist, you beg or borrow a room, restaurant or hall and simply mount your own exhibition. It's just what one does. Afterwards, we had a glass of Irish stout in a little bar round the corner, bizarrely named the Lockerbie bar, in honour of the dreadful Pan-Am 747 crash. Nobody behind the bar could explain the *connection*.

We stood on the stage of the breathtaking Roman amphitheatre at Vienne, and on the way back stopped off at Hauterives to see another extraordinary sight: the miniature re-creation of an entire medieval castle. Legend has it that a *facteur* or postman called Ferdinand Cheval spent thirty-three years of his working life collecting stones and pebbles on his round each morning to create the extraordinary Palais Idéal. It's just big enough, with stooped shoulders, to walk around inside. I found it quite bizarre – after Cheval's death it was hailed as work of great artistic genius – even Picasso visited it. Sal and I both felt Ferdinand should have had something better to do.

And at every spare moment we swam: by day, in the various rivers and tributaries of the Ardèche basin, basking in the tropical heat; by night, when the restaurant was closed, in the darkness and delicious chill of Marie-Elise's pool.

Christiane is genuinely upset when it's time for me to take Sal to Montélimar station. There are tears, as the two almost-sisters embrace for the last time. Christiane has baked Sal a dozen little *vol au vonts* for the journey home, and packs these along with a couple of bottles of red wine.

'It's been epic, just wonderful!' bellows Sal.

'Why are you shouting?' I ask.

'I'm nervous I'm never going to see Christiane again!'

There is the usual exchange of *unbreakable* promises: of course, Sal would return to Laurac just *as soon* as she can; and yes, Christiane and JB would love to come to London, just *as soon* as the restaurant quietens down.

I wonder whether they ever really will see each other again.

The drive to the station is touching, and depressing. There is a strange sense of imminent loss.

'I just want to say how much I admire you,' says Sal to me, quite suddenly. 'Just look what you've achieved. Most people thought your idea was crazy. But you've *done it*. Against the odds. L'Été Indien is a thriving, viable business with a golden future. You should be proud of yourself.'

And she leans across, and gently kisses me on the cheek.

She doesn't want me to wait for the train but I say it's the least I can do. So we wait, rather awkwardly, struggling for things to say to each other, as people do. The platform is crowded with people, laughing, hugging, kissing, crying.

Eventually, the sleek silhouette of the TGV appears through the shimmer of a heat haze.

The doors hiss open; we embrace. A whistle is blown.

And then Sally Ann is gone.

ONE MONTH LATER

~ 2 SEPTEMBER ~

Soho smells much better than I remember. Even now, there's a residue of the year's extraordinary Indian summer in the air. It's very mild. The restaurants and bars are spilling out of control on to the pavements; there's hardly room to move through the throng of tanned, happy drinkers. A different kind of music, Caribbean, Kylie or Mozart, greets one around every street corner.

This is a nation that suddenly seems *sentir mieux dans votre peau* – comfortable in its skin. And it's good to be back.

I meet Charlie in one of our old drinking haunts, the Toucan, round the corner from Soho Square. There is one pint of iced Guinness in his hand, and one for me on the bar. We greet each other briefly, and I take a long, lazy swig of the beer. I haven't enjoyed a smell or a taste like it for the best part of a year.

'How goes L'Été Indien?' asks Charlie.

I take another long draught of the glorious black stuff.

'We've had one or two problems.'

Charlie stares at me for a few moments, smiling, but with that slightly blank look in his eyes.

'You wouldn't believe how quiet it has become.'

I explain to Charlie that I'm able to get back over here for a few days' break because it's quiet now in L'Été Indien. The rest of July was good. August was better. But now the season is coming to an end. The grape harvest, which Christiane says always generates a good deal of trade, has come and gone, thanks to this extraordinary summer, weeks earlier than usual. So if I want a break, Christiane says, this is the time to take it; she, Edward and Ramsa can look after the shop. Many restaurants are already preparing to close for the winter. And maybe when the season starts to get chillier, and we head towards the shortest day of the year, the stomach of the average Ardèchoise turns against the spirit of gastronomic adventure and experiment, and seeks to return to the comfort and solace of the tried and trusted traditional fare.

Sally Ann is staying with her sister in York. Reza is in India.

'The first and most significant problem,' I continue, 'is that I just don't like being a restaurateur. The hours. The repetition. The paperwork. The fact you have to keep smiling. It's just not me.'

'That was perfectly obvious from the opening night, Farrell.'

'And I miss the Guinness.'

'Do you still hate the work?'

'Not so much.' The relentless daily routine of the restaurant has become so familiar that I can now do most of it with my eyes closed; and that makes it so much easier and less stressful. But more boring.

'Anything else?'

'It's all cost much more than we budgeted for.'

'What a surprise.'

This is sadly true. Our overheads are higher than when Christiane simply ran the place as Le Relais Fleuri. Edward, as the specialist Indian chef, commands a higher wage than a local French one. He has to be accommodated. And soon, presumably, he will be wanting to bring his family up from Nice.

And there is the rent to pay to the Tochous. And Christiane's salary.

Also, the start-up costs haven't been fully repaid. I was incredibly naive to think that this could have been achieved by now. We've been trading only eighteen weeks.

'So what's going to happen?' asks Charlie.

Eighty per cent of restaurants close within the first two years.

I am strangely, illogically, stubbornly reluctant to abandon the dream and hand Le Relais Fleuri back to the Tochous, even though this is the easiest and most obvious option. Next season, if we could just hang on in there over the winter, could be very successful. If we were making enough money, I could even find somebody to help run it for me.

Also, there's a matter of principle here. I don't court or relish failure. If I make up my mind to do something, I will go to almost any length to ensure that it's done to the best of my abilities. And I love France. I am determined to make L'Été Indien a permanent fixture in the Ardèche landscape, an animate and enduring tribute to the spirit of the pioneer, the adventurer that so inspired Reza in the first place. And Reza agrees. The problem is that neither of us, right now, has any spare cash and, sadly, it could be cash we need to keep the flame of L'Été Indien alive through the long winter months.

'So what's gong to happen?' asks Charlie.

'I might need to subsidize the restaurant. Just for a month or two. To see us through the winter.'

'How's that?'

'Need a decent documentary producer, Charlie?' I ask. 'I'm a safe pair of hands.'

THREE MONTHS LATER

～ 8 DECEMBER ～

An extraordinary lunch with Reza, Charlie and Manu, at the Star of India, Old Brompton Road, London SW5. Quite like old times.

L'Été is still very quiet, so I've been buzzing about all over the place getting what work I can to raise enough funds to keep the doors of the restaurant open. We're just about holding our heads above water. But only just. So arranging to meet up with the gang again is a welcome relief.

It's weird and wonderful to see Manu over in London for a few days. He's come armed with mountains of details of houses for sale in the south of France. Despite Reza's mental – and physical – scars, amazingly he too has decided he wants to buy a house out in the Ardèche. He simply *venerates* the region. I've suggested Les Fabres would be a great buy, and Reza says this is a very amusing suggestion. He wants something *habitable*.

Reza (who never drinks alcohol, remember) cracks open the champagne and we all drink our way through several bottles. Manu has a letter for me from Celine. I haven't seen her for months. She has a new boyfriend. She wants me to be the first to know. I'm touched. There's a photo – he looks terribly young, and impossibly handsome. But she looks happy, and so she should. It was an unforgettable year. Good luck to her. And good luck to his shins.

It all feels very strange over lunch. But *good*. The last time I was in the Star was in March, nine months ago, trying to persuade a reluctant Reza to invest in the first Indian restaurant to open in the Ardèche. Today he provides us all with a wonderful selection of curries for lunch. But I just tinker with the cutlery. My mind's elsewhere. To be honest, I'm off Indian cuisine. Just for a while.

After lunch, we retire upstairs, and Reza performs Schubert's Impromptu No. I. He plays it impeccably; not a single mistake. No long-term injury to the hands, then. Then I take over on his old joanna, thrashing out a few old pub favourites. I want to play 'I Am a Rover' but can't remember the chords. Or the words. Reza says that's a blessing. So it has to be 'On the Sunny Side of the Street'. Seems strangely appropriate, somehow.

At last Sally Ann arrives, hours late. She looks *sensationnelle*. Long, wild hair. Big, open smile.

I'd been extremely nervous when I originally asked Sal out over the phone, some days earlier. We'd become such buddies over the summer that any attempt to change the nature of our relationship was almost like beginning all over again.

'Howdy, Freckles, how's my beloved Ardèche?'

I hadn't heard her voice for weeks. A tingle ran down the spine.

'Up and down, with rather more emphasis on the "down". If I can just hold my nerve until the start of the new season, I think L'Été could be there forever.'

'You're a genius.'

'Sal, I'm coming to England for a few weeks.'

'Yes?' Her voice was getting louder.

'Shall we meet up?'

'Sure, what have you got in mind?' She was almost shouting now.

'Maybe dinner? Or you could suggest something good at the National?'

'Do you mean *on a date*?' She was bellowing so loudly I was holding the earpiece as far away as I could.

'Yes, sweetheart.'

'I was so nervous, I thought you'd never ask!' she said at length, struggling to bring her voice under control. 'What took you so bloody long?'

Since then we've scarcely been apart.

Reza pops open more champagne. Charlie says we should all arrange to have a party at his house in a few weeks' time, so we can watch the first of his programmes going out live on air on Channel 4. We can all watch it together. It'll be *fantastique*!

But I will be in France.

I don't want to hurt Charlie's feelings, but I really can't bear to go through the whole damned thing all over again.

Besides, time has moved on. It's been almost a year since I started the diary, and my New Year beckons. I've been working on another Big Idea. This one is an even greater challenge. It could also help revive the flagging fortunes of L'Été, allow me to *really* make my mark in the Ardèche, and change the world.

I intend to take up Christiane's suggestion, and stand as the next *maire* of Laurac.

Charlie thinks it's an absolutely *brilliant* idea.

❧

Recreate the experience of L'Été Indien,
with these exclusive recipes from Reza Mahammad

~ LEMON RICE ~

300 g basmati rice
Salt to taste
½ tsp turmeric powder
3 lemons
30 ml clarified butter/ghee/vegetable oil
10 g black mustard seeds
12–15 curry leaves
15 g Bengal gram lentils (chana dal)
Urad lentils (white lentils) – make sure they are husked

1. Wash and soak rice in warm water for about 15 minutes.
2. In a large saucepan, boil 1.2 litres of water and add salt, turmeric and the juice of 2 lemons.
3. Drain the soaked rice and add to the boiling liquid. Cook until the rice is just tender.
4. Drain in a colander. Gently transfer the rice back into the pot and cover.
5. In a frying pan, heat the ghee or oil until hot, then add the mustard seeds and curry leaves. Allow to crackle and pop. Add both types of lentils, and stir until they turn golden. Immediately add the juice of the remaining lemon.
6. Pour this mixture on to the cooked rice and cover.
7. Keep warm until ready to serve.
8. Just before serving, fluff out the rice with a fork.

~ FRENCH BEAN THOREN ~

This makes an excellent side dish for six people

500 g french beans
20 ml vegetable oil
5 g (1½ tsp) black mustard seeds
12–15 curry leaves
20 g root ginger, peeled and finely chopped
2 green chillies, slit, deseeded and finely chopped
100 g freshly grated coconut
5 g/1 tsp sugar
Juice of a lemon
60 g cashew nuts, sautéed with a teaspoon of oil until golden,
    then dried on kitchen paper
Half a bunch of fresh coriander, finely chopped

1. Top and tail beans, string if necessary, and cut into 1-inch lengths.
2. Blanch beans in boiling salted water for a minute. Drain and plunge into cold water immediately so they retain their colour. This will also stop the beans from cooking further. Drain and pat dry.
3. In a non-stick frying pan or wok, add the oil and heat on a high flame. Make sure that the oil is hot, then add the mustard seeds and curry leaves. As soon as they begin to pop and crackle, add the ginger and chillies. Stir-fry for a moment. Now add the beans to reheat and continue to stir.
4. Finally, add the grated coconut, sugar, lemon juice, cashew nuts and chopped coriander. Toss everything together and season with salt. Serve immediately.

~ CHICKEN KOFTAS ~

Serves six

For the koftas:

    6 chicken breasts (7–8 oz or 200 g each), trimmed of fat, cartilage etc.

    30 g root ginger, peeled and chopped

    30 g garlic, peeled and chopped

    2 tbsp coriander, chopped

    2–3 green chillies, chopped

    5 g salt

    5 g chilli powder

    5 g garam masala

For the stuffing:

    50 g raisins, washed and dried on kitchen paper

    3 tbsp mint, chopped

    2–3 green chillies, chopped

For the gravy:

    25 g root ginger, peeled and chopped

    5 cloves garlic

    2 tbsp vegetable oil

    4 green cardamoms

    1 blade mace

    1 star anise

    5 g each of powdered turmeric, chilli, garam masala and cumin

    50 ml tomato purée

    500 g yoghurt, whisked

    50 g cashew nuts

1. Cut chicken into cubes, add ginger, garlic, coriander, green chillies, salt, chilli powder and garam masala, and mix lightly.
2. Pass through mincer or finely chop in a food processor.
3. Turn into a bowl and knead the minced chicken to distribute the spices evenly. Chill for half an hour.
4. Mix the stuffing ingredients together. Make small round balls with the chicken and stuff each with a teaspoon of the stuffing. To make it easier, lightly oil your hands to shape koftas. Keep koftas in refrigerator until the gravy is ready.

For the gravy:
5. Prepare a paste of the chopped ginger and garlic with a tablespoon of water in a blender.
6. Heat the oil in a heavy saucepan or casserole dish, and add the cardamoms, mace and star anise, then the ginger and garlic paste, and cook for about a minute.
7. Add in the powdered spices and cook for half a minute.
8. Add the tomato purée and yoghurt, reduce the heat and simmer for about 5 minutes.
9. Gently add the koftas to the simmering sauce and cook for 8–10 minutes.
10. While the koftas are cooking, soak the cashews in hot water for 10 minutes and blend to a paste. Add the nut paste to the koftas and cook for a few more minutes.
11. Garnish with chopped coriander and serve immediately.